IN SEARCH OF
GAY AMERICA

▲ ▲ ▲ ▲ ▲ ▲ ▲ ▲ ▲ ▲ ▲

IN SEARCH OF

GAY AMERICA

WOMEN AND MEN

IN A TIME OF CHANGE

NEIL MILLER

▼ ▼ ▼ ▼ ▼ ▼ ▼ ▼ ▼ ▼ ▼

THE ATLANTIC MONTHLY PRESS

NEW YORK

Published simultaneously in Canada.
Printed in the United States of America.
First edition

Library of Congress Cataloging-in-Publication Data
Miller, Neil (Neil I.)
In search of gay America : women and men in a time of change / Neil Miller.
ISBN 0-87113-304-0
1. Gays—United States. I. Title
HQ76.33.U5M55   1989   306.7′66′0973—dc19   88-30502

The Atlantic Monthly Press
19 Union Square West
New York, NY 10003

First printing

Design and composition by The Sarabande Press

FOR STEPHEN

ACKNOWLEDGMENTS

I am deeply grateful to many individuals around the country who offered their advice and hospitality. Although I am not able to thank everyone by name, I do wish to express my appreciation to: Tim Angle and Ron Jouillian, the late Dan Bradley, Chris Bull, Colevia Carter, Kevin Cathcart, Craig Chapman, Kate Clinton and Trudy Wood, Ann DeGroot, Susan Denelsbeck, Mike Fain, Lesli Gordon, Darrel Hildebrant, Amy Hoffman, David Hollander, Toby Johnson and Kip Dollar, Larry Killian, Tim Kuchta, Lissa LeGrand, Jane Levin, David Lott, Joe Martin and Clinton Anderson, Brian McNaught, Tom McNaught, Joe McQuay, Peter Meyer, Lon Murphy and Tom Wrubel, John Nikalotos, Rick Notch, Cindy Patton, Canon Price, the Reverend Marge Ragona, Gloria Ramirez, Eric Rofes, Eric Rosenthal, Eddie Sandifer, Barry Sandler, Steve Savage, Denny Smith, Joseph E. Smith, Melissa Smith and Robin Rooks, Sterling Stowell, Gene Ulrich, Michael Watson, Wellesley College Lesbians and Friends, Nick Wilkerson, Jim Williamson, Carter Wilson and Ray Martinez, William Wright, and Roberta Wyn and Steve Hinshaw.

My thanks to Urvashi Vaid and Sue Hyde of the National Gay and Lesbian

Task Force for their help in directing me to people in various parts of the United States. Michael Bronski was an invaluable source of information and always challenged my thinking. Over the years, Richard Burns, Jim Marko, and Ken Rabb helped me in formulating the ideas and attitudes that led to this book. Ken Mayer kept me informed of the latest medical developments and issues of social policy surrounding AIDS. Katie Garate and Sue Hornik read portions of this manuscript and were generous with their time and comments. Kathleen Hirsch was consistently encouraging. Jonathan Strong and Morgan Mead nurtured this project from beginning to end: Jonathan was an immensely valuable critic, and Morgan, in addition to offering his insights, proved a loyal and patient traveling companion. Stephen McCauley's critical intelligence and judgement improved the book immeasurably. His companionship and affection sustained me during the writing of it.

I am indebted to my agent, Arlene Donovan, and to my editor, Ann Godoff, for her shrewd editorial sense and her confidence in me. My parents, Selma and Leon Miller, and my sister, Jane Miller, were extremely supportive, as ever. And were it not for the late Luis Sanjurjo, my agent during the early stages of this project, the book would never have become a reality. I will always be grateful to him.

CONTENTS

▼ ▼ ▼ ▼ ▼ ▼ ▼ ▼ ▼ ▼ ▼ ▼ ▼ ▼

CONTENTS

INTRODUCTION

In the summer of 1975, I took a job as the news editor of the *Gay Community News* (*GCN*), a Boston-based paper that was, at the time, the country's only gay and lesbian weekly. As editor, my responsibility was to fill the first five pages with gay-related news from Boston and around the country. I often wound up doing most of the writing myself.

The staff included six people, plus display and classified advertising managers. There was also a small army of volunteers—the artistically minded who did the layout and paste-up on Thursday nights; the "Friday night folders" who mailed out the paper after it was printed; and news and feature writers. *GCN* was a nonprofit organization and a collective. Each staff member received the same salary—sixty dollars a week. That came to forty-eight dollars after taxes. Fortunately, my portion of the rent for the apartment I shared with two other gay men came to seventy-five dollars a month. The apartment didn't have central heating (my room was warmed in winter by a space heater, which I was convinced emitted noxious fumes), but it was a five-minute walk from Harvard Square, with its bookstores and coffee houses and revival movie theatres. I put a Van Gogh poster on the wall above my bed and one of Lenin on the inside of my closet door. Needless to say, my parents, who wished I was in law school, were not pleased.

I have only a vague memory of the August evening I first walked into the offices of *GCN* for my job interview. The paper was then located in a huge second-floor loft that looked out on a downtown street populated by camera and jewelry stores. I recall sitting around a long table, surrounded by a group of earnest people, mostly women, who peppered me with questions. (*GCN* was one of the few gay papers where gay men and lesbians worked together, and it remains so today. At the time I began my tenure there, the other two editors were women.) Until that moment, I had never laid eyes on anyone who called herself a lesbian.

The competition wasn't exactly stiff—even at a time when some remnants of Vietnam era idealism persisted, few people were willing to work for sixty dollars a week—and I was hired. For most of the next month, I wandered around Boston with what felt like a low-grade fever. I took my temperature every few hours but it was always normal. Perhaps it was just the August heat. More likely, it was because I realized that when aunts, uncles, cousins, or the lady who ran the laundromat inquired what I did for a living, I would have to say I was an editor at the *Gay Community News*. No good gay activist should lie about that, although sometimes, I admit, I did.

I worked desperately to fill the news pages. There wasn't as much gay and lesbian news in those days, and it wasn't easy to find copy—especially in the middle of August, when little was happening, and especially when there was no money to pay freelance writers. In my first few weeks, we did one article on the court-martial of two lesbian WACs at nearby Fort Devens, another on the funding problems of a gay youth organization, still another on the convention of Dignity, the organization of gay and lesbian Catholics. Then, a patron of a gay bar in Springfield was severely beaten by the bar's bouncer. At our weekly staff meeting the advertising manager castigated me for our coverage. I hadn't called the police for their version of events. A gay and lesbian paper telephone the police! I hadn't considered the idea. But I soon got the hang of things.

Being news editor at *GCN* was my first "movement" job. My coming out as a gay person had been a relatively late one. I don't remember even hearing the word *homosexual* until my junior or senior year in high school. At the university I attended (I graduated in 1967), there was no gay group, no openly gay person I knew of at the time, nothing. I was unhappy but I never thought that it was because I was out of touch with my sexuality. When the drag queens rioted outside the Stonewall Inn in New York's Greenwich Village in June 1969 and launched the gay-liberation movement, I was somewhere in Iran or Turkey, heading back from a trip to India, where I had sat under a tree for three days with a holy man who wore a leather jacket and listened to ragas on a portable radio. I never even knew the gay revolution happened. Later, I spent a couple of years in Israel, teaching high-school English to the children of Moroccan and Iraqi immigrants in a development town near Jerusalem. In Israel it seemed as if everyone my age was getting married. Every woman on the street younger than thirty-five was either pregnant or pushing a baby carriage or both. All this happy Zionist hetero-sexuality proved too much even for me; once and for all, I realized it was fruitless for me to try to fit in. It was time to come home and come out.

And so, I found my way on that August night to the offices of the *Gay Community News*. I was tired of working in bookstores and teaching English to Venezuelan businessmen at Berlitz, my two jobs since returning from Israel. I fancied myself a writer. Nonetheless, my gay "qualifications" remained pretty meager. I had probably been in a gay bar only three or four times since I returned from Israel. My roommates, whom I had known for six months or so, were virtually the only gay friends I had. My gay sexual experiences consisted of a couple of short-lived relationships and a few one-night stands. Unlike a lot of gay men at that time, my sexual identity had little to do with sex. It soon had quite a lot to do with gay politics and the *Gay Community News*.

At *GCN*, I found a curious cast of characters. Our precocious ace reporter worked for nothing, tracking down every assault or murder in the city for a possible gay connection; he later developed a cozy relationship with his police sources and died mysteriously (his death was ruled a suicide) before he was 24. The features editor (and my arch rival in political squabbles) was a bisexual woman who was into S and M, later married, and once in an argument called me a sell-out because I owned a car. The business manager was a balding and overweight former small-town schoolteacher in his forties who dragged me to an interminable Red Sox game along with his sister from

Connecticut; we both had to pretend we were straight while his sister oohed and aahed at the handsome Red Sox outfielders. Also on staff were two men who called each another "Clara" and "Binky" and every other man "she." And then there was an older woman, a grandmother figure whose main concerns were bridge and perfect grammar and who was always complaining about misplaced commas.

If I was a movement "greenhorn," that changed rapidly once I began work at *GCN*. Tuesday night staff meetings were often the occasion for raging political debates and were sometimes the scene of carnage. *GCN* was the only gay and lesbian paper for hundreds of miles (New York City did not have a gay newspaper at the time). We had aspirations to cover the entire community — men and women; black, white, and Latino; drag queens and stockbrokers; gay Catholics and gay atheists. The conflicting claims of these disparate groups were one of the major reasons we were always in the thick of battle, battle that was sometimes exhilarating, more often exhausting. Should we accept an ad for a bar featuring a macho guy who asked provocatively "Are you man enough?" or was the ad sexist? Was abortion a gay and lesbian issue? Was nuclear power? Should we run a gossipy column of bar happenings? Did we dare criticize Massachusetts Representative Elaine Noble, the nation's first openly lesbian state legislator? Was there enough lesbian coverage, gay male coverage, coverage of Third World gays?

One of the most heated conflicts involved the decision of the Club Baths chain to run a series of male beauty contests in different cities around the country; a percentage of the proceeds would go to the gay newspaper in each city. To promote the events, called the Mr. Club Baths contests, the company planned to take out full-page ads in those same papers for several weeks running. That meant money, and for a struggling paper dependent for much of its revenue on small businesses and the notoriously unreliable bar advertising, it was welcome. (Club Baths always paid its bills on time.) Along with most of the women on the staff, I opposed the idea. A male beauty contest and the sexist objectification it involved was exactly what gay liberation was trying to get away from, we argued. If feminists picketed the Miss America pageant, how could a gay paper endorse, let alone profit from, the same kind of thing for men! If we did, how could anyone take the paper seriously? Above all, I wanted *GCN* to be serious. In my view, the paper should be the *New York Times* of the gay movement — with a left-wing slant, of course.

The staff voted against any involvement with the Mr. Club Baths contests. Our board of directors was aghast and overruled us, although no one was sure they really had the power to do so under the bylaws. The Club Baths ownership got wind of the whole thing, decided we were a bunch of crazies, and didn't advertise with the paper again for years.

Then there was the Susan Saxe case. In 1970, as a student at Brandeis University, Saxe (as we always called her, as if she were Callas or Pavlova) had become involved with a small band of political radicals. The group decided to rob a bank in the Boston neighborhood of Brighton, apparently to finance the revolution. During the heist, a policeman was killed. Saxe did not pull the trigger, but under Massachusetts state law she could still be charged with felony murder. She went into hiding and became a regular on the FBI's Ten Most Wanted list. Five years later she was apprehended on a Philadelphia street. At the time of her arrest, Saxe was quoted as defending her actions as those of "a revolutionary, a feminist, and an Amazon!" She was brought to Boston to stand trial.

To me, the Susan Saxe case was heady stuff, far more exciting than conventions of gay Catholics or seemingly futile efforts to get a gay and lesbian civil rights bill through the state legislature. Saxe was a nice Jewish girl from Albany, New York, who had gone to an elite school and had become involved with (I assumed) a bunch of misplaced idealists. I was a nice Jewish boy from Kingston, New York, an hour's drive to the south, who had gone to an elite school (Brown University) and had missed out on the revolution of the sixties. I liked to think, given the passions of the times, that I was capable of doing something as foolish as Saxe. I admired her. She was politically committed. And besides, she was courageous enough to proclaim she was a lesbian (or at least an "Amazon") when that fact was unlikely to help her in court. I figured no one was likely to rush to her assistance.

And rush to her assistance *GCN* did every week, in prominently placed, rather one-sided news stories, as she was transferred from one women's prison to another, as pretrial motions and jury selection dragged on. Staff meetings became even more raucous than usual; readers wrote angry letters, advertisers were in revolt, alarmed by our apparent support of a bank-robbing revolutionary. The coverage was my doing, and I stood firm. We were writing about an open lesbian's experiences with the criminal-justice system, I insisted. And besides, the trial would be over soon. We had given the case so much coverage that if we backed out now, we would look like fools. Finally, after a hung jury, Saxe's lawyers plea-bargained and she was sentenced to twelve to fourteen years in prison. (She could be paroled in six.) At *GCN*, everyone heaved a sigh of relief at the end of all the controversy.

Soon after, Anita Bryant and her anti-gay crusade in Miami dominated the news and we veered back towards the more acceptable middle of the road. We ran the first story in the gay press about the singer and promoter of Florida citrus products and her attempt to repeal the Dade County gay-rights ordinance. I clipped Anita's picture out of a glossy magazine and headlined the story, "Who Is Anita Bryant and Why Does She Hate Us?" The night that Bryant triumphed and the Dade County ordinance was overwhelmingly rejected by the voters, I was interviewed for the Boston TV news. "I am sure that if a Southern city had a chance to vote on the rights for blacks at the height of the civil rights movement, it would have voted that down, too," I said, rather grandly.

I stayed on a year longer at *GCN*. For a while, we were paid only half the time. Advertisements and subscriptions could never keep up with the printing bills and typewriter repairs and the rent, especially for a paper that prided itself on its independence and its determination to take on every sacred (gay) cow in sight. The managing editor left; so did the features editor. We couldn't afford to replace them, and I found myself doing all three jobs. I burned out quickly. As the year wore on, our finances returned to their usual dismal (but no longer desperate) shape. I annointed my successor, the reporter who had covered the Susan Saxe trial. It was time to go. I had been at *GCN* for almost two and a half years but it seemed like ten.

After leaving *GCN*, I tried my journalistic wings elsewhere. Eventually, I wound up as a staff feature writer at the *Boston Phoenix*, the alternative weekly that had grown fat and prosperous and considerably less alternative over the years (the paper's detractors referred to it as the "Yuppie weekly") but still offered its writers the freedom to explore their subjects, to take a strong point of view.

I began to settle down. Shortly after I left *GCN*, I became involved in a relationship that, despite ups and downs, has endured for almost ten years now. When I first met Stephen McCauley, a man of quick wit and a modest, self-effacing charm, he was delivering tickets for a Harvard Square travel agency and wandering from one graduate program to the next. In 1987, his first novel, *The Object of My Affection*, a romantic comedy about a relationship between a gay man and a heterosexual woman, was published to critical acclaim. Soon after, Stephen was appointed visiting writer at the University of Massachusetts in Boston. At about the same time as Stephen's book was appearing, we bought an aging two-family Victorian house in a working-class town just outside Boston. If buying a house wasn't suspect enough (at least according to the rigid ethic of "political correctness" that prevailed during my *GCN* years), we also became landlords—to a married couple with a ten year old daughter, and a cat, dog, rabbit, hamster, and parakeet.

Even as I moved into a neighborhood where bathtub Virgin Marys blessed the front yards and aluminum siding seemed an aesthetic requirement, where teenage girls still teased their hair into mounds that looked like cotton candy and the preferred bumpersticker read "Shit Happens," even as I mowed the lawn and wrote articles about kidney transplants and Cambodian refugees and new treatments for depression, I still kept my eye on what was happening in Boston's gay and lesbian community. I covered gay issues for the *Phoenix*, served on boards of organizations, and read *GCN* each week, muttering about what I would have done differently.

And, by the mid-eighties, the community was undergoing some dramatic changes. During my years at *GCN*, most gay men in town were closeted and apolitical; they looked down on the movement even as they benefited from its achievements. They lived in the Back Bay or the South End, went to the bars and the invitation-only parties of a social group called the Papagallos, to Provincetown in the summer. On the other hand, a large number of lesbians were separatists who identified with feminism and the emerging women's culture and would have little or nothing to do with gay men. There were some openly gay and lesbian mainstream figures, like Elaine Noble, but their numbers were small. And then there was the movement—those associated with *GCN* or the gay-liberation periodical *Fag Rag* plus assorted other activists—self-styled outsiders, anti-establishment types nearly all. I am oversimplifying to some degree, of course. There were plenty of people who didn't fit any of these categories and even more who were so deeply in the closet they couldn't be considered gay or lesbian at all.

It was in the autumn of 1985 at a dinner in a swank downtown hotel banquet room that the changes in the community crystallized for me. Some four hundred gay men and women had put down $150 each to eat fruit cocktail and rubbery chicken to benefit the Human Rights Campaign Fund, a political action committee that contributes money to candidates who support gay rights and lobbies Congress on gay and AIDS issues. Marion Barry, the mayor of Washington, D.C., gave the keynote speech. Congressman Barney Frank (who would come out as gay two years later) told jokes and took potshots at the Reagan administration. The poet and novelist May Sarton read a poem about AIDS written for the occasion. Almost all the men were dressed in three-piece suits and the women in tuxedos (the men greatly outnumbered the women, in part reflecting the economic gap between gay men and lesbians). As I scanned the room, the only casually dressed man I could find, besides myself, was an ex-*GCN* staffer named Tim Grant.

Many of the people at that dinner, particularly the men, had been brought there by the AIDS issue. Even in 1985, relatively early in the epidemic in Boston, AIDS had transformed the community, sobering it, bringing a sense of urgency. Many of those formerly closeted and apolitical men who had eschewed any connection with organized gay activity before the epidemic found themselves volunteering to be "buddies" to men with AIDS, doing fund-raising, disseminating safe-sex information. The most powerful organization in town with roots in the gay community was the AIDS Action Committee, the AIDS social-service organization that, within three years, would have a six million dollar annual budget and more than a thousand volunteers. Many of the gay activists of my generation who would have nothing to do with "the system" found themselves applying for government grants, advising public-health officials, serving on all manner of government AIDS task forces. (Later in the epidemic, AIDS was to bring gay people to the streets once again as direct-action groups like ACT UP protested against the federal government's "business as usual" attitude towards the epidemic.)

The people at that $150-a-plate dinner represented one end of the gay social and economic spectrum, of course. The fact that they were there and politically active marked an important change in gay life. But that was just part of a changing picture. Gays and lesbians were buying houses in formerly off-limits blue-collar enclaves of the city like Dorchester and Jamaica Plain, and my own downtrodden town of Somerville. Lesbians were having babies through artificial insemination. Gay men were trying to adopt kids, not always successfully. The bars were in decline; professional organizations (the Lesbian and Gay Bar Association, for example) and sports leagues (baseball, volleyball, soccer, even bowling) were proliferating. In Boston, there was a gay theatre, a gay chorus, a gay bookstore, a women's bookstore, and, by the mid-eighties, four gay newspapers (including an unreconstructed *GCN*, increasingly positioning itself to the left of the emerging political and social consensus).

At least in Boston, and at least among the white middle class, gays and lesbians were acquiring a new sense of security and self-confidence, were moving in from the margins. In part, this was a consequence of the aging of the gay baby-boom generation; in part, it was because of the gains of the movement. I was witnessing, as much as I hesitated to use the word, the mainstreaming of gay and lesbian life. Gay men and lesbians increasingly had many of the same options as heterosexuals while still being proud and vocal about being gay.

Yet, as these developments were taking place, there were discouraging signs as well. Anti-gay violence was on the rise, fueled by public fear of AIDS. The number of AIDS discrimination cases was outrunning the meager resources of the local gay legal group. In the midst of all the new-found security lurked a sense of insecurity: a fear of becoming ill, of one's friends becoming ill, of political backlash.

And AIDS aside, some things just didn't change. To be anti-gay was still acceptable in public discourse; even in "liberal" Massachusetts, you could make outrageous, if not scurrilous, generalizations about gays and lesbians you would never be permitted to make about other minority groups. A gay fireman was virtually run off the Boston firefighting force. The state legislature still voted down gay civil rights protections year after year. And the administration of Governor Michael Dukakis had promulgated the commonwealth's first executive policy to actively discriminate against homosexuals by essentially barring gays and lesbians from being foster parents.

Yet, despite the terrible toll of AIDS, the persistence of prejudice and stereotyping, the demonizing of gays by the religious right and its allies, something very significant was taking place. The gay community seemed to be following the pattern of assimilation of ethnic groups and other minorities that had gradually fought their way to some modicum of social acceptance.

As I wrote about many of these changes for the *Phoenix,* I began to consider some intriguing notions that stood in stark contrast to my previous political thinking. Because gays had been so marginalized, so relegated to the fringes of society, our sexual practices against the law (still so in twenty-five states, including Massachusetts), behavior that was viewed as conservative when applied to society in general might in fact be subversive in gay men and lesbians. Having a baby might be traditional behavior for a straight couple, but radical when the parents were two lesbians. It was even more so when the parents were two men. Moving to the suburbs, the ultimate in American conformity, might represent boldness and even vision for a gay man who thought he had no option other than to live within the narrow confines of an urban gay ghetto. Having a long-term, committed relationship, the norm for most heterosexuals, flew in the face of societal expectations when that relationship was between two people of the same sex. Gays and lesbians were openly living out all this conventionality, in sharp contrast to the tradition of closeted gays or lesbians trying to pass for straight on some unobtrusive suburban street.

Even as I was drawn to this rather heretical view of what was happening in the gay community, I was uncomfortable with it. For someone like myself, influenced by the radical edge of the sixties and nourished by those Tuesday night debates at *GCN,* it went against the grain to accept the idea that it wasn't the lesbian bank robber but the gay cop who might be in the forefront of the revolution. One could certainly make the case that this kind of assimilation ultimately strengthened questionable societal norms (suburbia, the nuclear family, monogamy) and ran the risk of the cooptation of gay and lesbian identity and culture. And I knew that as all this middle-class movement towards the mainstream was going on, there were still large numbers of gays—women, the poor, people with AIDS, Third World gays, drag queens, adolescents—who weren't part of the new, increasingly secure gay world. Nonetheless, a transformation was going on around me and in my own life as well. In the end, I was convinced it represented a new and essentially healthy stage in gay and lesbian life. The most important thing for gays and lesbians was to be able to be open and comfortable in our lives while having the same options as everyone else.

As I witnessed these changes in Boston, I wondered if the rest of the country was following the same path. I knew a lot about the gay neighborhoods of the large urban centers and the people who lived there but I knew next to nothing about cities like Louisville and Knoxville, about small towns and rural areas. I wanted to know, twenty years after the Stonewall riots, if gay pride and progress had finally begun to trickle down to the grass roots; if the options for living, working, and being belligerently ourselves that we had won in cities like San Francisco, New York, and Boston extended to the rest of the country, to the towns where so many of us had grown up, to minority communities, to mid-size cities. I wondered, too, as a gay man living in a relatively comfortable urban environment, if I might have something to learn—about survival, about community, and finding one's place in society—from people in less outwardly congenial places. And so the idea for this book.

When I finally began my research, I didn't want to take the well-trodden path through the urban gay ghettos. Acceptance and self-acceptance amidst the anonymity of cities like New York and Los Angeles and even Boston meant little, I was convinced. One had to travel beyond the large metropolitan areas on the two coasts to places where diversity was less acceptable, where it was harder to melt into the crowd, to take the true measure of gay and lesbian life in the United States. That was where the majority of gay people lived anyway, even if you didn't read about them in the gay press or see them on the evening news.

So I didn't go to the South End of Boston, with its large gay population, but to the suburbs; not to Houston or Dallas, with their large and active communities, but to conservative, Latino San Antonio; not to Atlanta, but to Birmingham; not to Manhattan, but to Memphis and Minneapolis and the coal towns of Appalachia. I didn't ignore the big cities entirely, of course. But I felt that the more time I spent outside them, the closer I would get to a real picture of whether the changes that I was seeing at home were taking deeper root, were becoming part of the larger cultural landscape.

It was impossible for me to go everywhere. I couldn't cover every facet of the gay community, every subgroup of the gay and lesbian population. I wanted to explore certain themes that interested me, that I felt made up the lives of most gay people—roots, relationships and sexuality, family and parenthood, work, religion, politics, the impact of AIDS—and to do so in a variety of geographic, social, and cultural settings. Above all, I wanted to document people's lives, to tell their stories. I deliberately sought out individuals who had some sense of gay and lesbian identity and some connection to a gay community, whether they were in the closet or not. A sense of identity and relationship to community were prerequisites, I believed, to any move away from the margins of society to a richer, more integrated life.

I made sure to talk to both men and women. To make political progress, I believe it is essential for lesbians and gay men to work together. And my own view of the gay community, beginning at *GCN*, had always been a co-sexual one. More than that, I thought that the experiences of gay men and women, though often dissimilar, could shed light on one another, offer perspective, understanding. I also suspected the two groups were increasingly less separate than they had been in the past.

I have also tried to write about AIDS—the suffering it has caused and the heroism it has brought, the effect of the epidemic on the way gay men live their lives, on their values, on their sense of community, on politics and activism. Clearly, in writing a book about gay life in the age of AIDS, the epidemic was very much in the forefront of my consciousness; AIDS affected, indeed transformed, so many aspects of gay male life and sometimes lesbian life as well. At the same time, I did not set out to write a book about AIDS. I have attempted to do justice to the profound impact it has had on so many gay people without letting the epidemic stand for the whole of gay life or the contemporary gay and lesbian experience.

A few other comments: I spent a year and a half researching and writing this book, beginning in the winter of 1987 and extending into the summer of 1988. I have interspersed my own experiences throughout, but primarily the book is about people I met as I traveled through the country. I made contact with some people I interviewed through gay organizations, others were referred to me along the way, still others I met through my own friends. Whenever possible, I have tried to use real names. However, I did believe it was important to tell the stories of individuals who, for whatever reasons, did not feel comfortable making their identities public. In cases where I have not used real names, I have indicated such by a pseudonymous first name only.

Above all, I have tried to be true to the experiences of the men and women I met. I make no claims to a definitive view. I talked to a wide range of people in different parts of the country and record their stories here in the hopes of offering a modest glimpse into the lives of some gay men and women twenty years after the beginning of the gay liberation movement. As much as I attempted to organize their stories into thematic categories, what I was left with in the end was simply the astonishing richness of individual lives.

Somerville, Massachusetts
September 1988

FARMERS,
COAL MINERS,
AND SMALL TOWNS

▼　▼　▼　▼　▼　▼　▼　▼　▼　▼　▼　▼　▼

SELMA, ALABAMA (POPULATION 26,684)

The dogwoods were in lush flower, and Jill and I were sitting on her front porch, drinking Dr. Pepper and greeting the neighbors as they walked by. "How y'all doing?" she asked, in an Alabama drawl. I nodded and smiled politely, reluctant to break the spell with my Yankee accent. It was a balmy Sunday afternoon in late March, when the rest of the country was just emerging from the depths of winter, and Selma seemed like some romantic dream of Southern small-town peace and comfort and congeniality. That impression persisted even as Jill and I lingered, in full view of passersby, chatting about what it was like to be a lesbian in Selma, Alabama.

Small towns and homosexuals are not supposed to fit quite so pleasantly and easily as they seemed to on that Alabama Sunday. In his 1971 memoir, *On Being Different*, the novelist and editor Merle Miller wrote, with only "slight exaggeration," that he had started packing to leave his birthplace, Marshalltown, Iowa, when he was two years old. For a gay person in a small town there were only two options, he believed: "Either they ran you out of town or you left before they got around to it." With a few exceptions—resorts that cater to gays like Provincetown, Massachusetts, and Key West, Florida, or liberal college towns like Northampton, Massachusetts, or Boulder, Colorado—gays and lesbians in smaller communities have rarely been open about their sexuality, let alone organized in ways that give them some visibility. Like Merle Miller, most homosexuals who grew up in the hinterlands believed they had to exile themselves to the urban centers if they wanted to live openly, or even discreetly, as gay people. Main Street was simply off-limits, except for brief visits home for birthdays, weddings, and funerals.

I grew up in a Hudson River town of about thirty thousand and assumed that once I graduated from high school I had no alternative but to leave and never look back. In the fifties and sixties, Kingston, New York, was dull and stifling, dominated by the Dutch Reformed church and the Republican party. (The imposing building that housed the Republican headquarters was appropriately nicknamed "the Kremlin.") My family was Jewish, and I was the only student out of twenty-eight in my sixth-grade class to vote for Stevenson over Eisenhower in the mock presidential poll held at my elementary school. By the time I reached adolescence, I was sure that life was elsewhere and that people who read books and went to the theatre and had "interesting" conversations (and didn't vote a straight Republican ticket) were elsewhere, too. Although I was quite unaware that I was gay at the time, some nascent idea of my sexuality clearly played a role in my conviction that I had to get out.

Nonetheless, like many Americans who grew up in the provinces and migrated to big cities, I have always harbored a secret fantasy to live my adult life over again among those tree-lined streets and people who seemed to accept you, not for any particular virtue or achievement, but just because you were born there and had always lived among them. Especially when life isn't going well, I long to hear once again the faint, soothing sounds of the cheering crowds watching baseball games on warm summer nights in Dietz Stadium, sounds that I could hear from my bedroom window and that have always defined for me the safety and comfort of my small-town boyhood.

So when I began my travels, I started in small communities, partly out of nostalgia, perhaps, but mainly because small towns are the building blocks of American society, where our values are formed, where the ephemeral notions—and the great social experiments—of the big cities are last to take root, if they take root at all. The anonymity of large cities has always been viewed as the precondition for an open and satisfactory gay life. If gays could make a life for themselves in the intimate atmosphere of smaller communities and be accepted as openly gay people there, I thought that the revolution would practically be won.

Selma is not just any small town. Its name meant something to almost everyone alive in 1965 when Lyndon Johnson called the voting rights marches there "a turning point in man's search for freedom" comparable to the events at Lexington, Concord, and Appomattox. The civil rights movement did not begin in Selma, of course. But the events there were some of the most visible manifestations of a whole new way of thinking: that minority groups could take the fight for freedom into their own hands. It was an approach to social change that led, within a few years, to the Stonewall riots and to the emergence of the last of the great causes of the sixties—the movement for gay liberation and gay and lesbian rights.

In Selma, symbols of the struggle for social justice are very much alive. The humpbacked Edmund Pettus Bridge over the Alabama River, where Martin Luther King's followers began the famous march from Selma to Montgomery (and where they were set upon by the Alabama National Guard), still stands. So does Brown's Chapel, with its twin red brick steeples, where Dr. King rallied his forces and mapped strategy. More than twenty years after the march, the street in front of Brown's Chapel had been renamed after Dr. King, and Dallas County voters had actually elected the first black county official since Reconstruction. Still, at the time I visited, no blacks had ever served on the county commission, in a county that is fifty-five percent black. Selma had its white and black sides of town, and Jill, my lesbian friend, claimed that whites stood out in front of at least one local church on Sunday mornings to prevent black folks from coming in to worship.

Some degree of racial progress has come to Selma, symbol of black aspirations and white intransigence. But gay liberation has hardly come at all. No gay-rights marchers have made their journey over the Edmund Pettus Bridge. Not one brave soul has ever stood up publicly and proclaimed, "I'm gay and I'm proud and I live here, too." In fact, singer Anita Bryant—a symbol of hostility to civil rights for homosexuals—actually came to live in Selma in the early eighties. That Bryant was received with open arms by the city's first families, who flocked to the elegant dress shop she opened here, is an indication of how people feel about gays in Selma. Bryant has since moved on, but the cause she fought for so passionately in Miami—that homosexuals should remain in the closet—is, I was to discover, an article of faith in Selma, Alabama. An article of faith, not the least among the town's homosexuals.

My image of Selma came from the newsreels of the sixties: of blood on the streets, of state troopers with night sticks and bullwhips assaulting civil rights marchers, of tear gas and a sheriff who wore a button that said "NEVER." The historian Howard Zinn, in his book *SNCC: The New Abolitionists*, wrote that Selma in 1964 looked "as if a movie producer had reconstructed a pre–Civil War Southern town—the decaying buildings, the muddy streets, the little cafes, and the huge red brick Hotel Albert, modelled after a medieval Venetian palace."

When friends I was staying with in Birmingham had said that Selma was "beautiful," that the town had just restored the Center for the Performing Arts, and that I should think about going there, even if just to see the sights, I was skeptical. "Selma, *Alabama!*" I exclaimed, just a bit rudely. They turned out to be right. Selma—white residential Selma, at least—is unexpectedly lovely. The city's "historic district" is an architectural gem—block after block of restored Victorian and antebellum homes, with towering water oaks and a profusion of the white, and red, and yellow flowering trees of early spring.

I had telephoned Jill, a former college classmate of one of my Birmingham hosts, and she had promised to gather a group of gay folks for me to talk with when I came through Selma. On my arrival, though, I discovered she had been overly optimistic. No one was willing to meet with me, she said, despite pledges of anonymity she had proferred on my behalf. Black Selma might as well have been a million miles away; she didn't know any gay people there. As for Jill herself, she would agree to be interviewed only if I changed her name, disguised her living situation, was vague about her work, and made no mention of any civic activities that might identify her. So my view of Selma, and my introduction to gay small-town America, became what I saw from one woman's front porch.

Jill was a spirited woman in her early forties with a warm, down-to-earth quality and a turn of phrase so folksy you'd think she must stay awake nights practicing Southern colloquialisms. She worked in Montgomery, the state capital an hour or so to the east, and lived in an old house she was still in the process of restoring. What I remember most about the house were its high ceilings and that it was crammed with books, mostly novels. (Her favorite author seemed to be Rita Mae Brown.)

Like the other gay people she knew in Selma, Jill was in the closet. None of her neighbors were aware she was a lesbian, except the woman who was her best friend. She hadn't told anyone at her job, and she had never set foot in the gay bar in Montgomery, out of fear of exposure. Nonetheless, her life sounded like the height of liberation compared with that of the gay men in Selma. All but one of the seven or eight gay men she was acquainted with had wives and, in most cases, children. In contrast, none of the three or four gay women Jill knew were married, and Jill herself had never felt she had to date men in order to cover up her sexuality. In Selma, it was easy to fit into the role of the unmarried Southern lady. Fitting into the role of unmarried Southern gentleman was apparently a more difficult proposition.

There were no gay bars in Selma, no gay, lesbian, or feminist groups, and no gathering place except Skeeters, the bar in Montgomery, fifty-eight miles away. "I'm not sure there could ever be a place here in Selma," said Jill. "Maybe I am wrong about that. Maybe it is paranoia. But I think it would not be tolerated."

Still, most of the white gay people in Selma that Jill was acquainted with knew one another. Although they were not a close-knit bunch, on occasion they had gone out together for a drink or dinner. Even in a town like Selma, gays have an uncanny ability to make contact. "You know the expression, 'It takes one to know one'?" asked Jill. "You just *know*, and once other gay people realize you are gay, they will make comments and you get to talking and they tell you things." But all this was terribly discreet. "It is not like the gay grapevine here because people are so far back in the closet, they are back behind several racks of clothes," she said. "Maybe underneath the shoes."

I suspected that one of the reasons that gay life was so far back behind those racks of clothes was because Selma remained dominated by old families. The New South with its managerial class and its migrants from other parts of the country had never arrived in significant numbers; Dallas County, of which Selma is the county seat, had one of the highest unemployment rates in the state of Alabama. Unlike Jill, who had lived in Selma for only twenty years (which meant little in a town where being a "local" was measured in generations), most of the married gay men were born and grew up in Selma. "Everyone in town knows their mommas, their daddies, their grandmommas," Jill observed. "Some of them have families that dug the river" (her favored expression to describe families who had lived in the town since before the Civil War).

In the interconnected and inbred world of white Selma, for gay men "having a wife and children or at least a wife is the only way to survive," Jill maintained. The men did have affairs with others of the same sex, she said, but "mostly under cover of darkness." In such an atmosphere, it was hard to imagine any gay relationships that would possess affirming qualities beyond the relief of sexual tension. "One gay man I know is extremely guilt-ridden," she said. "He absolutely craves doing it but he is so guilt-ridden it may not be worth it." Two men she was acquainted with, both prominent local business-men, had an affair, which had since ended. Their families were still friends and got together socially. Even if some people in town who knew about them might snicker, the same advantages of birth and social position that pre-sented these men no alternatives but to marry and to express their sexual feelings clandestinely protected their community standing. "Because they were raised here, because their mommas are known, and because their families have been here forever, it makes it different," she said. "I don't think anyone is going to walk up to these men and say, 'I know you had an affair with thus and such.'"

She paused and went inside the house to bring us another round of Dr. Pepper, leaving me in charge of greeting passersby. I just smiled and nodded politely and kept my mouth shut until she returned. "You know it is so hard to explain about living in a place like Selma," Jill continued. "It is so different from Birmingham or Montgomery or Tallahassee. People here love to gossip, as I'm sure they do elsewhere, but it is more obvious here because there are fewer people to gossip about and fewer people to hear it. So if there is a scandal in town, everybody knows about it. And if they don't know the true story, they will add a little something to it, make it up as they go along. That is one thing I don't like about Selma."

We talked some more and then Jill took me for a walk through the old section of town. We passed the Center for the Performing Arts, a splendid, if somewhat gloomy, example of brick Victoriana; Sturdivant Hall, the antebellum mansion that looked as if it should have a mile-long driveway of oaks leading up to it; and the nineteenth-century house where the movie version of Carson McCullers's *The Heart Is a Lonely Hunter* was filmed.

As we wandered through the town, Jill began to relate something of her own life. She had grown up in Birmingham and came to Selma shortly after graduating from college. A college friend lived in Selma, but her real reason for moving was to get away from her mother. She was convinced—and remained so today—that her mother could never accept her homosexuality. "I see her being dead on the floor, if I ever said to her, 'Guess what, mama, you've raised a queer.'" While Jill admitted she could be freer if she lived in Birmingham, with its Sunday evening lesbian potlucks, its women's bar and women's music production company, and its alternative bookstore, all those advantages took second place to the complexities of her relationship with her mother. "I would be worried that every five minutes, mama was going to turn up," she said.

Nonetheless, most of Jill's social life revolved around Birmingham, a couple of hours drive north by back roads through dense pine forests. She went there for an occasional women's music concert or just to visit friends. In that respect, her life was probably quite different than it would have been twenty years ago when the gay and lesbian community in Birmingham wasn't unlike that of Selma today. Access to a relatively open community like Birmingham clearly relieved some of the pressure of living in a closed one like Selma.

Jill told me that recently she had been romantically involved with a woman in Birmingham, a relationship that meant even more frequent commuting. She had no compunctions about bringing her friend to Selma for occasional weekends, though, feeling perfectly free to go out walking or to dinner together. And she insisted that if the opportunity arose she would be willing to have a lover move in with her, as long as they kept it quiet. "People might talk and people might wonder but I don't think there would be problems," she said. There was one lesbian couple in town, she noted, although they would deny it if asked; people knew, but she doubted anyone had put the question directly to them.

I asked her what would happen, though, if she were vocal about being a lesbian or if an openly gay male couple moved to town. That would be quite a different story. "Folks here in town would rather embrace blacks than embrace gays," she said flatly. "If someone was open about being gay, they would find themselves ostracized. People would probably sell them groceries, but then we have some chain stores here and they probably would sell to anyone! But as far as being invited places, or having much social to do in town, I think if they lived openly as a gay couple they would not."

Still, it would take someone "real special" to persuade Jill to move away from Selma, to leave the house she had renovated so lovingly, to give up the civic activities she participated in and the slow pace of life and atmosphere of friendliness she enjoyed. "I really like living in Selma," she said. "You know people. Folks ride by and wave at you when you are sitting on your porch. I like being involved in community things here. It is easy for me to do that in a small town. It would be harder for me to get involved in a place like Birmingham."

As we headed back to Jill's house, we stopped by Mallory Alley Wardrobe Inc., the dress shop that Anita Bryant had opened in an old clapboard house on a side street and in which she is still said to have an economic interest. A woman in a long dress was sweeping the front steps, and Jill inquired if we could come in for a look. But it was Sunday and the place was closed; Anita Bryant is, above all, a God-fearing woman (and Selma does have blue laws). "Y'all be sure and come back tomorrow though," the woman in the long dress called after us, flashing a big smile, and we went on our way.

One of the major ironies of living in Selma as a gay person has been the influence of Anita Bryant on the town. Jill was always ready to poke fun at her former neighbor, repeating Bryant's comments about how she feared "hordes of militant homosexuals" would follow her to Selma and camp out on her doorstep. Shortly after Bryant arrived, Jill had spent an afternoon on the porch of a friend who lived down the street from the Mallory Alley Wardrobe. "I was excited, I was revved up. I was ready to go," she laughed. "But not a 'horde' did I see."

In small towns, the personal connection usually wins out in the end, and Jill defended Bryant's influence on Selma. "Let me say this," she said of the singer and former beauty queen, whom she has met socially on a number of occasions. "She has raised money for the performing arts center. She did a number of benefit concerts here. For as badly as I hate her politics, she has done some good. I hate like hell to say so, but it is true."

The fact that Anita Bryant, that arch-proponent of gay invisibility, had done as much as anyone to change the quality of one lesbian's life for the better speaks volumes about being gay in Selma, Alabama. As I sat on Jill's front porch on a Sunday afternoon, I felt I had put my face up to a window on the gay past. For if times had changed for gay people in small-town America, there was little indication of it in Selma. And as pleasant and as relaxed as it seemed on that Sunday afternoon, I was eager to get into my car and follow the freedom highway north, to search for other smaller communities, less rich in charm and symbolism than Selma perhaps, but where life for gays and lesbians might be fuller and more open.

BUNCETON, MISSOURI (POPULATION 418)

n Bunceton, Missouri, I thought I had found such a place. Gerald E. "Gene" Ulrich, the town's openly gay mayor, was showing me around the storefront on Main Street, up from the feed elevator and down from the funeral home, that serves as Bunceton's city hall. The walls were covered with cheap panelling, the floor was linoleum, and the furniture consisted of a desk, a few metal chairs, a file cabinet, and a folding table for meetings. Water and sewer maps were piled in a heap on a small table near the door.

The mayor led me to the storeroom in the back where a little metal jail stands. It was a cage really, with a steel floor, a toilet, and enough space for one person. The jail was surrounded by cartons stacked on top of one another, as well as a huge stuffed Santa Claus and a pile of fake wreaths dug out every December to bring the Christmas spirit to Main Street. "People are not afraid of going to jail because they know we don't want to remove the junk," the mayor laughed.

The jail hadn't been used in years. In fact, since Gene became mayor in

1980, the city marshall had given out a grand total of two tickets, one for speeding and another to a resident for not keeping up his property. That's the kind of town Bunceton is—where farmers wearing caps and overalls sit on the front steps of the insurance agency on Saturday mornings talking about crops and the weather, where the bulletin board in the bank advertises the pit barbecue the Masons are putting on and the Harvest Festival at the United Church of Christ, where the lowing of cows and the barking of dogs are heard more frequently on Main Street than the sound of passing cars. Bunceton is a poor farming community that reflects the depressed economic state of much of rural America. At one time, it was a major shipping point for livestock, but it went into a decline when the trains stopped coming in 1937. The city's population had fallen from 1,000 in the fifties to 418 today—mostly farmers and retirees and folks who work in nearby factories.

What is notable about Bunceton is that the farmers and retirees and factory workers elected Gene Ulrich (pronounced Yulrick) as their mayor in 1980 and continued to reelect him by overwhelming majorities (an eighty-eight to six vote in one race). Gene is gay, and the citizenry knew it when they first elected him; if that fact was lost on anyone at the time, they certainly know it now. They vote for him despite the kind of publicity that this small town, like most small towns, would rather avoid—articles about its mayor in the *St. Louis Post-Dispatch* and the *San Francisco Chronicle*, even a few minutes on the ABC News program "Nightline." When I visited him, Gene was comfortably ensconced in the midst of his fourth two-year term and was preparing for his fifth race, the longest-serving openly gay mayor in America.

I had heard that Bunceton had a gay mayor, but I wasn't sure of his name. Before I left Boston, I put in a call to Bunceton City Hall, luckily hitting one of the ten days each month when someone is there so folks can come in and pay their water and tax bills. I asked for the mayor, and whoever answered the phone gave me Vic Williams's home telephone number. "Vic isn't home right now," I was told. "His wife, June, will answer, though. She's the town collector." I hung up, figuring something was wrong. Then, I recalled that whoever had told me about the gay mayor of Bunceton had mentioned that he owned the town florist shop. I called back and asked to speak to "the guy who owns the florist shop who used to be mayor." That was how I reached Gene Ulrich, who had never run a florist shop (that was apparently just someone's stereotype of gay small-town life that I had accepted without question) and was still very much the mayor. I never quite understood the mix-up, but it made Bunceton seem appealing. You could call City Hall and get the mayor's home number. When I finally did reach him, Gene sounded friendly and told me to come down to Bunceton and stay with him and his lover, Larry, as long as I liked. His sister, Mary Lou Craig, was a lesbian, and she and her lover lived in Bunceton, too. He was sure they would be happy to talk with me, too.

The easiest way to get to Bunceton is to follow Interstate 70 west from St. Louis for a couple of hours and turn south just past Columbia, where the University of Missouri is located. I found the interstate extraordinarily ugly and congested. So I got off at the first opportunity and took a meandering route through the wine country along the Missouri River to Jefferson City, the tidy state capital with its famous Thomas Hart Benton murals on the inside of the state house. A road sign announced that this was Lewis and Clark's route, and I took it as an omen of sorts. In my grandest moments, I fancied myself an explorer searching for worlds that were, if not exactly undiscovered, at least obscure.

West of "Jeff City," as the locals call it, the vineyards vanish. The landscape turns into rolling hills and green pastures, fields of corn, wheat, and soybeans, with nary a farmhouse to be seen. Along Missouri Highway 5 and the blacktopped Cooper County Highway B, I began to feel as if I had entered a perfectly preserved piece of rural America, sealed off from the outside world. Then, at last, there was Bunceton, the silver water tower and the high school (home of the Bunceton Dragons) perched on the hill off to the right.

Bunceton has one main street, and a *St. Louis Post-Dispatch* reporter once calculated that it took exactly thirty seconds to drive from one end to the other. The sidewalks are poured concrete and are raised high above the street in the old-fashioned manner; the buildings are one- and two-story brick and whitewashed structures, a few with ornate carved roofs left over from the turn of the century. There is the G and H General Store (with its own Dairy Queen machine), an antiques store (which seemed to sell mostly rakes and shovels), a beauty shop, a bank, a post office, a plumbing and heating supply store, a doctor's office, an insurance agency, and city hall. Residential neighborhoods lie on either side of Main Street — on the right, sloping up the hill as you enter Bunceton, is the white side of town; on the left the population is mostly black, although that is where Gene Ulrich and Larry live.

I had expected the mayor to be dignified and courtly, wearing a seersucker suit, perhaps a broad-brimmed hat. Gene Ulrich was not cut from that romantic cloth, however. When I pulled into the driveway of his modest, one-story bungalow just off Main Street, Gene greeted me, dressed only in a pair of shorts. (It was a particularly hot day and must have been ninety-five degrees inside.) Gene had had the house built for his parents in the early seventies. There was an American eagle over the outside door and a large backyard with maple and apple trees. The first thing you saw as you entered the living room was a piano with two hymnals on the music stand, flanked by a painting of Gene's deceased Siamese cat, grey against an electric blue background. Off to the left was a console TV over which hung a large framed picture of Jesus. Gay culture was represented by Michelangelo's David, three feet high, on the floor by the kitchen door and a copy of *Gentlemen's Quarterly* on the coffee table.

Gene was forty-three and looked younger—tall, thin, with a mustache and a head of grey curly hair that had been allowed to grow out in all directions. He had a deep Missouri twang and the relaxed, down-to-earth manner one expects in a small-town politician. He had a kind of rural eloquence, as well, and opinions on every subject under the sun—from aid to the Contras to nuclear power to the problems of Bunceton's water and sewage systems.

Larry, his lover of fifteen years, was in the kitchen when I arrived, putting together a spaghetti dinner. He was the household chef. Larry told me that on the nights when he works and doesn't make it home for dinner, Gene won't prepare anything that doesn't come out of a can. A sandy-haired, slightly out-of-shape ex-marine, Larry worked in the composing room of the daily newspaper in nearby Boonville. My strongest impression was one of him slumped in a chair in the living room, watching wrestling matches on TV and trying to get a jump on his Christmas presents by knitting an afghan.

That weekend, Larry found himself preparing meals for more houseguests than he had expected. A friend of Gene's, a man who had once been his lover (I was told he was bisexual) and whom Gene hadn't seen in twelve years, had shown up unexpectedly a few hours before I arrived. He had been living in Florida and had been in prison for unexplained reasons; his chest and arms were covered with tattoos. He was considering moving back to the Bunceton area and was somewhat astonished to see that his old buddy was now the mayor. Gene was delighted that he had come. Back in 1972, he had talked Gene into placing a personal ad in the *Advocate*, the national gay publication. Gene met Larry through the ad. That alone made this man an important figure in Gene's life.

His friend's arrival meant the mayor wasn't able to offer me his undivided attention, but he was eager to take me on an "official tour" of Bunceton the morning of my second day in town. In his blue polo shirt, dark blue bermuda shorts, and sunglasses, Gene cut an odd figure among the farmers in their caps and overalls we passed on the side of the road. We drove up to the Masonic Cemetery, a well-tended spot on a hill just above the town, with exotic cigar trees and a panoramic view of the surrounding countryside. Gene's mother and father are buried there. When we arrived, Vic Williams, the town marshall, and a younger man were cutting away at the peonies. Gene chatted amiably with them about the condition of the cemetery and the unseasonably warm weather and kidded the young man about his upcoming marriage.

He showed me one of his major accomplishments as mayor—a five-acre city park on the outskirts of Bunceton, well-equipped with swings, slides, benches, and a pavilion. Gene's name will appear on a plaque to be erected on the site. Making the park a reality took some political skill, Gene assured me. "You can't come into these small towns and change them overnight," he said, a reference to his predecessor as mayor, who became irritated at public opposition to his plans for revitalizing Bunceton. "You have to make these changes gradually, and you have to make them so they don't involve changing the place physically. Small towns like things to stay the way they were one hundred years ago." He explained there had once been a park on the spot, but in recent years the property had been owned by the Bunceton Bridle and Saddle Club, a group of farmers who had neglected it. Vandalism had occurred over the years and the only thing that had remained was the shelter. Gene persuaded the farmers to donate the acreage to the city and established a five-person park commission ("my park board" as he referred to it) to run it. "This is the first time the city has grown in area in ninety-seven years," he said proudly.

Next, we visited Gwen Wright, a sixty-two year old black woman and Bunceton native. She had been an unsuccessful candidate for the city council a few years back and was one of Gene's closest friends. Gwen was a lively woman with a wry sense of humor, despite her recent back and cancer surgery and the death of her husband nine years ago. She informed us she had spent most of the morning making wine and apologized if she smelled like one of the local taverns. She and Gene occupied themselves by listing the black families who had remained in town—Gwen and Alberta, Debbie, Millie, Juanita, Frankie, Helen, the Roland family, Mr. Young (he moved back from the city), Kay Hopkins (Marilyn Hopkins's sister), and on and on. Gwen adored Gene. "He is the tops," she said. "The other mayors said they would do things for the black side of town, but they never did. Anything that has ever been done on the black side of Bunceton, Gene did since he was mayor. New water lines, fixed all the houses, tore all the raggedy ones down. I am living in a mansion now," she assured me and shook with laughter.

It wasn't until late in the day that I finally got Gene to tell me something of his background. He was born in central Illinois in 1944, the son of a farm laborer who settled in Cooper County, which includes Bunceton, when Gene was seven. While he was growing up, the family lived on farms and in towns with archetypal American names like Prairie Home and Boonville, where his mother ran bars and restaurants. The family moved into Bunceton proper in 1964, when Gene was twenty. His sister Mary Lou would later tell me that as a boy "Gene never brought books home to study. He didn't have to. He was brilliant. And he could squeeze a buffalo nickel until it yelled. He was that good with money." When his father became disabled and the family was forced to go on welfare, Gene dropped out of high school to help support them. For two or three years he worked ten-hour days as a farm laborer, making fifty cents an hour.

Long hours and low wages drove him off the farm and into the factory, first at the Bobbin Manufacturing Company, which manufactures shoe heels, where he worked for nineteen years, making his way from the assembly line to foreman. At the time of my visit, he was the plant supervisor at a small company that made industrial sponges in nearby Sedalia. "Moonlighting" is something a mayor of Bunceton has no choice but to do; the job pays exactly three dollars a year.

For Gene, coming to terms with his sexuality was apparently not very difficult even in rural Missouri. He realized he was attracted to other boys as early as age twelve and dated girls throughout high school and into his twenties, although he had affairs with men on the side. He related that as he was going off to his draft physical, his mother advised him, "There is a box you can check to avoid the draft." When he saw the box marked "homosexuality" on the military form, he understood. "It reached out like someone had slapped me," he recalled. "Mom knows." Gene didn't check the box, despite his mother's advice, and went off to Vietnam. By the time he put that personal ad in the *Advocate* and received a response from Larry, Gene was back working at Bobbin and living in Bunceton. Larry was running a beauty shop in Springfield, Missouri. The two began to correspond, met on Labor Day 1972, and Larry moved in with Gene in Bunceton a month later.

Gene and Larry's life wasn't very different from that of their neighbors. Like almost everyone else in Bunceton, their days revolved around work, the TV (which seemed to be on from morning to night), and church (Gene was active in a struggling gay church in Columbia, and Larry attended a Methodist Church in Boonville).

And like most of their neighbors, Gene and Larry were married, joined in "holy union" by the minister of a gay church in Oklahoma City a few months after they met. Gene and Larry's was the first of several gay marriages I was to encounter in the heartland, a phenomenon rarely found in larger cities, perhaps because the pressure to fit in is not as strong there. "My mother had pounded a lot of religion into us as kids and I wanted the Lord's blessing on our relationship," Gene told me. Gene believed that marriage has much to do with the longevity of their relationship, even though gay unions had no legal standing in Missouri or anywhere else in the United States. "I am a religious person myself and I believe anything that is blessed by the Lord has to work," he said. "We have gotten along together real well for fifteen years and we will spend the rest of our lives together."

And like most of his neighbors, Gene wouldn't consider living anywhere except Bunceton or one of the nearby towns. "A lot of people would say it is boring here," he admitted. "But I like it. I like the peace and quiet. I have no desire to live in a bigger city. Now, Larry likes big cities. He likes Springfield (population 133,000). If I could ever live in a big city, Springfield would probably be the one because it is so clean. But I have no desire to live in a big city." Urban life, he suspected, "may have a lot to do with relationships breaking up. You have more opportunities for people to go astray. Maybe that is another thing that has helped our relationship, because we are pretty much to ourselves here."

Except for membership in the Lion's Club, Gene had never really been involved in civic affairs until 1980. That year the incumbent mayor, a school teacher named Ralph Bowman, announced he was leaving town and would not seek another term. In his statement of withdrawal, he made several remarks suggesting that Bunceton was hostile to progress, comments Gene saw as derogatory to the city. So Gene decided to jump into the race. "I saw things were not getting done," he said. "I wanted to look after the elderly. I wanted do something for the black community, which was very neglected. I saw my opportunity to change things, to get involved."

A few days before the April 1 election, Bowman changed his mind and entered the race as a write-in candidate. He defeated Gene sixty-four to forty-six. But Bowman had made a crucial error. Even as a write-in candidate, he was required to file his candidacy by five P.M. the Friday before the Tuesday election, and he had neglected to do so. As a result, Gene Ulrich was elected mayor of Bunceton on a technicality. He had spent less than fifty dollars on his campaign. "What was really ironic was that I knew nothing about that law," said Gene. "The city marshall and the county clerk could have covered it up, and I would never have known."

Gene claimed that his first opponent had told him, "If you get elected, half the council will resign." That never happened, but the role the gay issue played in that first race isn't entirely clear. What is clear is that Gene and Larry had been together for eight years at that point, and most of the townsfolk knew of the nature of their relationship. "Of course, we don't walk down the street holding hands or kiss in public," Gene said. "I don't believe in that. I don't believe straight people should do that either. That is the way I was raised. But where you saw one of us, you usually saw both of us. So everyone I'm sure was aware of the situation."

Shortly after he was declared the winner, a reporter for the *Missourian*, the University of Missouri student newspaper in Columbia, thirty-five miles away, found out he was gay and asked to interview him. The *Missourian*, which is distributed outside the campus like any standard daily, had been tipped off by someone from Gene's church. Gene agreed to the interview, on the assumption that the newspaper wouldn't circulate outside of Columbia. But the day the *Missourian* ran the story headlined "Bunceton Citizens Elect Mayor Who Is a Respected Homosexual," the paper decided to do one of its periodic drop-offs in nearby communities. Bunceton was one of them, and its citizenry realized for the first time that the governing of their seemingly inconsequential municipality was of wider interest than they had imagined.

Media coverage grew. Gene was featured on a "Nightline" segment about gays in politics, and national reporters were jamming microphones in front of people's faces on Main Street asking them what they thought about their mayor's sexual orientation. The Baptist minister in Bunceton was interviewed on "Nightline," saying some unflattering things about Gene's "lifestyle," but most everyone else was positive—at least publicly.

Gene remembered the Wednesday night he appeared on national TV: "Larry and I would always drive to Columbia on Wednesday nights for Bible study. That night, our local station made a remark at the end of their news— 'Stay tuned, as one of our local communities is being aired on national TV.' Usually, when we came home from Bible study, the town would be dark, most everyone would be asleep. That night every house had light on."

Gene was worried, but while neighbors may have shaken their heads in dismay after watching the show, no one directed any criticism to him personally. He said the only negative reaction came from one local man who called the ABC affiliate in Columbia, demanding to be interviewed. The man asserted that the sole reason Gene was elected was because of support from the black community. But when the station sent a black reporter to interview him, the man backed off and wouldn't talk.

In the election that followed, Gene was reelected by a two-to-one majority over a candidate who had been born and raised in Bunceton and was "kin to half the town," in Gene's words. "They could have ousted me then," he said of that second race. He added, "I can't say that people here are liberal, I can't say they are broad-minded. I am sure the town didn't like all that publicity. But they didn't say anything; they sat back to see what I would do. After I was elected the first time, their attitude was 'He is doing good, leave him in there.'" In 1984, Gene won a third term by an eighty-eight to six vote, and in

1986 was elected to a fourth term by eighty-eight to fifty-six over a candidate who said in an interview that Gene was doing a good job but needed some competition.

My impression was that Gene had indeed been doing a good job for Bunceton. He took credit for a number of accomplishments: the elderly housing project on the edge of Main Street, the block grant for $263,000 to revitalize the black side of town, a new well, water lines, a truck for the fire department, cable television, and that new city park. He managed to use his position to keep potential opponents off balance, appointing the Baptist minister (the successor to the one who criticized him on "Nightline") to the park board, for example. "The minister is very friendly," said Gene. "I am sure in the back of his mind he believes what the Baptists believe. But that doesn't interfere with him volunteering or accepting any position I give him."

One thing Gene hadn't done was to raise gay issues in Bunceton. He never proposed a gay-rights law, for instance, claiming the city's very broad anti-discrimination ordinance was sufficient. When he was asked to testify on behalf of a gay-rights proposal in Columbia, he declined, saying "It is not my right to tell Columbia people how to run their town." He favored the ordinance, he told me, but thought too much of an issue was made of it, with "newspapers and TV involved and the staunch Baptist preachers upset. I think a lot of things can be done quicker and a lot easier with a lot less hoopla."

All in all, the consensus was that Gene was the first mayor of Bunceton in years to have taken the job seriously and, above all, to have produced results. That explained the overwhelming majorities he was able to pile up each election. In the "Show Me State," he had done just that.

Nonetheless, I didn't get the feeling that Gene was "Mr. Bunceton." He didn't glad-hand his way down Main Street; people weren't rushing up to him with this question or that problem. Maybe that's not how things are done in Bunceton. But I speculated that perhaps he was viewed more as politically essential than personally popular, and that the fact that Bunceton had been in a state of economic decline for years might have been a major factor in the town's support of Gene. Bunceton badly needed leadership and vision and was willing to accept it from whatever quarter.

I soon found out that the election and reelection of a gay mayor was no indication that Bunceton was any beacon of tolerance towards homosexuals. Nor did it signify a change in the views of many of Bunceton's citizens towards gay people in general, especially those who didn't grow up in Cooper County, Missouri, as Gene had. "There are still a lot of prejudiced people in Bunceton," said Walter, a gay man who moved to town a few years earlier and discovered that fact first hand.

Walter grew up in a small town northeast of Columbia, went off to Chicago to live, and then returned home to take care of his ailing father. He now worked as a financial counsellor at a hospital in Columbia. He met Gene at the gay church in Columbia, told him he was looking to buy a house, and Gene encouraged him to look in Bunceton. Three years ago, when he was in his mid-thirties, Walter bought a one-story Victorian house on Main Street for four thousand dollars. He had been remodeling it room by room, sanding floors and stripping woodwork, painting, wallpapering, filling the house with the antiques he had collected over the years. When I came to visit, he had just finished an afternoon of home improvement and was still dressed in paint-spattered overalls.

Walter said that when he first moved to Bunceton he expected to find a town full of "open-minded, good-hearted people." After all, Bunceton had elected a gay man as mayor. Instead, he received harassing phone calls at night and was yelled at from passing cars. Eggs were thrown at his house. Someone lit a firecracker in the back of his car, destroying the seat.

When a friend of Walter's named Howard moved from Chicago and bought a house a couple of doors away, his reception was even less welcoming. According to Walter, the woman who sold the house to Howard found out after the fact that he was gay and tried to go back on the sale, even going before the city council to attempt to stop the deal. Then Howard started receiving harassing phone calls, too. Part of his problem may have stemmed from a genuine mix-up. At about the time Howard put down the money on his house, the minister of the gay church in Columbia was visiting Gene and Larry in Bunceton. The minister walked around town in his clerical collar, and rumors circulated that he was going to start a gay church in Bunceton. Townspeople apparently believed this man was Howard and that the house Howard had bought was going to become the church. Bunceton, they became convinced, was about to become a heartland San Francisco. It was a fear that proved unfounded: since Walter and Howard, no other open gays or lesbians have moved into town.

All this soured Walter on Bunceton. "I pictured a real friendly town," he told me bitterly. "I think it is friendly — to people who have lived here all their lives and to straight people from the outside." The harassment had died down, but Walter remained estranged from the town and was afraid he had sunk too much money into a house he might not be able to sell. I wondered if some of Walter's alienation might be self-inflicted. He did his banking in Columbia and food shopping in Boonville, which meant he hadn't gotten to know Bunceton very well and the townspeople hadn't gotten to know him. Neither side had had the chance to overcome suspicions and preconceived notions.

Another source of Walter's unhappiness was his inability to find a lover. He was involved with the gay student group at the University of Missouri in Columbia and went to the gay bars there — in search of a monogamous relationship, he said. But he hadn't found one yet, complaining that the people he met in the college town tended to be too young, too transient. His friend, Howard, was his main source of support, and, although Walter was friendlier with some of the neighbors now, Bunceton remained the focus of much of his discontent. "I wish I had bought a house outside of town, maybe on a farm, away from gossipy neighbors," he confided.

My talk with Gene's sister, Mary Lou Craig, and her lover, Nancy Sloan, revealed another side to Bunceton, as well. At forty-one, Mary Lou had a thin, lined mountain face. She wore her hair slicked all the way back, and was dressed in a work shirt, slacks, and cowboy boots. A large crucifix dangled from her neck, and she wore a leather belt with a big silver buckle. She was, to say the least, vibrant — the kind of person who is delightful in small doses, undoubtedly exhausting in larger ones. Because of a deteriorated disc, Mary Lou didn't work, except for mowing lawns and delivering papers (she told me she had been named Newspaper Carrier of the Year). She was married twice before she settled down with Nancy. Her brother claimed she had only worn a dress twice in her life, "once at Dad's funeral, once at her first wedding. Maybe she wore one at her second wedding but I'm not sure."

Her forty-seven year old lover, Nancy, seemed her opposite—large, sub-dued, dressed without flamboyance in a yellow baseball jersey, checked trousers, and sneakers. She worked driving Mary Lou on her paper route and doing odd jobs. Nancy grew up in California, was married twice (like Mary Lou), and had five children, all of whom lived with relatives in Nevada and California. Her family were fundamentalist Christians who had succeeded in preventing her from having much contact with her children. Nancy gave up custody of the children to her family at a time when she had a great many personal problems. "I could kick myself one hundred times over for giving up the children," she said. The loss of her children might have much to do with what I perceived as her somewhat downcast personality.

Nancy and Mary Lou met at a bar in Boonville, where Nancy had a job singing. The couple "tied the knot," as Mary Lou put it, in a ceremony on Valentine's Day 1982, in the gay church in Columbia. It was the third "marriage" for both of them.

Although the two women seemed quite comfortable in Bunceton, Mary Lou admitted there are some people "who look downwards on the gay situation," as demonstrated by the incident that had taken place the previous summer. Mary Lou, Nancy, and Gwen Wright, the heterosexual black woman who was Gene's good friend, had formed a musical threesome called the "Oriole Gang" and sang in "colored" churches. (Mary Lou always used the word *colored* instead of *black*.) As a result, Mary Lou and Nancy began attending services regularly at a black church in Bunceton. During one Sunday service, with no advance warning, the minister called Mary Lou and Nancy to the pulpit. They complied. Then, according to Mary Lou's account, he proceeded to lecture them in front of the congregation, condemning them for being lesbians, and imploring them to "Go and sin no more."

At that point, Mary Lou said she wished she had "run out the door and got a rock for the preacher to cast the first stone." Instead, she and Nancy seem to have stood there without saying a word. Mary Lou, the kind of person, I suspect, who doesn't like to admit very often that she is vulnerable, said the incident hurt. Describing the black church as "spirit-filled," she said, "That church was my home away from home." But small towns have an intimacy that outsiders can only find baffling, and a few months later the two women went back to the same church when another minister was preaching. Unbeknownst to them, the minister who had condemned them was sitting in the congregation. After the service, he came up and hugged them.

AIDS had been a main topic in Bunceton, according to Mary Lou, although there hadn't been any known cases there or in the surrounding towns. The previous summer, when Gene had a gall-bladder problem that the doctors had trouble diagnosing, the local gossip was that he had AIDS. Mary Lou and Nancy had received some of the AIDS backlash, even though lesbians are at minimal risk for the disease (only two or three cases of AIDS among lesbians had been documented nationwide at the time, and it was unclear if they in fact had been transmitted through lesbian sex). One of their neighbors warned people to stay away from them and not to drink out of the same glasses as they did. Despite the misinformation, AIDS education did not seem to be much of a local priority. Gene, who served as chapter chairman of the Cooper County Red Cross, said he sent letters to area schools offering information about AIDS, but no one expressed any interest.

By the time I had arrived in Bunceton, gossip about Gene had stopped (once his gall bladder was removed, he was fine). But that was not to say that AIDS rumors wouldn't surface again at some point in a town where talking about other people was a major occupation. And Walter described Bunceton's attitudes this way: "If I were to get AIDS, I'm sure the neighbors would burn this house down."

The mayor, of course, tried to put the best face on the difficulties of gay-straight relations in Bunceton. For gay people, Bunceton represented a "live and let live situation," he said. But clearly, growing up there and being coupled off in a domestic arrangement that resembled that of one's neighbors made it easier for gay people to be accepted. And I found it interesting that both Gene and Mary Lou seemed particularly close with the blacks in Bunceton, indicating they might unconsciously feel more affinity with another "out" group than with the town at large.

Being gay did put some constraints on Gene's political ambitions, a pattern I was to see repeated in other parts of the country. Although he was active on boards and in organizations outside of Bunceton, Gene had no illusions of aspiring to higher office. He had planned to run for state senator in 1988 but changed his mind. Finances were one consideration. But he also feared that his sexual orientation wouldn't play beyond the people who knew him well. "In a district election like that, I am sure there would be a lot of controversy," he said. "And the way candidates sling mud, I know there would be a candidate out there who would make an issue of my personal life." His ambition now stopped at another term as mayor of Bunceton, which, in fact, would make him the longest consecutively serving mayor in the city's history. (In April 1988, running unopposed, Gene was elected to his fifth term.)

In our final conversation, I asked Gene if he felt what he was doing had a significance beyond Bunceton. Did he, as the only openly gay mayor of an American small town, view himself as an example to other gay people? That wasn't the way he saw things. He had run for mayor of Bunceton, he emphasized, because he wanted to change the way the town was being managed, not because he was gay or wanted to make a statement to other gays and lesbians. It was true that the gay community in Columbia and across the state (he believed he was the only openly gay public official in Missouri) considered him a role model. "I don't think I'm that important," he said. "I am just a human being like anyone else. I am glad my tenure as mayor turned out the way it did. It is a very positive thing for the gay community to look at. But, as for being important, I don't look at it that way."

I didn't entirely agree. I thought that not only was Gene someone for other gays and lesbians in smaller places to look up to, but he was also a symbol of people's ability to overlook their prejudices when someone they might be disposed to dislike or dismiss had a positive impact on their daily lives. Nonetheless, Gene Ulrich's modesty and unpretentiousness were qualities I particularly liked about him. He was a person with a sense of his strengths and his limitations, without grandiose dreams of acting on a stage with more than 418 people on it. He was just the mayor of a small rural town and there he would stay as long as the voters wanted him. Perhaps his reduced expectations and ambitions were the trade-off for being openly gay in rural America. Still, it was a trade-off that seemed good for Bunceton and most likely, in the end, good for Gene.

MORGANTOWN, WEST VIRGINIA

(POPULATION 27,605)

was hanging around Morgantown hoping to meet a gay coal miner. Located a couple of hours' drive south of Pittsburgh, Morgantown is the home of West Virginia University. It is also at the center of one of the largest coal-producing counties in the state. A few months earlier, I had spent an afternoon in the town of Bluefield in the south of West Virginia. There, I had seen railroad flatcars brimming with coal, a line of cars that seemed to extend for miles.

The sight of all those coal cars captured my imagination. I had been reading *The Road to Wigan Pier*, George Orwell's account of his visit to the industrial north of England during the Great Depression. In that book, Orwell argued that coal was the very foundation of our civilization. "In the metabolism of the Western world the coal miner is second in importance only to the man who ploughs the soil," he wrote. Despite the development of other fossil fuels, the increasing mechanization of the mines, and the transformation of the United States and Western European nations into service economies, Orwell's observation was still largely true. As I viewed that line of coal cars outside Bluefield I felt as if I was peering into the engine room of some great ocean liner; on the upper decks everyone was playing bridge or shuffleboard or having an elegant dinner, but this made the whole thing work.

I wanted to spend time in West Virginia, to meet gay people who worked in the mines. But of all the places I was to visit on my travels, making contacts there proved the most challenging. It took several evenings of telephone calls from Boston, mostly to women's groups, before I reached someone gay, let alone someone gay who would agree to talk. I was finally given the name of a graduate student at West Virginia University (WVU) named Sarah. Not surprisingly, she lived in Morgantown, the university town and the only place in the state with much of a gay community. When I phoned her, she assured me she could introduce me to a number of gays and lesbians in Morgantown.

Did she know any gay coal miners? I asked. No one came to mind right away but she would ask around.

Set in the middle of steep hills and narrow valleys, hugging the banks of the Monongahela River, Morgantown is the America I assumed had vanished twenty years ago. From the town, you can see coal mines in the green hills above; just across the Monongahela are blue-collar suburbs where the miners live. My first impression of Morgantown was that it had the topography of San Francisco and the buildings (brick, circa 1880) of Worcester, Massachusetts. High Street, the main shopping street, climbs up the hill to the university and is crowded with beefy football players and women who look like cheerleaders out for pizza or soft ice cream. Football is king in Morgantown: students wear T-shirts that proclaim "American by birth, Mountaineer by choice" (a reference to the WVU team), and the stadium/athletic complex is the most impressive structure in town. At the university bookstore, *Playboy* occupies a special rack next to the cash register; the magazine had apparently rated WVU one of the top "party" schools in the country.

But there is another side to Morgantown — the nooks and crannies and little alleyways that Orwell might have found in the north of England; three of the best used bookstores I've seen anywhere; a tiny Japanese cafe where you can play backgammon and eat fried tofu. In fact, the town has a quaint sixties ambience. Someone said that people in Morgantown had just discovered that bell-bottoms had gone out of fashion and I didn't doubt it. There is an innocence about the place I found appealing.

I was staying at the Hotel Morgan at the foot of High Street. The hotel had recently been renovated, and each surface re-covered with some kind of synthetic material. There were marbelized plastic walls and acoustic-tile ceilings. Even the elevator was sheathed in vinyl. A rack of clothes, apparently belonging to the hotel boutique, stood outside all day under an awning. The night clerk was a black man wearing a wig; he was rumored to have once been Liberace's lover. The graffiti scrawled next to the elevator on the floor where my room was read, "Never trust a Jew." When I told people I was staying at the Morgan, they looked at me as if I were out of my mind. But in some strange way I grew attached to the Morgan. It was convenient, and from my fifth-floor window I had a sweeping panorama of the sea of brick buildings up High Street to the university and the surrounding hills.

I met Sarah, my contact, at Maxwell's, a High Street restaurant that attracts a bohemian crowd, including many gays and lesbians. Decorated with ceiling fans, fake Tiffany lamps, and lots of plants, it is the kind of establishment that serves broccoli omelettes and avocado and sprout sandwiches. The male waiters wear their hair in ponytails. The food is good, everyone is very friendly, and you can sit there forever without being asked to leave. In the late evenings, when most of the dinner customers have gone, the manager puts Count Basie's "One O'Clock Jump" and other fifties jazz tunes on the stereo. I spent a lot of time in Maxwell's during my visit to Morgantown, and many of the locals seemed to do the same.

Sarah, who was thirty, had big blue eyes and brown hair down to her waist and exuded a New Age earnestness. She was studying Appalachian history. Sarah grew up in Michigan in a fundamentalist Christian household and had come down to West Virginia to escape her family when she was nineteen and coming out. She fell in love with the green hills and with another woman, and she has never left. When I met her, she and her lover had been together for more than ten years.

Sarah told me that Morgantown had a large women's community that had grown out of women's studies classes at the university. There was a feminist lending library called Sisterspace and a women's coffeehouse that took place once a month at Maxwell's. A women's music festival had been held a few weeks before, with local fiddlers and singers and square-dancing. (The expressions *women's community* and *women's music* usually meant lesbian, but with some heterosexual feminist overlay. Women's music, popularized by artists like Cris Williamson, Meg Christian, and Holly Near, initially combined folk style with overtly lesbian lyrics and genderless love ballads. Over the years, it has played a formative role in creating lesbian culture.)

In the past few years, many lesbians, including Sarah, had become interested in women's spirituality. She told me that a group of about fifteen women had been holding full-moon rituals on the farm just outside of town where she and her lover lived. When the organizers asked Sarah if they could use the property, her first response was a cynical "Oh, Lord!" Now, she was changing her view. The rituals—mostly consisting of chants, bonfires, and centering and visualization exercises—were forging a stronger sense of community, she said. I pressed Sarah to be more specific; instead she became vaguer still. "Some women in the group see it as goddess worship but I'm not into that," she said. "But there is a general sense in the group and within women's spiritual circles as a whole that we need to get into a more feminine frame of mind to make the world more secure. I am not sure how far I go with that. But it is pretty sweet to go out and do meditation with a group of women."

Sarah had invited two gay men involved in an AIDS education group called the Mountain State AIDS Network to join us. She had never met them before (someone had given her their names), a sign of the lack of interaction between the lesbian community and the gay men in Morgantown. Roger Banks, who headed the Morgantown AIDS group, was a graduate student in public policy at WVU. He looked like a young, handsome Truman Capote. Roger had grown up in Logan County, one of the most poverty-stricken regions of the state. Life there, he said, consisted of coal-mining and the church. His father had been a coal miner, and Roger grew up believing that homosexuals—himself included—would wind up in hell. He had been kicked out of his fraternity at West Virginia Wesleyan College because he was gay, and in the ensuing uproar (he was assaulted by another student armed with a club) he almost had to leave school. The incident radicalized him, he said. His lover, Richard, was a quiet, neatly groomed man with a mustache. He had moved to Morgantown from Massachusetts a few years earlier and worked in a finance company.

Roger and Richard didn't have much good to say about gay life in West Virginia. Gay men in the state had low opinions of themselves, said Roger. They held minimum-wage jobs and had no career aspirations and lived to go out and get drunk on the weekends. Richard suggested the reason for this was the environment they had grown up in. Gays were constantly being told being gay was wrong, that they would never amount to anything; they wound up believing it. Alcoholism was a major problem, they told me. There was little gay male life in the town outside of the one gay bar, which was a dismal place. The campus gay organization was virtually defunct; the local gay Metropolitan Community Church was functioning, but it was a small group that seemed to revel in moving from crisis to crisis. Roger thought that gay men felt they were unable to change or influence the forces that shaped attitudes in West Virginia, so they turned on other gay people and gay organizations, battling among themselves. "The most positive thing a new person in town should do is to get away from the gay community," Roger said.

Given the poor self-image of many gay men, AIDS presented a large problem. Roger and Richard were concerned that people didn't care enough about themselves to practice safe sex. There had only been twenty-seven cases in the state at that point, but they expected a significant increase. "We may wind up with a good number of cases because of low educational background, poor hygiene, and low self-esteem," Roger said. "You still have cruise areas, bar scenes, one-night stands. There is the thinking that we have iron walls around the state."

Meanwhile, their group was doing the best it could to disseminate information about the disease—setting up hotlines, doing presentations at university dorms. But the state hadn't given them any money yet, and the organization had a tiny budget and no office space. As a result, they were banking on controversy to arouse interest and awareness. They had found an opportunity a few months before when a man who had tested positive for HIV (human immunodeficiency virus, generally believed to be the cause of AIDS) was denied access to a public swimming pool in the small town of Williamson. In order to provide accurate information about AIDS transmission, two members of their group and an official from the state health department had gone down to the town and had insisted on swimming in the pool with the infected person. The town then shut down the pool.

I listened skeptically to Roger and Richard's dismal view of gay men in Morgantown. More than anything, they seemed to be expressing class and education prejudice. Yet by the time I left West Virginia, I had heard the same thing from so many people, both natives and out-of-staters, that I assumed it must be true to some degree. For her part, Sarah appeared increasingly dismayed. When Roger and Richard talked about jealous gay men "infiltrating" relationships and trying to break up couples, she noted how supportive other lesbians were of her and her lover's relationship. "We recently had our ten-year celebration of being together, and we did it almost more for our friends than for us," she said. "They were so excited to see success in a couple who are doing well and are sane and stable." And when Richard observed that gay men in West Virginia had a hard time viewing women as equals, Sarah's face fell. "Gay women would welcome men with open arms," she said, a pleading tone in her voice. "They would care about them."

The following day, I went to visit Sisterspace, the feminist lending library that functions as a kind of community center. It is located on the eighth floor of a High Street office building largely populated by lawyers' offices. Sisterspace occupies a large room with comfortable couches and chairs, a stunning view of the Monongahela River, and close to one thousand books and periodicals. There, I chatted with a lesbian social worker named Elise who was a member of the Sisterspace collective.

Sarah had told me that, of all the women she knew in Morgantown, Elise was the most politically minded, a reputation apparently stemming from her anti-apartheid activism and her involvement in a group opposed to U.S. intervention in Central America. Previously, she had been active in a local organization called the Committee for Individual Rights. The group had been formed when a West Virginia kindergarten teacher was forced to resign from her job because she was rumored to be a lesbian. The case became a *cause célèbre* and went to the state supreme court, which upheld the woman's dismissal. As an outgrowth of its involvement in the case, the Committee for Individual Rights had received a two-year grant to fund educational programs and gay and lesbian organizing throughout the state. Although the organization was inactive at that point, a portion of the grant money had been used to establish Sisterspace.

However outspoken she was in her political views, I found Elise to have an unassuming manner. A short, dark woman, she spoke with quiet reserve. Today more than half of the ten or fifteen women who ran Sisterspace were lesbians, she said. But the collective had never been viewed as a lesbian organization. Elise felt that because they avoided that label, Sisterspace and the Morgantown's women's movement in general were able to provide a secure environment that could nourish a lesbian community in a hostile part of the country. "Women can hang out at Sisterspace and feel more protected because it is not just a lesbian organization," she told me. "When gay men come out and become organized, they don't have this sort of protection. And being 'out' in a community like this is very risky." Elise proceeded to ask me a host of questions about gay men around the country. Were they very organized? Politically minded? What did I think about the gay men in

Morgantown? One reason for her interest, she told me, was that Sisterspace had received funding to start a telephone hotline that would include referrals for gay men and AIDS information.

When I got back to my hotel, I received some bad news. The following day was the West Virginia–Ohio State football game. To my astonishment, the Hotel Morgan was raising its rates by fifteen dollars for the occasion. It was Labor Day weekend and the town would be packed, the desk clerk told me; the police were setting up roadblocks on High Street. I wanted to ask him about the Liberace connection, but I was too embarrassed. At the desk, there was a message for me to call Sarah.

When I reached her, she told me she and her lover were planning to go camping for the weekend. Would I like to stay at the farm and keep an eye on things? And, by the way, she also had a lead on a lesbian coal miner. She would try to arrange a meeting the following day. I was delighted and bid the Morgan good-bye with considerably less regret than I had anticipated.

Sarah and her lover lived fifteen minutes from town in an old farmhouse on 250 acres. There were steep hillsides and green meadows, a pond, and little abandoned shacks with corrugated roofs. Cows wandered around (their landlord grazed his cows on the property), and there were cow pies everywhere. It seemed the perfect spot for full-moon rituals. The main house was shabby but inviting, with hooked rugs, a wood stove, overstuffed furniture, and a stereo with records ranging from women's music artists Cris Williamson and Margie Adam to Ella Fitzgerald and Billie Holiday.

It was the ideal retreat from the football weekend, and I longed to stay on. But the coal miner, a woman named Jan who had left the mines just a few months before, had agreed to talk. The next morning, as I drove up to the ranch house Jan shared with her lover, Barb, in a blue-collar suburb of Morgantown, I was entering a world far removed from meditation exercises in the full moon and Cris Williamson records on the turntable. Jan's neighbors were all working-class families, miners, mechanics, and glass-blowers. From her back porch, you could see the blue and white markings of a coal mine on one of the nearby hills.

Jan greeted me warmly. She was a short, compact woman and, not surprisingly, gave the impression of physical strength. She spoke softly, but with deliberation and feeling. At first, I found her a little timid. I had trouble imagining her holding her own with the male miners or bargaining with management (she had served as a union official). But Jan was commanding in her own quiet way. When she spoke about injustice in the mines, her voice rose with passion.

As Jan went off to make tea, I noticed that her living room was the mirror image of Sarah's farm. It was country, all right, but new country. The room was dominated by a large, unpainted bookcase filled with knickknacks, dried flowers, and duck decoys. Everything was designed to give a rural flavor—a wood stove, a framed poster of a quilt, a ceiling fan, a rocking chair with an embroidered cushion. Copies of *Country Home* and *Horticulture* and the *L. L. Bean Catalog* were piled on the coffee table. The room was pleasant enough, but its quaintness was all new, all imitation. It seemed almost as if Jan and her lover were trying to mimic the back-to-the-land style of Sarah and other Morgantown lesbians, while still making the decor store-bought enough to be acceptable to their suburban neighbors. To me, it symbolized some uneasy middle ground between two worlds.

Jan came to West Virginia in 1968 to work as a mental-health volunteer in the VISTA program, the domestic version of the Peace Corps. She stayed on to study history at West Virginia University, mainly because tuition was cheap. Shortly after she arrived in West Virginia, she met her lover Barb; they had been together for eighteen years.

In 1974 and 1975, the coal industry began hiring women for the first time. Jan was interested. The mines paid well and she needed the money; she had been working at low-paying jobs for a long while and was trying to put Barb through graduate school. The prospect of working in the mines stirred her sense of political commitment, as well. "A lot of people were telling me, 'This is where it's happening,'" she recalled. "That it wasn't in the civil rights movement, not in the peace movement. It was getting involved in basic industry. The workers would make the difference." She made the rounds of the coal-company business offices. It was winter and she was working as a nurse's aide. She would show up at the company offices at six A.M. on cold and snowy mornings to put in her applications and take the required tests. Eight months later, in October 1975, she got a telephone call from one of the largest coal-mining companies in the area. They had a job available, if she was interested. "Can I give two-weeks' notice?" she asked. "Come on Monday or don't come at all," she was told. So began almost twelve years in the mines.

Jan worked several hundred feet below the surface in what is known as "high coal," the bituminous coal that is high in sulfur and is used for producing electricity. Walls of coal stood six to eight feet high and passageways were about fourteen feet across, she told me. Everything in the mines was highly mechanized; huge continuous mining machines filled the passageways. In the section where Jan worked, a continuous miner—a thirty-ton machine with a drum and large teeth—would cut a block of virgin coal. A loading machine followed and picked up the coal and loaded it into hoppers on a buggy behind it. The buggy transported the coal to a belt, where it was unloaded and sent to underground railroad cars. Jan's job was to drive the buggy back and forth and unload the coal. She also worked as a classified roof bolter, shoring up the passageway after the coal was cut.

Her early years in the mines were exhilarating. Only five hundred women were employed in the entire coal industry, and Jan was one of the first. She was a celebrity, a woman literally breaking new ground in a nontraditional field. Reporters were continually interviewing her. "I got a lot of attention," she recalled. "I was special."

Still, it wasn't easy being a woman in the mines. Many of her co-workers were just out of high school. They could be crude, she said; some felt they had to show off when a woman was present. The older miners, many of whom remembered the struggles of the twenties and thirties when Mother Jones was organizing in the mines in northern West Virginia, were the most supportive. To them, you were a coal miner first and a woman second, said Jan. If she faced sexual harassment, it was primarily from company officials, not from other miners.

As a woman, Jan felt she had to prove herself. The men were surprised at how much weight she could lift, she said: She could pick up a ninety-pound bag of Portland cement and walk a distance with it. "I'm short but I'm strong," she said proudly. "I worked very hard at that time. A lot of us did. The company sort of works that out of you. They burn you out so that you don't even want to give it a good day's work anymore."

Interestingly, the people most uncomfortable with women in the mines were not the miners themselves but their wives. Once, a woman who had found out that her husband was riding to work with Jan called her on the phone. "Stay away from my husband," she told her. Jan found another way to get to work.

Jan was taking home a real paycheck for the first time in her life—ten thousand dollars a year (considered a good salary in West Virginia in 1975) plus benefits—and this overcame many of the difficulties. So did the strong sense of camaraderie that developed underground. "You work as a small crew," she said. "You have difficulty communicating because of the situation—the noise, the lack of good lighting. You have to learn to work together, to trust one another, and to bond. And you do bond."

But Jan was not just a woman in a previously all-male industry, she was also a lesbian who lived with another woman. Despite the closeness of working together under difficult circumstances, she felt that she couldn't share her personal life with her co-workers. She was convinced that they would ridicule and ostracize her if they knew she was a lesbian. As far as she knew, none of the male miners were gay. The miners got rid of tension and anxiety through horseplay that often involved physical contact—good-natured wrestling, shoving, sometimes even goosing. The men protected themselves from any misinterpretation of that kind of expression by making anti-gay comments. "I wanted to share more," she said. "I wanted them to feel they could just pop over to my house. A lot of them did. I was a union officer, and they did come to pay their dues. They knew where I lived, but I couldn't just say 'Come over and have a beer.' I didn't feel I could do that."

If, as Jan feared, the other miners couldn't or wouldn't accept her as a lesbian, she had a hard time accepting it herself. She developed an elaborate system of denial. Barb wasn't really her lover, she rationalized, but just a friend she was helping through graduate school. (They had become romantically involved in 1969, six years before she went to work in the mines.) "I didn't admit how much I needed her," she said. "I thought I was the strong one. I didn't realize that I wasn't, that my life would actually collapse without her." She told the guys she worked with that Barb was just renting a room from her.

In a community rigidly divided between town and gown, Jan strongly allied herself with the other miners. She looked down on academics and white-collar workers who "didn't know what really having to put in a day's work was like." "I developed some really rotten attitudes," she admitted. As much as she claimed to have moderated those views, today she still referred disparagingly to the university community as "the chrysalis over there" or "the incubator." The group she had held in such contempt included many gays and lesbians towards whom she might otherwise have gravitated. In those days, she looked down on gay couples for other reasons, too. She was convinced that gays lived very "licentious lives"; they were totally self-indulgent. It didn't matter, of course, that she didn't actually know any gay couples. She had been raised Catholic and, in retrospect, blamed the Church for her attitudes. "I had the worst stereotypes," she said. "I was just as homophobic as the people I worked with."

Being a woman and working in the mines did make her sexual orientation suspect to a certain degree. Sometimes, the guys she worked with would tell her "there are rumors about you being a lesbian." She would deny it fiercely. One time she recalled asking a couple of co-workers if she could ride to work with them. One apparently objected; later, the other told her that his friend had refused to ride with her because she was gay. She remembered becoming very upset. Nonetheless, suspicions about her sexuality didn't prevent her co-workers from electing her union representative.

In retrospect, she thought more people were aware of her homosexuality than she was willing to admit at the time. "You can't be in this community and not have people know who you are," she told me. "You see the guys all over the place. I was with Barb a lot. She would say things to me like 'People don't think about it that much. They get to know *you*.' I didn't believe her. It never occurred to me that people might not object."

One night in 1980, Jan was at work, bolting the roof of an area from which coal had been cut. She was having trouble with a bolt, and in attempting to steady the drill she was using, she fell and broke both forearms. They were very bad breaks, and the doctor didn't think she would ever go back to the mines.

After several months, she did go back. But she used the intervening period to return to school to finish her undergraduate degree. And she entered therapy. It was the therapist who broke through Jan's denial system, helped her to work on issues of self-esteem, and told her she was bigoted about other gay people. In therapy, Jan gradually learned to be more accepting of her lesbianism. Still, she had never been open about it with other miners. Today, she finally had a few gay friends, although not a great number, and occasionally went to Sisterspace. "I wouldn't say I am comfortable now with being gay," Jan said. "But I did leave the mines."

When I asked her about the political commitment that had led her to work in the coal industry, the conversation took an unexpected turn. One of the reasons she had gone to work there was because she had been a member of a political organization that she didn't want to name. "Being a person in a basic industry is very important to that group," she said. "So they considered me important. I received a great deal of attention from this political organization. I wasn't doing organizing. I found out right away that was impossible. But I was able to let them know what miners wanted, what they needed."

She wasn't involved anymore, she went on. In fact, the issue that had driven her away was homosexuality. Eight or nine years into her involvement, she was considered for nomination to one of the organization's central bodies. But that nomination never took place. Shortly after, a labor organizer explained to Jan that she had been passed over because she was a lesbian. It was the first time that she had realized the depth of the group's anti-gay prejudice. She was devastated. Continuing to work with them was impossible, she felt. Still it took several years of soul-searching before she could bring herself to break ties. "I wanted to be involved," she said. "I really do feel they have some very good things to offer. But how can you work with a group that is ashamed of the basis of what you are? My relationship with Barb is the closest relationship of my life. I'm committed to this relationship. It hurt a lot."

"Was that the Communist party?" I asked.

"Yes," she replied.

Despite her disillusionment, she said she was still in some communication with the Party. She tended to blame its anti-gay attitudes on the New York headquarters. Chicago always seemed a better place, she said. But she had made the break. She recalled a meeting she attended at which someone described the members of the Communist group in Houston as "a bunch of fairies." At that point, another comrade stood up. "That is not the Party's stand on homosexuals," he stated. "We consider it a disease." That, Jan noted, was the moderate point of view. "I began to see that if I wanted to be in the Party, I would have to deny myself," she said. "It was the same with the mines."

I noted that all the major forces in her life seemed arrayed in opposition to her sexuality. "The Big Three," nodded Jan grimly. "The Union, the Church, and the Party."

Jan stayed on in the mines until 1987. She was making $33,000 a year, a salary that was hard to give up. She still identified heavily with the other miners, and loved her union work. "The guys didn't know how to deal with the company people," she told me. "They are very angry and they feel stepped on. I got a great deal of satisfaction defending these people and seeing them win once in a while. And it was very infrequently we won." Jan began to realize her union work was becoming the only thing she really liked about the job. The actual coal-mining began to seem increasingly stressful and depressing. The excitement of being one of the first women in the coal industry had long passed. The Communist party, which had been one of the reasons she had gone down to the mines in the first place, had rejected her and she had rejected it. And as she became more accepting of her lesbianism, the dissonance between her personal life and her work life loomed larger. It was time to go.

When I met Jan, she had been out of the mines for only a few months. She still wasn't sure she had made the right decision; she missed the other miners, the solidarity. She had worked for a while at a group home for mentally retarded adults but hadn't liked it. Now she had enrolled in a nursing program at a nearby college. She was extremely worried about whether she would make it through. The work was overwhelming, she said. The sense of security and purpose that had characterized her life in the mines had vanished; the future was uncertain.

After another cup of tea, she excused herself and said she had to begin studying for an exam the next day. I headed back to my New Age paradise. Morgantown, it seemed, was divided against itself. There was the division between town and gown, between the blue-collar workers and gays, between gay men and gay women. In her own way, Jan had tried to bridge some of those gaps and failed, even if the banner she had been waving was hardly one of gay liberation. She herself had said "I have often wondered what happens if you grow up in these working-class communities and feel you're gay. What do you do?" More than ever, I was convinced that if the gay movement was to have broad social impact, if it was to avoid being dismissed as parochial and middle class, it had to find some way of reconciling itself with the kinds of people Jan lived beside and had worked with.

As I got back to Sarah's farm, it was beginning to rain. The cows in the field in front of the house glared at me as I passed; I almost stepped on a pile of cow shit as I approached the front door. Now, I found the whole scene more troubling than serene. The "real world" was out there in those blue-collar suburbs or hundreds of feet under the ground where huge machines sheared back the coal and gay people weren't welcome. No wonder gay working-class kids got out or drank too much and lived only for the weekend. The farm was just a New Age version of an urban gay ghetto. I put a Billie Holiday record on the phonograph, lay down on the couch, and fell asleep.

OGILVIE, MINNESOTA (POPULATION 374)

missed the Minnesota State Fair by three weeks. As an easterner living in a large urban area, I am not particularly conscious of state fairs. And I never assumed that the beef and poultry barn or the cattle barn of a state fair would be a particularly good place to observe gay and lesbian life.

I was wrong. At the Minnesota State Fair, held at the end of August at the St. Paul fairgrounds, a brown and white fifteen hundred pound bull belonging to Al Philipi and John Ritter was named the 1987 state champion. Al and John are two gay dairy farmers who live sixty-five miles north of the Twin Cities. At the awards ceremony, they received a wooden plaque in the shape of the state of Minnesota with the state seal embossed in gold. Tears were streaming down Al's face, John told me.

In the Twin Cities of Minneapolis and St. Paul, you can't help but be aware of the state's agricultural roots. The farm is always just a generation away, despite the air of urban sophistication, the experimental theatre and the recording studios and the take-out Szechuan restaurants, the punk rockers and the long-haired graduate students pedalling their ten-speeds down Hennepin Avenue as if it were Harvard Square. The connection to the land is as true for gay people as anyone else. Karen Clark, the openly lesbian state representative from an inner-city district of Minneapolis, told me with pride that she had grown up on a farm in southwestern Minnesota; she advertised her rural background in her campaign literature. On the office wall of Allan Spear, the gay state senator and chairman of the Minnesota Senate Judiciary Committee, were large framed photographs of Floyd Olson and Elmer Benson, the two agrarian reforming governors of the thirties elected on the ticket of the Farmer Labor party. So when the managing editor of *Equal Time*, the gay newspaper in Minneapolis, suggested I interview one of their editors who lived on a farm and whose lover was a full-time dairy farmer, I was eager to do so. Orwell had written that the coal miner was second in importance to the man who plowed the soil. I had found the first after much travail; two genuine dairy farmers were as close as I expected to get to the second.

When I arrived at Al and John's farm, late on a Saturday afternoon, autumn was beginning to wane, though it was only September. The leaves had turned to dull yellows and oranges, the cornfields along the side of the road were a russet brown, the days were crisp and clear, and the nights felt colder. Al and John were in high spirits. They had just returned from an overnight trip to the Guernsey Breeders Association cattle sale in Hutchinson, Minnesota, a few hours' drive away. Their friend Paul Leach, a gay dairy farmer who lived an hour to the north, had come by to do the milking and keep an eye on things. Al and John had bought three new cows in Hutchinson, and their prize-winning bull had been displayed on the cover of the auction catalog. John told me later that Al hadn't slept for the entire week before the auction.

Al didn't tend to sleep much anyway. He had put his cows on an unusual schedule, milking and feeding five times in each two-day period, at nine and a half hour intervals, with the schedule changing every other day. The cycle began with a milking at midnight; other milkings followed at nine thirty the next morning and seven in the evening. The next day he milked at four thirty in the morning, at two in the afternoon, and once again at midnight. (Most farmers had a saner schedule, milking regularly at five in the morning and five in the evening.) Al started on this routine to increase cash flow. "Your operation can either get larger and generate more product," he said, "or you can generate more product per unit." Buying more cows was just too expensive, with prices ranging from $750 to $1,600 a head, so Al opted for getting more milk out of the cows he had. The arrangement seemed to work, with production up eighteen percent since they had started on the new schedule. One result was that Al and John had a coffee pot going twenty-four hours a day, and Al took frequent catnaps.

I had never been on a dairy farm before and didn't realize how demanding the work could be. John and Al had fifty cows, twenty of which were milking. Almost all their livestock was brown and white Guernseys, and the two farmers were extremely partial to the breed. Guernsey cattle, they told me, tended to produce higher solids in their milk, which was good for making cheese. Their farm produced six hundred pounds of milk each day, which John and Al sold to a dairy cooperative that resold it to small cheese plants in Wisconsin. Each milking and feeding lasted about two and a half hours.

The evening I arrived, I fell asleep before the midnight milking (or "melking," as John and Al pronounce it) but was at the barn promptly at nine thirty the following morning. There, in a sweatshirt, jeans, and high galoshes, John was lugging a forty-five pound steel milking unit from cow to cow and transferring the milk to a big steel vat at the entrance to the barn; then he washed and cleaned the cows' teats, swept the stalls, and shoveled manure. Paul, the visiting farmer, was in charge of the feeding. Al was shoring up a broken stall and giving the cows a dessert of beet pulp.

Like a proud father, Al introduced me to every cow by name, personality, and production value. First came Lilly, lone Brown Swiss among Guernseys, a cow Al described as "heavy, aggressive, good producing. She will finish with 21,000 to 22,000 pounds of milk this year." Then, Honors: "a people cow." Isabel: "on her first lactation." Teardrop: "Our gay friends love her. She has incredibly beautiful eyes." And so on, through fifty cows, eight crested Polish chickens (whose coloration made them look as if they were wearing hats), sixteen lambs (Al hoped to increase that number to one or two hundred soon; both the wool and lamb market had been up recently), two lavender angora rabbits (whose fur could be spun into yarn), and three horses. Never far away was Nellie, the diminutive white poodle who made a rather humorous farm dog.

Al compared looking after his cows to bringing up fifty children. "They are very dependent on humans and very individual," he said. "With them, there are tremendous difficulties and tremendous disappointments. They can have structural problems, heart attacks. You play doctor and nurse to them. They can lay down and die one day for no apparent reason. In this business, the profit margins are slim, the tension and stress can be awful." The rewards made it all worthwhile, nonetheless: "the renewing experience" of calving, the "tremendous joy" of working with animals.

Al was an unusual combination of urban camp sensibility and country style and values. He wore two earrings in his left ear and a bangle on his wrist; his shirt was open almost to his navel. He gave his cows names like "You Tell 'Em Dorothy" and "Fashion Design" and called one sheep "Dottie of Fergus Falls" (after an ice-cream commercial). He divided the cows that weren't milking into three categories: "debs, minnies, and nymphettes." Inside the farmhouse, gay paperback gothics and mysteries filled the shelves. Three movie-theatre seats provided living room furniture, someone's idea of trendy but not particularly comfortable "gay" decor. On the dining room wall was a photograph of someone standing in the barn dressed in black stockings, lace panties, and black jacket, with a cow looking on incredulously in the background. On closer inspection, the person in the photograph turned out to bear a striking resemblance to Al. Also on that wall was the wooden plaque Al and John's bull won at the State Fair. "1987 Minnesota State Fair Grand Champion," it read.

Al, at thirty-seven, was the dreamer, the impractical one, living out his passion—his love of animals. John, at thirty-two, complemented him—he was solid and forthright, bringing sense, balance, and some hard-headed financial realism to the operation and to their life together. When Al described the cows as "a commodity," John assured me, "He doesn't really mean that. He picked up that phrase from me." Unlike Al, John had a life beyond the farm. He commuted five days a week to the Twin Cities, where he worked as a reporter-editor for *The Farmer*, a monthly magazine that covers midwestern agriculture. He also worked part-time as regional news editor for *Equal Time*, the gay and lesbian paper. While Al called dairy farming "my career," John considered himself a journalist first and a farmer second.

Weekdays, John left for work at seven in the morning, often not returning until as late as eleven in the evening, especially if he was doing a story for *Equal Time*. Sometimes he could be gone for days at a stretch covering South Dakota, his beat. John's absences left the management of the farm almost completely in Al's hands. Al became the one to negotiate with the banks and the dairy cooperative and the salesmen who came to the farm to sell feed and semen, to talk to the veterinarian and the county agent. He spent his days like most other dairy farmers in the Midwest: milking and feeding cows, cleaning barns, hauling manure, mowing lawns, confronting crises, and grabbing a few hours of sleep when he could.

Al and John had been dairy farmers for four years and lovers for eight and a half. They leased a five-acre farm near the town of Ogilvie, where the exurbia of Minneapolis gives way to the bait shops and mobile homes of Kanabec County. One demographer recently annointed the county the next area for growth in Minnesota, but there were few signs of development yet, at least in the area where Al and John lived. Ogilvie, the nearest town and where the two did their shopping, looks as if it is out of a painting by Edward Hopper. The country is flat and cheerless, crossed by Highway 65, the route that hunters and fishermen from the Twin Cities take to their cabins on the lakes farther north. The farms are poor and relatively small; the visitor misses the intimacy of the rolling country of Iowa to the south or the dramatic expanses of the wheat belt of the Dakotas to the west.

There was nothing particularly bucolic about John and Al's Blue Spur Farm. They didn't grow their own feed or even have a vegetable garden. The farmhouse, located virtually on the highway, was plain and slightly run-down. Just behind the house, the cattle barn, with its characteristic grey-shingled silo, was badly in need of paint. Connected to it was a tin-roofed, functional structure for the dry cows and baby heifers and a shed for the lambs. A few acres of pasture behind the barn completed the picture.

I went off with John and Paul, the visiting farmer, in John's pickup to have dinner at the Sportsman's Cafe, the nearest watering hole, about ten minutes down the road at Mora. Sportsman's was a joint with a large counter in the middle and booths along the side wall. It was open twenty-four hours a day to serve fishermen and hunters and state troopers, and John knew all the waitresses, women in their forties and fifties who have spent their lives standing on their feet. "Where's your friend?" one of them asked John as soon as we walked in. "I haven't seen either one of you in weeks."

At Sportsman's, we ate homemade oyster stew and pecan pie, and John drank several cups of coffee to keep awake for the late-night milking. John told me that he and Al had both grown up on dairy farms—Al in northern Minnesota, sixty miles from the Canadian border, where his father raised Guernseys; John to the west of the Twin Cities, where his family still raised Holsteins. John had always intended to get away from farming; the work was too hard. He met Al at the wedding of a mutual friend in Grand Forks, North Dakota. At the time, John was living in the Twin Cities and working on a newspaper; Al was farming with his father. Soon after, Al moved down to St. Paul to live with John, working in retail clothing stores.

But the attractions of urban life dwindled, and the focus of their lives began to shift back towards the farm. John moved into ag-journalism, writing for *The Farmer*, partly because he was frustrated by the long hours of news writing but also because of Al's continuing interest in the subject. More and more, they began to fantasize about returning to a rural setting, if not to farming itself. Their friends refused to take them seriously, dismissing the idea as "cute" or "a nice little dream." Al and John bought some horses and moved just outside St. Paul. A few cows wouldn't be too much trouble, they decided, and then they moved out even farther. John was somewhat reluctant; he is the cautious one, after all, and also the one who really wanted to get away from farming. But Al pressed, and John gave in.

John stressed that in returning to the farm, he and Al had made a conscious effort to do things differently from most gay farmers in the past. Traditionally, he said, in order to stay in agriculture, gay farmers either married someone of the opposite sex or completely sacrificed any possibility of a relationship. Whatever their strategy for survival, they remained in the closet. Although John and Al weren't going to advertise their homosexuality, they were determined not to hide it either, letting people draw their own conclusions instead. "I have run into people in town who thought we were brothers, even though our names are different," said John. "They are more comfortable thinking that way." Some people were suspicious, he admitted, and others knew they were gay and didn't approve, sometimes telling them so directly. But he thought that to half of them, the possibility of his and Al's homosexuality "doesn't occur at all."

Al agreed. "Most farmers are more interested in how the livestock in our farming operation performs," he told me later. When a story about them as gay farmers (including photos) appeared on the front page of the daily newspaper in nearby St. Cloud, there was no visible reaction from their neighbors.

Their friend Paul had had a more traditionally closeted experience, however. He was a sweet and unassuming man in his late twenties, with curly brown hair and a neatly clipped beard. Four and a half years ago, while living in the Twin Cities, he became the lover of an older man. The two bought a farm together in a predominantly Finnish area about two and a half hours north of Minneapolis. The older man had died of lung cancer a few months before; Paul still spoke of his lover in the present tense. Paul stayed on at the farm with only three small calves, rebuilding a barn and hoping to establish a viable livestock business. Paul said the main issue for the neighbors had not been the couple's homosexuality but the fact that he and his lover were German Catholics, not Finnish Protestants. "First they thought my lover was my father until they realized we didn't have the same last name," he said. "Then they thought I was just his hired man." Now, his neighbors were beginning to wonder. "They are thinking, 'This is weird. The hired man is still living there,'" Paul observed. Just a week before, in the small town nearby, he had heard someone mutter "There goes a queer," as he was leaving a store. "I presume they were talking about me," he said. "I guess I'm 'out' now."

For their part, Al and John had not been particularly active in the organization of local Guernsey farmers, but this was changing. The award their bull received at the state fair and the fact they were advertising their livestock in the Guernsey breeders' magazine had given them increased visibility among local farmers. Now, "people notice us," said John. "The ad gave people an opportunity to say something to us." In fact, the following week Al and John were holding a potluck picnic at their farm for the Northeast District Guernsey Breeders Association. They expected about twenty dairy farmers to attend.

There had been one disturbing episode, however. Al had been coaching the 4-H county dairy cattle judging team, composed of kids aged fourteen to sixteen. One parent complained to the county agent who supervises the 4-H that Al was gay. The agent apparently failed to back Al up, and Al resigned as coach. He hoped to be invited back the following year, noting that the kids involved in the organization had been supportive. But John, always the more realistic one, was doubtful this would happen.

In the process of living in the country, they had increasingly discovered other farmers like themselves — a gay male couple nearby who raised sheep, a lesbian couple who had dairy goats, and two other men with a hog farm. Three years ago, Al and John took out a classified advertisement in *Equal Time*, announcing they would be at the state fair and inviting other gay people to stop by the cattle barn and say hello. They were startled by the constant stream of visitors. This summer, *Equal Time* published John's "Gay Guide to the State Fair" as its cover article. One result was that Paul came by the cattle barn, introduced himself to them, and all three became fast friends.

The fact that John and Al were open about their sexuality put them in a pivotal spot in helping to develop a close-knit rural gay community in Minnesota. (John and Al, it should be noted, were not the first gay farmers in the state to come out publicly. Dick Hanson, farmer, farm activist, and member of the Democratic National Committee, was openly gay and quite well-known. Hanson died of AIDS in late July 1987.) "Unless you are willing to be 'out,' it is hard to connect with people," John observed. "A lot of these gay farmers thought they were the only ones doing this." Now Al and John's social circle was shifting. Although they remained close with many of their urban gay friends, especially those who were interested in what they were doing, only a special occasion could persuade them to trek into the Twin Cities.

To me, one of the most interesting aspects of John and Al's return to the farm was that it had brought about a reconciliation with their parents. Several years ago, when John first told his parents he was gay, they were traumatized, he said. But out of seven sons of a farm family, John was the only one currently involved in agriculture. For his father, who was still operating the family farm, the return of his gay son to the land was "the least expected thing," said John. His father had been supportive of their operation and both father and son tried to help each other whenever possible, trading advice and material assistance. As John noted, they were both in the same business and faced the "same questions and troubles."

None of Al's two brothers and two sisters were farming either, and his parents had retired. But family ties to the land remained strong. One sister, who lived in Denver, was "absolutely thrilled," he said, when their bull won the state fair championship. Although she lived in a city, she was eager for her children to have some connection with the family's rural roots. "And it just so happens that in our family Uncle Al and Uncle John are the only ones who are farming," her brother pointed out.

The ability of both sets of parents to identify with Al and John's occupation appeared to provide a counterweight to their difficulties in accepting their sons' homosexuality. If they had lived in the Twin Cities and worked at jobs their parents couldn't identify with, the gay issue might loom larger between the generations, Al and John thought. John noted that from the time he went to college until he began farming, he had had little in common with his family. That certainly wasn't true these days. "As far as sexuality goes, they accept it but they are not supportive," he said. "But they are supportive of the rest of my life."

Al and John maintained that living on the farm had strengthened their own relationship as well, and noted they had been together the longest in their circle of gay couples. John believed that doing what they wanted to do with their lives—in Al's case, farming, in John's, a combination of farming and journalism—gave their relationship a strength it might not have had if they had sacrificed their aspirations and opted for a more conventional urban gay life. The fact they were business partners as well as lovers provided another tie; it would take months to dissolve their financial bonds. "This is not just a personal relationship, but an economic one, too," Al said.

Although they had left the big city behind, they were reluctant to cut their links to the larger gay world. They had been exploring the notion of combining farming with managing a gay-oriented bed and breakfast. (By the end of my travels, I was convinced that running a B and B is the dream of half the gay men in the United States.) The farm they currently leased wouldn't be appropriate, so they were looking at property slightly closer to the Twin Cities. "It is a dream," John admitted. He also conceded that combining milking cows and raising sheep with changing sheets and cooking breakfast for guests might turn out to be more than they could handle. Nonetheless, they were just not the kind of farmers who want to be "isolated and secluded," as John put it. The presence of a large and active gay community in the Twin Cities offered them a connection and a potential for involvement that other gay farmers who lived farther away didn't have.

Few urban gays were following in Al and John's footsteps. The dismal state of the farm economy argued against any major migration back to the farm; large numbers of farmers, both gay and straight, were packing up and leaving the land, as it was. And many gay men and lesbians who grew up on farms and in rural areas didn't necessarily recall their formative years with fondness. "You grow up on the farm and as you realize your sexuality, you feel you just don't fit," Al told me. "You don't fit in at Sunday church dinners or the PTA or picnics. You become frustrated and you search for others like yourself, and they are not real visible in a rural area. So you tend to leave."

But the pull of one's roots is a powerful thing. "As you mature," Al added, "you tend to go back."

After leaving Al and John's farm, I headed north through the Minnesota lake country. Autumn seemed even more advanced: leaves covered the ground along the highway, and the lakeside cabins were deserted. In that somewhat melancholy landscape, my mind drifted back to an evening I had spent a few months earlier outside of Knoxville in the lush Tennessee June.

I had come to east Tennessee to observe Knoxville's gay-pride events. While hundreds of thousands of gay men and lesbians were marching in New York and San Francisco and Boston, the celebrations of Knoxville's Ten Percent (KTP), the city's gay organization, were far more circumspect. There was no procession down Gay Street, one of the major downtown arteries. But there was a picnic at a state park on a lake created by the Tennessee Valley Authority, and that was where I met Cynthia Creech and Carol Nelson. They invited me to their house for dinner the following evening.

Cynthia and Carol lived less than thirty minutes from downtown, but once you leave the sprawl of Knoxville proper the landscape turns rural very quickly. This is particularly true near Louisville, southwest of the city, where the two women live. Cynthia met me at the Amoco station near her house. I followed her home, through narrow winding lanes so shrouded in greenery that I had no idea what lay on either side of the road. Their house, built by Cynthia and a former lover on the property where Cynthia's family had lived since she was ten, was strikingly beautiful. The outside was covered with shingles of natural wood. Huge hickory trees surrounded the house, giving a sense of being totally protected and enclosed. The inside was all earth-tones and stained woodwork and polished floors, with an air of comfort and affluence. There were paintings of Cynthia's dogs on the walls and stacks of *National Geographic* on the coffee table.

As we dined on salami and cheese sandwiches and Coca-Cola, conversation ranged over a number of subjects—Cynthia and Carol's coming to terms with their sexuality, Carol's former marriage, their own six-year relationship, and Knoxville's gay group, in which they had been active for a year or so. Cynthia, who was thirty-eight, worked as an assistant to a federal bankruptcy court judge in Knoxville. She was lanky and athletic; in her madras blouse and khaki slacks, she reminded me just a little of a young Katharine Hepburn in *Pat and Mike*. Carol was tall and in her thirties, with a helmet of blondish-brown hair, glamorous and self-possessed. She had been working as a surgical assistant in the operating room of a Knoxville hospital and was now buying into a crafts shop owned by a gay male friend, soon to be located in the city's fanciest mall. Being part-owner of a small business would permit her to be more open about being a lesbian, a freedom she never allowed herself while working in the macho atmosphere of a hospital operating room.

After dinner, Cynthia became more confiding. She told me that her dream since childhood had been to have a small, diversified farm. Recently, she had read an article in a magazine about a breed of lineback cattle that was in danger of dying out unless someone rescued them. All that remained was a herd of seventeen cows in Massachusetts. The cows were unusual because they had never been cross-bred with any other livestock. For that reason, she said, they were heartier and didn't need the high-protein diets and air-conditioned barns that most hybridized cows require. They were an anachronism that didn't fit into the streamlined agribusiness that dominates the American dairy industry.

She wrote to the owner of the cattle expressing an interest in buying them. Out of the three thousand letters of inquiry he received, Cynthia was the person to whom he chose to sell them. She bought the herd sight unseen. "I am a big believer that everyone should give something back to the world in which they live," Cynthia told me when I asked what motivated her interest in the idea. "That coupled with the fact I think cows are the neatest people on earth. Earth and animals have always given me a spark."

Despite their reputation for heartiness, the cattle arrived in Tennessee three months later sick and undernourished. Everyone who saw them was convinced they were going to die. But Cynthia nursed them back to health and they were now doing well; some had even calved. A geneticist had come over from Virginia Polytechnic Institute to help develop a breeding program. Cynthia was renting some nearby pasture for the cows (except for the bull, which lived on her property) and was looking for a permanent piece of land for them and the farm she had always wanted.

"Let's go and take a walk," Cynthia suggested. Darkness was rapidly coming on, and the evening was warm. The three of us passed the white frame house about one hundred feet away where Cynthia grew up and her mother still lived. Her mother had finally accepted the fact that her only child was a lesbian, although when Cynthia first told her years ago she immediately sent her off to a psychiatrist. "Still, in the back of her mind she thinks it may be OK for me because I'm her daughter," Cynthia added with amusement. "I am not sure she thinks it is OK for anyone else." Now, her mother dropped in every Sunday morning for breakfast with Cynthia and Carol. Her mother raised canaries—she had sixty of them—and I could make out the cages through the lighted windows.

As the darkness deepened, we paused at a green hillside, framed once again by hickory trees. Just in front of us were two cows and the bull of Cynthia's newly acquired herd. Towards the top of the hill, two deer were quietly grazing. Fireflies dotted the night with fine points of light; the air was thick with the scent of freshly cut grass. We stood in silence. Then a young calf scampered up the hill and the deer fled. The moment had passed; we walked back to the house in the darkness and said our good-byes.

Cynthia and Carol, the would-be farmers in Tennessee, and Al and John on their working farm in Minnesota represented to me a kind of reconciliation—with their roots, their families, with many of the values of the larger culture, and, above all, with their deepest selves. As John had noted, ten years ago it would have been virtually impossible for them to work on the land as openly gay people. They would have had to make a choice: either to stay in a rural area and remain hidden, cut off from any source of positive affirmation as gay people, or to move in to the city, be openly or discreetly gay, and forego those powerful inclinations towards a rural life. Today, while they obviously had to make some accommodations, the choices were significantly less stark.

There is always the danger of sentimentalizing the virtues of small-town and rural life, of course. And one could argue that these people weren't leading a traditionally rural life at all, that they were just an example of urban gay freedoms spreading outwards to exurbia. Perhaps Al and John could lead a fuller gay life because their farm was within driving distance of Minneapolis, one of the cities in the United States most accepting of gay people. Cynthia and Carol, after all, lived on the outskirts of a mid-size city, where there was a gay and lesbian community that held a pride week every June, even if it didn't parade noisily down Gay Street.

Still, I was accustomed to assuming that a gay life required a pulling up of roots, a breaking with the past—with hometown, family, with church and synagogue. I was finding the opposite. Perhaps that shouldn't have surprised me. Obviously, gays and lesbians in small towns and rural areas, even relatively openly gay people like Al and John and Cynthia and Carol, would have an affinity with the world in which they lived, a strong sense of allegiance to it. Nonetheless, it came as something of a revelation.

If their lives represented a new direction, it was a fragile one, delicate, like Cynthia's herd of cows; it could be easily undone by homophobia, by AIDS backlash, by simple economics, by self-doubt. Meanwhile, I was heading for territory where that kind of full life might be far more difficult for gay people. I was off to the remote, proud Dakotas, where everyone knew everyone and where living outside of social norms required courage and determination.

While at John and Al's, I had casually mentioned that I was looking forward to going to North Dakota because the fall foliage would probably be at its peak. I would have the chance to enjoy two autumns—one in the northern Midwest and one in New England once I got home. That idea gave Al a good laugh. "There's not much chance you'll see leaves changing in North Dakota," he said. "It's all prairie there. There are hardly any trees."

FARGO, NORTH DAKOTA (POPULATION 66,042)

arrived in Fargo after dark because I was having car trouble. I was driving a baby blue 1968 Mercedes 280 SL that belonged to a friend of mine who lived in Denver. He needed someone to get the car from the East Coast to the Rockies and didn't much care how long it took; I offered my services. Still, the car, which had leather seats, a tape deck, and even a compass (in case I got lost on some lonely prairie road) was a constant source of embarrassment and worry. Until a few years ago, I had owned a rusting yellow 1972 Volkswagen bug. The windows never seemed to go all the way up or down, there was a hole in the floor, and I had to stuff newspaper in the space between the front window and the convertible top to prevent the rain from pouring in. Once, on a trip to visit my parents, the muffler gave out and by the time I reached their driveway, the car sounded like a DC-3 about to take off. When my father offered to sell me my mother's Oldsmobile compact for modest monthly payments, I agreed, convinced I had achieved the height of luxury—until I encountered the Mercedes.

But I was nervous about the car. What kind of impression would I make showing up in a Mercedes at the home of some dedicated but impoverished gay activist? Would people think I was an elitist and immediately distrust me? Would I be perceived as "politically incorrect," shallow, and spoiled? I found myself constantly making apologies, explaining that the seats were uncomfortable, that the tape deck was drowned out by the noise of the motor, and that the car guzzled gas at an alarming rate. The truth was that no one seemed to have the slightest interest in the kind of vehicle I was driving.

Trouble had actually started in Minneapolis a couple of days before. First, the battery died. Once that was taken care of, someone skidded into the rear end on a rainy afternoon, smashing a taillight. The car was battered but driveable, and I was convinced my friend would never forgive me—if I even got it back to Denver. Then, as I approached the resort town of Detroit Lakes, Minnesota, fifty miles southeast of Fargo, the engine began to smoke. It was about five thirty on a Sunday afternoon and I figured that my luck had finally run out. Who in Detroit Lakes would be able to fix an aging Mercedes sports car at that hour on a Sunday? I would be marooned there for days. I was directed to Grover's, the only open service station in town, where the mechanic told me the alternator belt had worn out. Miraculously, he had one in stock that fit. He spent a couple of hours trying to figure out how to install it while running out to pump gas, and I nervously gobbled Milky Ways and watched the sunset on the prairie. In the end, the entire misadventure cost me $11.79. I figured it would have cost ten times that in Boston and drove away in triumph, convinced if anyone deserved to drive a Mercedes sports car across the country, it was me.

So it was late by the time I got into Fargo. Teenagers were driving up and down Broadway burning rubber, and the enormous marquee of the downtown movie theatre was flashing "F-A-R-G-O" in green, yellow, and red neon— torch-like, lurid, and beautiful.

As I drove around aimlessly trying to find a cheap hotel, cruising teenagers would pull up beside me at stoplights in their Plymouths and Mustangs and glare, then race around the corner squealing their tires. I guessed I was competition—a new car in town. Finally, I decided to toss monetary considerations to the winds and checked into the pricy Radisson Hotel downtown. It had been a long day; I didn't want to go to the outskirts to find a cheap motel, and most appealingly, the Radisson had a parking garage where I could stash my car for the duration of my stay.

In Fargo, the railroad tracks are at the end of the downtown business section, where Broadway hits Main, and freight trains seemed to pass through every five minutes. Long after the local hot-rodders were off the streets, the romantic wail of train whistles dominated the night, filling my room. It was all very soothing, and I enjoyed the best night's sleep I had had in days.

The next morning I had breakfast at the VFW club (the only breakfast places open on Broadway seemed to be run by the Veterans of Foreign Wars or the American Legion). As I was having my fried eggs and coffee and reading the Minneapolis and Fargo papers, the waitress informed me breakfast was on the house because of slow service. The unexpected free meal made me disposed to like Fargo right away. But I liked it for other reasons, too: the friendliness of its inhabitants, its unpretentious feeling, and the charm of its architecture. The city's two- and three-story brick and sandstone turn-of-the-century commercial buildings reminded me of uptown Kingston, where I grew up, before they ruined it by putting up trendy arcades. Fargo had escaped that fate. There were some modern structures (the Radisson, Prairie Public Television, city hall, some banks), and there were skyways connecting them in the manner of the Twin Cities, but that didn't detract from the town's cozy feeling.

All I really knew about Fargo before arriving was that the mayor had been strongly supportive of gay rights and that there was a struggling gay bar in town. Mostly I came because it seemed to fit the bill as a prototype of a typical American small city: the combined population of Fargo and its sister city, Moorhead, Minnesota, was about 95,000; the city was economically dependent on agriculture and therefore maintained strong connections to the countryside around it; and the nearest metropolitan areas were Minneapolis and Winnipeg, Manitoba, each four and a half hours away, which indicated that Fargo probably had a strong identity of its own and certainly could not be considered a suburb of anywhere else.

I figured that going to see the mayor was as good a place to start as any, and the meeting was easily arranged. I called up his secretary, gave her a vague idea of what I was doing, and I was scheduled in for the next day. I found Jon Lindgren, then in the middle of his third four-year term in office, to be a gentle, rather charming man in his late forties, with bright blue eyes. An economics teacher at North Dakota State University in Fargo (his wife was also a college teacher), he seemed far more like a professor than a politician. The afternoon I saw him, he was off to an Eddie Murphy concert in Minneapolis, where his daughter was in college. "It is amazing," he said, "Here I am living in Fargo, North Dakota, and in a few hours I can be watching Eddie Murphy on stage."

It was difficult to believe that someone so mild-mannered was always in the midst of confrontation, usually with the other members of the five-person city commission. During his first term in office, Lindgren ordered the city to approve a permit for the Women's Health Clinic (which performed abortions) after the commission had refused to do so. He had fought a long battle with the majority of the commission about whether to build a bridge in downtown Fargo (the mayor opposed it). Now, he was quarreling with other commission members over whether or not to hire a city manager; in the middle of this latest fracas, the commission had voted to reduce the mayor's salary by thirty-nine percent.

In June 1984, the mayor issued an official city proclamation announcing Gay Pride Week in Fargo, in recognition of the contributions of the city's gay and lesbian citizens. The city commission promptly repealed it. Thus began one of the most acrimonious episodes of Lindgren's political career. A city commission meeting to discuss the proclamation (and the abortion issue) attracted such an overflow crowd that it had to be moved from the commission chambers to the civic center. Sermons thundered from the pulpits of Fargo's conservative churches, and a prayer vigil was held on the steps of city hall. The following June the mayor did it again (proclaiming Gay/Lesbian Awareness Week on that occasion), and the city commission promptly rescinded the proclamation. In 1986 and 1987, the mayor reissued the proclamation, but something had changed. The commission made no effort to rescind it; the opponents no longer had the votes. In 1986, midway through this controversy, Lindgren was reelected to a third term with fifty-nine percent of the vote; one of his rivals had been the severest critic of the gay proclamation.

The proclamations and the public debate surrounding them were "the most satisfying things that I have done in my ten years as mayor," Lindgren told me. He said it hadn't adversely affected his political standing, even though he might have lost some votes. The public, he contended, admires political figures who express their views, even if they are different from their own. So expressing *any* view probably had some political benefit. And only through confrontation, he argued, through bringing out all sides of an issue and not going the route of compromise, could the truth emerge. This seemed to be the cornerstone of his philosophy.

Had the proclamations and the ensuing debate changed things much in Fargo? He thought so. The city had turned the corner on its attitudes towards its homosexual citizens. "A significant number of people realize there is a gay community here, that they aren't hurting them at all." he said. "To me that is progress. Whether or not life has improved for the average person in the gay community, I'm not sure. I hope it will. That would be the ultimate accomplishment."

What impressed me most about Lindgren was that he had been such a forceful advocate for gay rights not in an effort to appeal to a large and vocal gay constituency, as has been the case with politicians in larger cities, but because he seemed genuinely to care about the issue. The ten thousand member Assemblies of God church in Fargo, which believes that homosexuality is sinful (the minister's brother served on the city commission, where he strongly opposed the gay proclamations), was clearly a much more powerful political force in Fargo than the still almost entirely closeted gay community. So if political calculations were involved in the mayor's decision, he would have come down against any gay-pride proclamation.

As we were about to leave, I pressed Lindgren. Why take the risk, why take such an uncompromising stand on an unpopular issue, year after year? And why did he feel that it was the most satisfying thing he had done in his three terms as mayor? "It wasn't an argument about money or management," he said, as he put on his overcoat. "It was an argument about real people and how their lives are affected. In my view of the world, I guess, the most important progress is in issues like civil rights. It isn't in the computer revolution or Star Wars. It is how has the life of the average human being improved over one hundred years. I think the biggest progress then would be in civil rights issues and laws. That being my view, this [gay rights] is also a big issue and any progress made in it is important."

Not surprisingly, one of the mayor's staunchest supporters in Fargo was Lenny Tweedon, owner of My Place, the city's gay bar. Lenny kept a scrapbook filled with newspaper clippings and pieces of memorabilia collected over the past five years on the subject of My Place, the Fargo-Moorhead gay community, and himself. The first thing he showed me the afternoon I met him was a handwritten note that the mayor passed him the night his application to open a bar came up before the city commission in January 1983. "I am supporting your application without asking you for any side considerations like a free beer," wrote Lindgren. "I would accept a free beer, however." Whether or not the mayor got his beer, I'm not sure. But Lenny said that the mayor had gone to bat for him over licensing issues before the city commission on several occasions. When someone tossed a grenade into the bar (it did not contain explosives), it was the mayor who called Lenny the next day to voice his concern and check on how the police had handled the incident. "Had Lindgren not been the mayor, I would be closed by now," Lenny maintained.

From the outside, My Place looked more like a fortress than a drinking spot. A former Catholic War Veterans clubhouse located a short walk from downtown, it was a large, windowless, one-story building completely covered with metal siding. You entered through a back door by the parking lot. A local architectural critic who gave out yearly "orchids and onions" designations for the best and worst architecture in Fargo awarded the building a well-deserved "onion" a few years ago.

Nonetheless, the inside of My Place was roomy and surprisingly pleasant, at least by day. There were two rows of booths, a bar on one side (with Hula-Hoops above it for decor), and a dance floor with strobe lights on the other side. As you walked in, there was a pool table and, next to the bar, pinball machines. Posters of Marilyn Monroe, James Dean, and the movies *Rebel Without a Cause* and *Psycho* adorned the black walls.

When I stopped by My Place in the middle of the afternoon, Lenny was sweeping up. Lenny didn't fit my image of a typical bar owner, whom I perhaps unfairly associate with payoffs to the cops, watered-down drinks, and the habit of turning up the music so loud the customer has no choice but to order beer after beer to dull the pain. At thirty-three, Lenny was open and boyish-looking, with a broad grin and the beginnings of a double chin. He radiated earnestness and sincerity, church and youth work and community service. He grew up in Fargo, put political posters on his bicycle while delivering the local newspaper as a kid, and watched city commission meetings while his junior-high classmates were out playing baseball. Still in the closet, he ran unsuccessfully for city commission in 1980 and 1982. Until he opened the bar, he worked as personnel manager at a local supermarket.

Before Lenny bought My Place, there was no gay bar in Fargo. In the seventies, one bar in town did have a gay section but the place burned down. After that, some Fargo gay men would hang out in the parking lot of a bar called The Flame or at a Chinese restaurant which became a disco late at night, or at Roger's Sandwich Shop on Broadway. Social options for lesbians were limited to private parties. By the early eighties, a group called the Prairie Gay and Lesbian Community was running monthly dances in motel function rooms to provide some social outlet for both men and women. At that time, Lenny had come out and was serving as president of the group. Despite the dances, he felt there was really no place for gay people to socialize in Fargo. So he took a bold step and bought the workingman's bar that was now My Place, telling no one except the mayor that it was going to cater to homosexuals. He started off by holding gay dances on Saturday night when the bar, which got a big after-work crowd, was usually empty. He had hoped to keep the regular afternoon customers, but once word got around about the Saturday night dances, "the straights basically cleared out," he said.

Opening a bar that gays could call their own was "a brave and courageous act," according to local gay activist Mark Chekola. A professor of philosophy at Moorhead State College, Chekola stressed the importance of the bar to the local gay population. "In a small community like this, you are known," he emphasized. "If you are gay and dating a man [or a woman] you feel on guard in public. Few places are anonymous. The bar is a safe space in that respect." When I was there, My Place was the only gay bar in the entire state of North Dakota, attracting patrons within a radius of one hundred miles — from Fergus Falls, Minnesota, in the south to Grand Forks, North Dakota, in the north, as well as occasional stragglers from Bismarck, the state capital three hours to the west. It was also a place where men and women mixed, unlike many gay bars in larger cities. "The men and women tend to get along pretty well," Lenny told me. "When we first opened there was an invincible line down the middle that divided men and women. So we rearranged the furniture to create new routes. We try to get them to intertwine a little bit." He admitted, though, that some women had been "slacking off lately," viewing the bar as male-dominated. Lenny, in fact, had a personality clash with one woman employee who wanted him to play women's music instead of the dance music that he favored and that she considered "male." Lenny refused to budge, and I suspected he had no idea what women's music was.

The bar tried to function as community center and a health education center. Recently, a fund-raiser for the Minnesota AIDS Project was held there, with entertainment provided by female impersonators who had left town and moved to the Twin Cities. On two occasions, the local health department offered patrons anonymous HIV testing at the bar. Condoms were available ("They are just starting to pick up," Lenny said), and a table with brochures about AIDS was the first thing you saw as you came in the door.

But My Place had its problems, too, both as a community center and a business enterprise. It had never been able to draw Fargo's middle-class gay professionals, so essential to forging a cohesive community. "We don't tend to see a gay doctor or banker come in here," admitted Lenny. "Gay professionals will go to The Cities [Minneapolis–St. Paul] for the weekend as opposed to coming in here and running the chance of being seen." One gay man suggested that the bar tended to attract "flaming kids" (there are three colleges in the Fargo-Moorhead area: North Dakota State, Concordia, and Moorhead State). When I telephoned a lesbian college professor named Anne to arrange an interview, she had little positive to say about My Place. Lesbian professional couples rarely went to the bar, she told me. "Of the five or six lesbian couples I socialize with, only one would think of going there," she said, adding, "It is not an atmosphere I enjoy. When I go there, it is only out of a sense of community. Here, the bar can be the only option."

Although I wasn't in town on a weekend night when the bar might have been livelier, I found My Place rather dismal: on both a Monday and a Tuesday night a handful of people were sitting around, the place was dark, the music loud. What had seemed pleasant and expansive at three in the afternoon seemed unappealing, even depressing, at ten in the evening. Both Anne and Mark Chekola bemoaned the demise of the monthly dances sponsored by the Prairie Gay and Lesbian Community in the days before My Place opened. "I liked the dances," Anne said. "There was a broader spectrum of people there." Mark suggested the bar hastened the decline of the Prairie Gay and Lesbian Community, which sponsored lectures and discussion groups in addition to the monthly dances. "The bar really hurt," he said. "It became hard to get people out to more serious stuff."

Perhaps their criticisms were just a hankering for the old days. Or perhaps they had outgrown the bar or just weren't the kinds of people who enjoyed bars to begin with. But the impression I got was that there wasn't a close and active community in Fargo anymore, just a group of people who happened to drink together at the same watering hole. Even Lenny complained that the members of the community were not politically involved, that "as a whole they don't get too excited about anything."

Still, when declining business led Lenny to announce he would close My Place on December 31, 1986, there was an outpouring of support. As a result, he kept the bar open another two months to see what would happen.

Finally, he decided not to close after all, but to move to a location with cheaper rent when his lease expired several months down the road. There seemed to be a clear consensus among Fargo gays and lesbians that the bar might not be ideal, but no one was willing to let it fold.

It wasn't surprising that despite Anne's reservations about My Place, we wound up meeting there. It was the one spot where we could talk comfortably, she had conceded on the phone. Anne was a forty year old North Dakota native who made it on her own and was proud of it. A heavy-set woman, she was smart and tough-minded, active in civic affairs and a classical music buff. She grew up in a small town west of Fargo and, an only child, was raised "without traditional feminine expectations," she said. "My mother was widowed twice and is a very independent person. She never believed that marriage was the greatest state in the world. She never asked me, 'When are you going to get married?' She always expected I would go to college."

To me, Anne personified many of the dilemmas of being a single gay professional in a mid-American city the size of Fargo. She didn't exactly hide that she was a lesbian, although she wasn't apt to volunteer the information either. People in Fargo were naive about homosexuality, she maintained. "Anyone who has an eye to see would know in three minutes. Others are oblivious. I am amazed at how many simply don't know." She had never told her mother she was gay. "We are good Scandinavians," she said. "We don't talk about most anything, certainly not anything personal and emotional."

Anne seemed alienated from other lesbians in Fargo; her primary ties were to two gay male couples and to heterosexual feminist women whom she has met through her community involvement. There were not many lesbian professionals in Fargo, she said, and fewer who shared her interests. The most visible lesbians, she said, were the softball crowd, a group of mostly younger women with whom Anne had little in common. Others were coupled off or involved with a private network of family or friends. There were no lesbian social groups, none of the regular potluck get-togethers I found in some smaller cities, no music, poetry, or cultural events. At one time, there was a group that got together to discuss lesbian literature but it didn't last long. All that remained was the bar.

She told me (and Lenny concurred) that for many lesbians and gay men from smaller towns in North Dakota, Fargo was a transition point. They stayed for a while and then headed out for the bigger cities with larger and more open gay communities, particularly Minneapolis–St. Paul. Those who did come to Fargo from larger places, for whatever reasons, tended to leave. "Women who want to be surrounded by other lesbians will migrate," she told me. And she had seen a lot of people move away. All this coming and going seemed to offer still another explanation as to why Fargo did not have a particularly close-knit gay and lesbian community.

For those who stayed, being a lesbian did not constitute their primary self-definition, she said. "To survive here you have to have more than one identity. You focus less than in big cities on one element of yourself, like being gay. Here nothing is a single identifier. I am a teacher, a lesbian, an activist, a person interested in music. And I need to spend time with people who affirm all these."

She liked living in Fargo because she felt she had control of her life and could have an effect on the world around her. "You can be involved in lots of things and really have an impact on life in Fargo," she maintained, unlike a big city where you have to devote yourself single-mindedly to one interest or activity in order to make a difference. So she was involved—with the rape crisis center and the National Organization for Women, to name just two organizations. Her life consisted of an early morning meeting, then errands, teaching, then more meetings, ending in late-night telephone conversations with friends in various cities. "It is very liveable here," she said. "I have interests. I have friends."

She admitted that she would enjoy living in a place with more lesbians who shared her interests. And she also conceded that, although she had been involved in relationships in Fargo and in commuting relationships with women in other cities, she would have a greater possibility for making and sustaining relationships in a city like Minneapolis. But giving up her life in Fargo for the possibility of a relationship in a larger city was a trade-off she was unwilling to make. "Given all the things I can do here, and with my connections outside, I have seen nothing that makes me crave moving to a larger city," she said.

The bar never picked up very much, so we went back to Anne's apartment for a nightcap. It was a comfortable place with books and plants everywhere; we could have been in Minneapolis or Boston or New York's Upper West Side. The living room was lined with shelves of classical albums, arranged alphabetically. There she talked more personally. She confided that she was involved in a relationship with a woman in Minneapolis who described herself as heterosexual. The woman had told her that as much as she cared for Anne, as far as she was concerned the relationship would always be platonic. Anne's friends told her this woman would change her mind, but Anne was increasingly less optimistic. It was becoming evident that the relationship would remain one-sided. Still, she was reluctant to give it up. "I am not sure quite what to do," she said, pausing for a moment and gazing out the window at the starlit North Dakota night. "I have a better time with her than with anyone else I have ever been with."

Her relationship with an apparently straight woman seemed emblematic of the "half-a-loaf" approach to life that Anne, despite her proud self-sufficiency, seemed to accept. Like Jill, the woman I had met in Selma, frequent traveling and commuting relationships gave Anne the opportunity to take part in the more open lesbian culture in larger cities, while remaining in the closet at home. Access to that larger world made a major difference to her. She delighted in telling me about visiting friends in Omaha and going on an all-lesbian cruise down the Missouri River. Yet, despite the obvious richness of many aspects of her life, I felt there was something missing. Perhaps it was the isolation that educated people experience in smaller communities; maybe it was the difficulty single people, gay or straight, have in finding potential mates in towns where everyone appears to be married or coupled off. But perhaps what seemed to be missing in Anne's life had other roots as well: the constrictions of being unable to be open about her sexuality at work, in certain civic activities, or with her mother; and the lack of an affirming gay world and cultural framework in which she could interact every day, in which her sexuality could be taken for granted.

Yet what would happen in Fargo if you didn't take the half-a-loaf attitude, if you insisted on being openly gay in all aspects of your life, at home as well as out of town? That, it seemed to me, was the test of the mayor's contention that Fargo had made significant strides in its attitudes towards gays.

And in a community where most gays and lesbians remained in the closet, the one person I met in Fargo who most exemplified this more open, noncompartmentalized approach was Lenny Tweedon. Owning the local gay bar had transformed Lenny's life in many ways. It made him the de facto spokesperson for the gay community in Fargo, a role that he seemed to enjoy. It forced him to come out to his parents, who have been generally supportive, even though they write to him from their home in Arizona telling him about supermarket jobs available there.

What was most striking, however, and seemed the greatest indicator of change in Fargo was Lenny's relationship with his church. Lenny had been on the church council of St. Mark's Lutheran Church for six and a half years before he bought My Place. Once he opened the bar and it was publicized in the newspaper as catering to gays and lesbians, he began to stay away from church, fearing it would be too uncomfortable. The absence was painful for him. He told me that sometimes he would drive down to church on Sunday morning and sit in his car, debating whether or not to go in. "Then," he said, "I would go back home."

Finally, Lenny returned to St. Mark's. He ran for church council and lost. Then, when a vacancy occurred, he was appointed to the council by the pastor, who was very supportive of gay rights. Lenny was reelected twice and six months before had been elected president of the twelve-member council, a position that entailed running council and congregational meetings and sometimes serving communion.

As council president, Lenny clearly wanted to have an impact. He was attempting to push things through that had been talked about for years but never accomplished—purchasing a computer, installing an elevator (St. Mark's had a large number of retired members). Under his leadership, the church had finally bought the computer, and the pastor who had been telling him to slow down on promoting the elevator was starting to get excited about that, too, he said. Lenny was also putting his political skills to good use. The computer and the elevator were favored projects of certain council members; by supporting them so vociferously, he was making allies. "I am probably very ambitious," Lenny conceded. "Other council presidents would just say 'What did we do last year? Let's have the spaghetti dinner again.' I am proving myself to the congregation. I am trying to show that even though I am gay I can still be a good council president."

How Lenny's tenure as church council president would turn out was still in doubt. But what he accomplished or failed to accomplish was probably less significant than the fact that he had been elected to the position in the first place. Back in 1981 the St. Mark's Church Council had voted—after heated debate—to deny meeting space at the church to a gay group. Lenny, who was on the council but in the closet, remembered the church secretary saying to him one day, "Did you see those two guys who just came in? They are faggots." At that time, he made no reply. Six years later that same church had a gay council president running its meetings and serving communion.

Just after he became president of the church council, Lenny told the pastor he was concerned that some people might be reluctant to receive communion from him. The pastor replied, "If they don't like it, they can stand on the other side of the church." If Lenny's experience was any guide, and if the declining opposition to the mayor's gay proclamations was any further indication, fewer and fewer people in Fargo were insisting on standing on the other side— whether in church or in the community in general. In Fargo, as in Bunceton and other small places, people seemed willing to accept gays when they got to know them on a personal basis and they didn't feel threatened by a large gay presence. While that might not translate into general acceptance, it was a first step towards progress.

WOLVERTON, MINNESOTA (POPULATION 200)

Gays and lesbians in Fargo still talked about "the incident" even though it happened several years ago, not in Fargo but in the tiny community of Wolverton, Minnesota, which straddles the North Dakota border about twenty miles to the south. There, in the yellow brick schoolhouse they had bought and were in the process of restoring, Mark Nelson and John Oliver held a gay dance. Some of the townspeople got wind of the gathering and invaded the hall. Although there was no violence, the events that evening alarmed the largely closeted gay community, and forced Mark and John into a dramatic, public coming out. Today, the two men had converted the school-house into a successful restaurant—gift shop—senior-citizens' center called District 31—Victoria's. They had made their peace (mostly) with the town, and the town with them, but it had not been easy.

Some of the gay people I talked with in Fargo had been in Wolverton that night in January 1982 and encouraged me to meet Mark and John. "They should be at the bar tonight," Lenny Tweedon had mentioned the afternoon I interviewed him. "They always come in for a drink after their health club on Mondays." I waited around at My Place, but Mark and John must have left before I arrived or maybe they were unable to face the idea of a workout and skipped the evening's activities altogether. So I telephoned them the next morning. Tuesdays were a slow day for them, they said (the restaurant served dinner Wednesdays through Sundays only), so why didn't I drop by just after lunch? A little before noon, I started for Wolverton.

As you head from Fargo to Wolverton down Highway 75, along the tracks of the Northern Pacific Railroad, you drive through some of the richest farm-land in America. On either side, green fields of sugar beets and yellow fields of soybeans stretch to the horizon. The landscape is completely flat, with hardly a tree in sight, only a solitary line of telephone poles. It reminded me of the scene in Alfred Hitchcock's *North by Northwest* in which Cary Grant is fired upon by enemy agents from a crop-dusting plane, with nowhere to hide except a field of corn. To Hitchcock, the prairie was barren, limitless, frightening, a place where human beings were utterly vulnerable. I would understand that vulnerability a little better after visiting Wolverton, but as I drove that day I felt instead an overwhelming, almost transfiguring beauty. In the blazing autumn sunlight, against those endless spaces, everything took on a heightened intensity. A yellow school bus, an orange tractor standing by the side of the road seemed to be communicating something important, something never quite comprehensible.

In the midst of this, Wolverton emerged, dreamlike, out of scale. To my eye, already distorted by the prairie, the church steeple and the water tower at the entrance of town appeared like the gates of some half-forgotten city always on the verge of being swallowed up by the landscape. Reality reasserted itself when I reached downtown Wolverton, which extends for a block or two along the highway. On one side of the road are the grain elevators, the mainstay of the town's economy, and the railroad cars. On the other side are the Truck Stop Cafe, the post office and fire station, the general store and the hardware store, and the American Legion post. The residential streets, off to the right, are shady, with gravel pavement, modest frame bungalows, and the brick and stucco Lutheran Church. Overall, though, the feeling Wolverton gives is one of being exposed, open to wind, weather, the roar of passing trucks, and the silences of the prairie.

At the entrance to the town, behind the service station that Mark's father ran for years, stood Mark and John's schoolhouse, just out of view. District 31–Victoria's was a large, handsome, two-story building with rows of tall, graceful windows on both floors. It was built in 1906 and is listed in the National Register of Historic Places. There was a sweeping green lawn in front and the town park just behind. An American flag waved from a flagpole, just as it had when school was in session.

Mark was up on a ladder, patching the roof. He climbed down and ushered me into the former school library, now the reception area, and went off to wash tar off his hands. John would be along in a minute; he was still presiding over lunch, he explained. The library was an elegant room, with high ceilings, beautiful painted woodwork, and green and red velvet Victorian sofas and chairs. Bookshelves dominated the room, as in the old days, with some of the books left over from the old school library.

Once the lunch crowd had gone, Mark returned, bringing John with him. An older man poked his head in; my view was blocked and I couldn't make out much beyond a large cigar. The visitor was Mark's father, now retired and active in the senior-citizens' center headquartered in the building.

Mark was born and raised in Wolverton and never left (he attended elementary school in the very building in which we were sitting). Blond and good-looking, he had the poise and reserve of a diplomat. He received his degree in architecture from North Dakota State University in Fargo and worked in a Fargo engineering office until a year before. Now, he devoted himself full-time to the restaurant and had his own architectural office upstairs. John, the son of a Fargo physician, was born in Newfoundland, Canada, and moved to Fargo in 1973. He was tall, with thinning brown hair and an expressive face. There was a warmth and exuberance about him; I was sure he made the perfect restaurant host.

John, who avidly followed politics, was discoursing on Ronald Reagan's nomination of Robert Bork to the U.S. Supreme Court, which was big news at the time. An active Republican while in college, he had turned against his old party and informed me proudly that he voted against Reagan both times he ran for president. "This is strong Reagan country," he said. "Everyone at *that* church [pointing at the Free Evangelical Church across the way] and everyone at *that* church [the Lutheran church down the street] voted for Reagan."

Mark and John became lovers in 1980 when John was a senior at North Dakota State University, majoring in sociology, and Mark was working in his Fargo engineering office. John moved to Wolverton to live with Mark and, the following year, the two bought the deteriorating schoolhouse. By the time of the incident, they had renovated much of the structure and had hosted a couple of banquets. Their intention was for the building to serve as city hall and a center for the town's senior citizens, in addition to being a restaurant; in fact, the older folks were scheduled to move into their quarters the day after the trouble happened.

To understand the events that transpired that evening in 1982 and in the weeks that followed, one has to go back still further, to the previous summer and fall. Mark, thirty at the time, had served for two terms as a member of the Wolverton City Council and had been on the council of the local Lutheran church for seven years. He was the pride of his family, a solid citizen who hadn't moved away to Fargo or Minneapolis, as had many of his high-school classmates. That summer, Mark had given up his city-council post in order to run for mayor. The incumbent mayor had told Mark he wouldn't seek another term and assured him he wouldn't stand in his way. Then came an unpleasant series of occurrences. Mark and John subscribed to the *Advocate*, the same national gay periodical in whose personal section Bunceton mayor Gene Ulrich had met his lover Larry ten years before. The *Advocate* always came in a plain brown wrapper to protect closeted subscribers like Mark and John. That summer, their issues began arriving with the envelopes slightly torn to suggest inadvertent damage. Then they arrived torn more blatantly, and finally, opened completely. After a while, the tampering ceased. Meanwhile, rumors began to circulate in Wolverton: that Mark and John planned to turn the old schoolhouse into a nightclub [a report that particularly upset members of the extremely conservative Free Evangelical Church, located directly across the street]; that Mark was gay. Then, just as in Gene Ulrich's first mayoral race in Bunceton, the incumbent changed his mind at the last moment and entered the race. On election day, he defeated Mark by two votes out of the slightly more than one hundred cast. In this case, however, there was no technicality to elevate Mark into the mayor's chair.

As a result of the rumors and pre-election shenanigans, a number of the townspeople began to look warily at Mark and John and the District 31 schoolhouse. Mark had his political enemies, too—the cliquish "bar crowd," as he referred to the mayor and some members of the city council who hung out at the Truck Stop Cafe. They didn't care in the least if he took a fall.

During this period, Mark was also active in the Prairie Gay and Lesbian Community, the Fargo-Moorhead group whose monthly dances provided the major gay social events in the days before My Place. Mark suggested holding the January dance in the old schoolhouse he and John were fixing up in Wolverton. People would feel comfortable there, he reasoned, because it was far enough from Fargo that those in attendance wouldn't have to worry about being recognized attending a gay event.

On that Friday evening in January 1982, the caravans of Fargo's gay community headed down Highway 75 to Wolverton. The dance turned out to be one of the group's most heavily attended, and midway through the evening, everything was going as planned. John was tending bar and Mark was acting as host; many of the guests were dancing. Then came a knock at the front door. When the person stationed at the door opened it, he was confronted by the mayor of Wolverton, members of the city council, and a crowd of outraged citizens, demanding the right to enter. He informed them it was a private party; they countered with a flyer publicizing the dance. Although he still told them they couldn't come in, they pushed their way through. Most of the crowd milled around in the front lobby, while the mayor inspected the other rooms, trying to ascertain exactly what was going on in the old town schoolhouse. "We've got trouble," Mark told John, who promptly telephoned the sheriff. Half an hour later, two deputies showed up and politely asked the townspeople to leave. They did so.

For Mark, the incident didn't end there. When the townspeople arrived, he had tried to stand in the background. He had hoped his neighbors wouldn't assume he was gay, merely hosting the event. That was a vain hope, and soon word was all over town. As it happened, Mark's parents were spending the weekend in the Twin Cities. His mother had known about Mark's homosexuality for years, but he had never told his father. So on Monday, an abashed Mark walked over to the service station where his father worked to tell him he was gay, before his father learned it from half the town. "Why didn't you tell me earlier?" was his father's only reply. Mark's father, in fact, turned out to be a major bulwark of support in the days that followed. "My father took on the whole community to protect his son," Mark said.

The pastor of the church where Mark was a member of the council proved far less sympathetic, however. According to Mark's account, the minister called him to his office and informed him that when he was in the military, "We used to use homosexuals for target practice." Soon after that meeting, the pastor sent a letter to the bishop of his diocese, members of the church council, the mayor of Wolverton, and Mark's parents. The letter informed them that Mark was a practicing homosexual, recommended that he have nothing to do with the town's youth, and suggested he should resign from the church council. Mark could continue to sing in the church choir and take communion, though. The letter, which Mark said was also circulated at a basketball game in town, stated explicitly that Mark and John were lovers. Mark claimed that the pastor had no basis on which to make this statement. The pastor had never asked him directly if he was gay or about the nature of his relationship with John, he said.

Mark was devastated by the turn of events. Fargo activist Mark Chekola, who was involved in Lutherans Concerned, an organization that lobbies the Lutheran church to be more accepting of gays, arranged a meeting for Mark with the bishop. Mark remembered the bishop as warm and understanding. At one point in the conversation, he asked Mark why he wanted to remain on the church council. "Faith without works is nothing," Mark replied. That was the right answer, but the bishop's major concern, it appeared, was to avoid controversy. He urged that Mark resign from the council in order to "heal the brokenness," a phrase that Mark has not forgotten.

Mark then wrote a letter to the church council, offering to resign if requested to do so. In the letter, he described what it was like to discover he was gay in a small town and related the jokes he had had to put up with while in high school; he also tried to put the most positive gloss possible on the Lutheran church's views on homosexuality, which was no easy task. A special meeting of the church council was called. The church secretary read Mark's letter aloud to the council and, as she reached the end, burst into tears. But Mark complained that the pastor "turned the whole thing around" by making it appear as if Mark were offering to leave the council of his own free will. Finally, the council decided by a one-vote margin (with Mark abstaining) to ask him to resign. After the decision, Mark's uncle, the president of the council, embraced him. Mark never returned to the church council, rarely went to church afterwards, and complained bitterly that the pastor had made no effort to reach out and "heal the brokenness."

Five and half years after these events, little hostility towards the two men was evident, though battle lines were still drawn to some degree. All of Mark's family had been supportive at the time of the trouble and remained so, except for one uncle, "a religious fundamentalist and a conservative Republican," in Mark's description, who continued to have nothing to do with his nephew. A woman in town who demanded of Mark, "How can you do this?" the night of the incident was now a good friend. Nonetheless, members of the Free Evangelical Church never quite reconciled themselves to a gay-owned business across the street. When District 31–Victoria's appeared in a directory published by *Equal Time*, the Minneapolis gay newspaper, listing businesses where gay people were welcome, the church was outraged. Accusing Mark and John of advertising in a "pornographic magazine" (a description that hardly applied to the serious-minded *Equal Time*), the Free Evangelicals pulled their aerobics classes from the schoolhouse and canceled a music festival for evangelical youth scheduled there.

"It has been a roller-coaster ride," conceded Mark. "After the big incident, there was such sincerity. When people said, 'How are you?' they really meant it." John added, somewhat more realistically, "People who were our good friends are still our good friends. People who didn't care for Mark in the first place still don't like him."

After we had talked for a while, Mark and John took me on a tour of the premises, starting with the upstairs banquet rooms (for weddings, birthday parties, and family reunions), the art gallery, and the gift shop, which specialized in crystal, brass, and handcrafted items. District 31–Victoria's was the major employer in Wolverton (after the grain elevators), they told me, with twelve to fourteen people working there. Ladies' groups and garden clubs traveled down from Fargo for lunch, and young professional couples came in for dinner.

We retraced our steps downstairs into the former first- and second-grade classroom, where elegant dining was offered five nights a week. The room was furnished with black chairs, white tablecloths, and a grand piano (a pianist entertained in the evenings). There was also a smaller dining room used for breakfast and lunch; customers consisted mostly of farm and construction crews, plus those ladies' groups from Fargo-Moorhead. Although neither Mark nor John did the cooking, they managed the place, waited on tables, and developed many of the recipes. "We are trying to move beyond meat and potatoes," said Mark. "Dining experiences in the Fargo-Moorhead area are evolving, and we are trying to be on the crest of the wave."

Mark and John lived a quiet life, largely dominated by work. Their weekly ritual of stopping by My Place for a drink was new for them. When they heard the bar was in danger of closing, they decided to patronize it regularly to show support. "We have met tons of people there, some of whom we hadn't seen in years," said John. "We were more part of the community before we started the business. It was so absorbing."

They also were beginning to make connections with other gay people in the surrounding area. A high-school classmate of Mark's recently approached him at the restaurant after dinner and asked to speak with him in private. The man was breaking up with his lover and needed some advice. "I had known him for twenty years and had no idea he was gay," said Mark. Recently, another young man who worked for a very conservative farmer near Wolverton took Mark aside, informing him in hushed tones that he too was gay. "When people say they want to talk to me, it is always about one thing," Mark chuckled. Today, Mark and John said gay people in the area were increasing their interaction with one another. "It is getting exciting out here in the country," said Mark. "People aren't moving away as much as they were. And some people are moving back to the area after seven or eight years," a trend he suggested might in part be related to AIDS. "People think there is safety here, that they won't get AIDS here," said John. "There are fewer [sexual] contacts."

One of Mark and John's major activities outside of managing the restaurant has been to take care of the city park, located just behind the schoolhouse. It had a tennis court, slides, seesaws, and a pavilion. Mark had designed the park himself during his tenure as Wolverton park commissioner prior to all the controversy; his father landscaped it. He and John do the mowing and weeding, taking care of the property "as if it were our own," in John's words.

Mark had considered moving to Minneapolis after he graduated from college, but decided to stay in Wolverton because he was afraid that his best friend and cousin—with whom he would have shared an apartment—would find out he was gay. Today, he was a strong booster of Wolverton, critical of his high-school classmates who had the disloyalty to move to Fargo. There was no reason they couldn't work in Fargo but still live in Wolverton, he insisted. John concurred. People who moved from Wolverton to Fargo didn't lead their lives any differently than they would had they stayed in their hometown, he claimed. "They still work in their yards and go out a little bit," he said. "If they lived in Wolverton, they would do the same thing. The only difference is that you can't order out for pizza and can't get movies [from the local convenience store that stocked videos] after ten at night."

They insisted that by staying in Wolverton as openly gay people they were making a difference. "Most people in Fargo-Moorhead know the restaurant is run by gay people," said Mark. "We are making a contribution because people say, 'These guys are doing something for themselves and their community.' Hopefully, they will say, 'Maybe it doesn't make a difference.' This is where the advancements are being made." For his part, John argued that the "gay ghetto that you find in large cities doesn't do anything for gay rights. People become so immersed in it they don't realize there is any need to protect what they have."

I was intrigued by a number of similarities between the role Gene Ulrich played in Bunceton and the one Mark and John played in Wolverton. In Bunceton, it was Gene who took credit for senior housing; in Wolverton, Mark and John were the ones who established a senior-citizens' center. Gene's major priority was a park; so was Mark and John's. Gene had paved the streets, torn down unsightly houses, and remodeled older ones through the federal block grant he got for Bunceton; Mark and John had restored the town schoolhouse and turned it into a community center of sorts.

Mark was even plotting his political resurrection. He was talking about changing the Wolverton town council and filling it with people not associated with the "bar crowd." A run for mayor at some time in the future was a real possibility, he said, although at present, he was too busy. John was sure he would win easily. Being civic-minded was the way these gay men coped with being gay in small town America and, once the initial resistance was overcome, it mostly appeared to work.

"Any dances planned soon?" I asked facetiously as I was about to leave. The response, as I expected, was no. Mark and John have a business to run, after all. But if they did have a gay dance, they were sure they wouldn't receive the same reaction they did on that night in 1982. "I don't think anyone would be surprised or would care," said John. Mark was a little more cautious. "A few people might kick up a fuss," he conceded, perhaps referring to the church just across the street or to his political adversaries down at the Truck Stop Cafe. But most of their neighbors, he believed, would just let it go by. "People in this area," he said, "have really grown up a lot in the last few years."

BISMARCK, NORTH DAKOTA

(POPULATION 44,485)

As I traveled through the heartland, one of the things that struck me was how little AIDS was discussed, how remote it seemed. Sometimes, I felt that the gap between urban and rural gay men, between the East and West coasts and the small towns in the vast middle of the country had the most to do with the atmosphere of crisis that prevailed in the major cities and the relative calm among gays in the rest of America. In Fargo, for example, Anne told me that AIDS was still viewed as "a problem of New York and San Francisco." Lenny Tweedon, who probably had a better sense of the gay male community in Fargo, thought the disease had reached the margins of consciousness but had still not made a real impact. "What I have heard lately is people saying, 'My friend in The Cities [Minneapolis–St. Paul] just found out he has AIDS.' So it is hitting near home but not at home."

Gay men were now much more cautious, Lenny thought, but much of the increased caution seemed to be focused on the great gay world beyond Fargo. The locals would go to Minneapolis–St. Paul for the weekend and would go to the bars but be careful not to go home with anyone. And Lenny related that when a visitor from San Francisco showed up at My Place, most of the other patrons would have nothing to do with him because of fear of AIDS. His response was: "Did you ever think that because he comes from San Francisco, he might in fact be more educated about AIDS than most of the guys who come here?" My Place did give out condoms, but the concept of safe sex, the prevailing ethos in the larger cities, seemed as remote as the disease itself.

Although the death that summer of well-known gay farmer Dick Hanson brought home to many in rural Minnesota that AIDS was not just an urban phenomenon, Mark and John in Wolverton still claimed "there is safety here." They talked as if the virus had no incubation period, as if rural and small-town gay men never went off to the bars and the baths of the larger cities. Part of the problem was that the few cases that occurred often didn't become public knowledge. Fargo-Moorhead activist Mark Chekola confided that a former lover had recently died of AIDS in Fargo. The man had never revealed to his doctor that he was gay, and his death was never attributed to AIDS. "It was completely covered up," said Mark. Clearly, this kind of refusal to acknowledge the truth contributed to a mood of evasion and denial.

Bismarck, North Dakota, was one of the least likely places to encounter AIDS in middle America. At the time I visited North Dakota, in late September 1987, exactly five cases of AIDS had been reported to health authorities in the state, making it, along with South Dakota, the lowest of all fifty states. Altogether, thirty people in North Dakota had tested positive for exposure to HIV. I had assumed the majority of those cases would have been in Fargo; Bismarck was smaller, more isolated. But Bismarck was where I met Darrel Hildebrant and stayed with him for four days. A year previously Darrel had tested positive for antibodies to HIV; three months before my arrival, he had been diagnosed with ARC (AIDS-related complex), the "milder" form of AIDS and the condition that often precedes the development of the full-blown disease. Darrel had made his condition public. In fact, he had been dubbed "the Rock Hudson of North Dakota."

I wasn't aware of any of this on the warm fall day as I drove along the interstate on the two hundred mile journey from Fargo west to Bismarck. All I knew was that Darrel was a librarian who had recently formed The Coalition, a statewide gay group, and had started a collection of books on gay and lesbian subjects, which he called the Lambda Library.

Although Fargo calls itself the "gateway to the West," it is actually Bismarck that deserves that label. East of Bismarck, the landscape is classic prairie—flat, treeless, with fields of wheat and sunflowers, all yellow and brown in the fierce autumn sunlight. West of Bismarck the landscape becomes rougher, less congenial, with desolate hillsides and great buttes rising like pyramids out of the plain. Horses graze on barren ground, and the cottonwoods stand in clusters for warmth and companionship.

Bismarck is dominated by the eighteen-story state capitol building, which was built after the old capitol was destroyed by fire in 1930 and which reminded me of pictures I had seen of Moscow University. Although the population is relatively small, Bismarck is a sprawling place, with a number of characterless modern subdivisions. Even the governor's mansion is a fifties-style ranch house on a broad avenue. You don't stroll around Bismarck. You drive your pickup to work, to the Ground Round for a hamburger, to the mall to shop at J.C. Penney's or Dayton's. Ethnically, Bismarck is homogeneous: I never saw a black or Hispanic person, although there were some American Indians, many of whom lived on nearby reservations. Economically, it was depressed; with the drop in oil prices and the collapse of the energy boom in the western part of the state, two newly constructed hotels had already filed for bankruptcy.

Darrel met me downtown. He was on his way home from the Bismarck Public Library, where he had worked for thirteen years, mostly as a children's librarian. Darrel was forty and rather ordinary looking, with thinning brown hair, a mustache, and a scraggly beard. He was full of optimism and good cheer, and by the end of my four days in Bismarck I found him an inspirational figure, almost a saintly one. On first impression, though, he just looked like the average guy down the block, which is as it should be with saints, I suppose. He liked to describe himself, with a twinkle in his eye, as "a shy country boy."

I followed him to his two-story colonial townhouse condominium, a five-minute drive from downtown. He had originally bought the condominium with his wife, to whom he had been married for thirteen years. They had split up five years before, and he was now living there with his lover, Maurice Hlavacek.

No one would mistake Maurice, at twenty-eight, for a shy country boy, even though he grew up in Bismarck. He has dark hair that stands straight on his head, punk style, a pierced ear, and he usually wore a necklace and bangles. He always had a cigarette dangling from his mouth. Maurice loved to cook and take care of people, and Darrel said that he had put on thirty pounds since Maurice had moved in several months before. Maurice was constantly bringing us trays of coffee, pizza, cookies, and cakes and making hearty dinners—beef roasts and meat loaves. Beyond that and showering his white poodle, Missy, with endless affection, Maurice tended to be friendly but uncommunicative.

Maurice told me he loved Darrel, but Darrel sometimes made it sound as if he had taken Maurice in as an act of kindness. In any event, they seemed to have struck a bargain of sorts: Darrel would give Maurice a place to live, look out for him, and support him financially, while Maurice would serve up immense quantities of red meat and keep Darrel as healthy as possible. Somewhere, too, there was affection and companionship. It seemed to me not unlike most American marriages.

One day, Maurice asked me to drive him to the mall. He was wearing a green fishnet shirt and baggy trousers, a necklace and bangles, and his hair seemed to stand up on his head straighter and more defiantly than usual. He wanted to go to Dayton's, the Minneapolis-based department store, to return an Izod shirt he had purchased five years before but had apparently never worn. "They will take back anything at Dayton's. They always give you cash and they never ask for the sales slip," he assured me. He was right. Maurice doesn't walk, he strides, as if he has something extremely urgent to do and doesn't care who might be in the way. I had trouble keeping up with him. As he made for the customer-service department, pushing his way through racks of sports shirts and jeans, I found myself lagging far enough behind to observe the reactions of other customers. Everyone in the store seemed to be doing double takes, stopping in their tracks for a look at him. "Now I've seen everything," one teenage girl told her companion. "He is even wearing a necklace." One woman muttered to another, "Not even in The Cities, dear, not even in The Cities!" I don't deny that Maurice might have attracted some attention in a larger and more sophisticated place. But the way people in Bismarck reacted, it seemed to me, said something about how unaccustomed they were to anything out of the ordinary—and how downright hostile they were, as well.

In fact, a week before, Maurice had been asked to leave the Ground Round, a popular lunch place, ostensibly for wearing an earring. He spent a couple of hours one morning trying to get through to the chain's headquarters to file a complaint. I encouraged him. Most of the gay people in Bismarck looked at Maurice with a mix of awe and disapproval, and while you could dismiss him as someone who desperately craved attention, I admired him nonetheless. I figured to dress the way he did in Bismarck, North Dakota, took a great deal of courage. If anyone in Bismarck was on the front lines of gay liberation, it was Maurice.

I spent much of my time in Bismarck sitting around Darrel's basement. It reminded me of my study at home. There was a cozy nook with a rocking chair with an Indian blanket thrown over it and a writing desk. The Lambda Library was also there, just a built-in bookcase filled with hardcovers and paperbacks and neatly arranged piles of the Seattle and Minneapolis gay newspapers. On top of the bookshelf was a row of leather hats from the days when Darrel was involved in the leather scene, and against one wall was a bunch of department-store mannequins belonging to Maurice. It was there, over a period of a few days, that Darrel related the story of his transformation from small-town librarian to habitué of the S and M bars to gay and AIDS activist.

He had grown up on a sheep ranch on the Montana border, not far from the famous Elkhorn ranch where Theodore Roosevelt took refuge after the death of his wife. Darrel always was attracted to men; oddly, he thought it was because of his interest in fashion. He rationalized that he wanted to look like them, not go to bed with them. "Our parents always made us the best-dressed kids in school," he recalled. He married at twenty, while a student at

Dickinson State College, and for ten years he and his wife had a very happy marriage, which he said he "wouldn't have given up for anything." He worked as children's librarian and puppeteer, traveling around North Dakota and the rest of the country with his life-size puppets (he once performed at the Kennedy Center in Washington, D.C.), putting on ballets such as *The Nutcracker, Cinderella*, and *Hansel and Gretel.*

When he had been married for ten years, he met a man at a national library conference and tumbled into bed with him. Terrified, he packed his bags the next day and fled before the conference was over. After that came two years of what he called "pure guilt." But the experience was too strong to be discounted; it had touched something basic in him. He corresponded with the man and finally got up the nerve to suggest they share a room together at another conference. Thus began a long-distance affair—and Darrel's introduction to the world of leather and S and M. Three years later, he divorced his wife (whom he said was still his best friend) and became involved in a five-year romance with another man in Bismarck.

The two had an open relationship, and Darrel would fly off to the East Coast for conferences, puppet shows, and sex. "I learned fast," he said. "I was like a kid in a candy store. Full leather and S and M were more my angle than anything else," sexual inclinations he attributed to growing up on a ranch with its rough existence and macho style. In the mid-eighties, he was spending time in bars like New York City's Mineshaft, closed now but in its heyday known for its open sexual activity. "I was having the time of my life," he said. "I knew about AIDS and yet I didn't. Nothing was said here in the Midwest."

In one city, he met a man in a bar who invited him home, and then kept him tied up for two days in a darkened basement as part of an S and M ritual. "He would come home at noon, use me, and off he would go," said Darrel. "I loved it. I didn't have any idea what time it was. At first I was scared. And then I got to trust the man. I knew he wasn't going to do anything wrong. I liked the suspense of it all and the excitement."

For the boy from Beach, North Dakota, the bright lights of Manhattan provided as much excitement as rough sex in dark places. He related arriving at the Broadway musical *La Cage aux Folles* in a horse and carriage; he wore a black tuxedo and the friend who accompanied him was in white tux and top hat. They had front balcony seats, with elderly couples on each side. At intermission, one of his neighbors elbowed him. "You guys sure know how to put on a damn good show," he said.

In July 1986, Darrel tested positive for antibodies to HIV. After the initial shock of his test result, it took him three months "to get my ducks in a row," as he put it. He immediately stopped having unsafe sex and called anyone he had had sexual relations with to urge them to get tested. He telephoned his father, whom he had never told he was gay, to give him both pieces of news. "The *Early Frost* thing," he noted, in reference to the highly praised made-for-TV movie. Although he hadn't been involved in anything resembling gay activism before, he now set up his basement library. He started putting pressure on the North Dakota AIDS Task Force to take a more aggressive stance. When the gay community representative on the Task Force resigned, Darrel was appointed to take his place. From his first Task Force meeting, he became convinced that it was necessary to develop a framework to disseminate AIDS information within the gay community. The result was The Coalition, formed in February 1987. Seven months later, The Coalition had thirty-five members who held weekend get-togethers that included meetings, workshops, and an evening social function. It established a support group for people who tested positive for HIV infection or were diagnosed with ARC or AIDS, and had held a safe-sex workshop for the gay community and another workshop to educate social workers about AIDS and HIV.

During this period, Darrel made his antibody status public (he had not yet been diagnosed with ARC). He wanted to be very honest with the gay male community, he said, to offer the "shock value" of "Hey, someone has been exposed to it—get tested and know where you stand." But when an article about The Coalition, including Darrel's name, appeared on the front page of the *Bismarck Tribune*, Darrel's boss at the library was upset. According to Darrel's account, the library director informed city commissioners and library board members that Darrel was gay and HIV-positive. A special staff meeting was called, where Darrel talked about his sexuality. The state AIDS coordinator also appeared, explained how HIV was transmitted, and gave assurances that Darrel was not contagious. Nonetheless, Darrel was convinced that the purpose of the meeting was not to educate the library staff but to humiliate him into resigning. If that was the case, the plan backfired. His co-workers rallied around him; even the high-school students working part-time at the library gave him a tape of the song "Lean on Me." Darrel stayed on, but was transferred from his position as children's librarian to head of adult programming and public relations. (Two months after my visit he quit his job, charging that library officials had forced him out through harassment and constant reviews of his work.)

For Darrel, 1987 was not a good year. In February, his car was hit by a tractor-trailer while he was on his way to work. He broke his neck and spent a month in the hospital; his doctors believed he would be a quadriplegic. His lover, terrified of having to take care of someone in that condition, left him. It was the husband of Darrel's ex-wife who came to the hospital each day and fed him.

Despite the prognosis, Darrel recovered normal use of his arms and legs. He returned to work and to his activism with The Coalition and the AIDS Task Force. Soon after, he met Maurice. But Darrel wasn't feeling well. He complained of fatigue and swollen glands and occasional disorientation. No one in Bismarck could figure out what was wrong. He flew out to San Francisco to consult a doctor. There, in July, he was diagnosed with AIDS-related complex.

His accident and the diagnosis of ARC appeared to increase Darrel's energy and enthusiasm. He kept up a busy schedule of public speaking around the state. His name was in the newspaper so frequently that the *Bismarck Tribune* headlined a notice of a talk he gave "Hildebrant Speaks"; no elaboration was necessary. Sometimes his exuberance seemed to run away with him: for example, he was negotiating with the Catholic bishop of Bismarck about helping fund The Coalition hotline, and was trying to bring Elizabeth Taylor to North Dakota to host an AIDS fund-raiser (the actress had once stated she intended to visit all fifty states to crusade against AIDS, he said). I was skeptical, but if anyone could pull off the unexpected, Darrel could. His message was a simple one. "We are in a unique position here in North Dakota," he repeated over and over again. "We are number fifty of the fifty states in terms of AIDS. We are sitting in a window. We can see the whole United States out there, see all their mistakes, what is going on, how the virus is spreading. And we still have time to do something about it here."

Unlike most gay and AIDS activists in other states, he strongly supported antibody testing for heterosexual couples applying for marriage licenses. Male homosexual activity was so undercover in North Dakota and there were so many married gay men, he was convinced that AIDS would hit families in the state, not the gay population. "Married gays go out for 'slam bang, thank you, ma'am' sex with other guys and then they go home and have sex with their wives," he noted. "So they can pass the virus on to their wives and their unborn children. I think AIDS will affect families because the married men are the ones who go to the bookstores and the rest stops. That is the way society is here."

A week after my visit to Bismarck, Darrel was scheduled to address a workshop of health professionals, where he would reveal that he had ARC. He had already told them that someone with ARC would address the group, and said "people's eyes lit up" at the prospect. But no one realized the person in question was actually Darrel. (His declaration, he told me later, was greeted by three minutes of stunned silence.)

The fact that Darrel was well known throughout the state for his puppeteering (he had performed at the state fair for twelve years running) put him in a good position to raise consciousness about AIDS in North Dakota. People needed to know someone with ARC or AIDS for reality to hit home, he insisted. It was one of the members of the state AIDS Task Force who told him, "You are going to be the Rock Hudson of North Dakota." Darrel rather liked that title. "If that is what it takes, that is what it takes," he said.

I asked him what explained his transformation, why he hadn't chosen to enjoy what remained of his life and nurse his health instead of driving hours across the prairie to give "AIDS 101" lectures to a handful of people huddled in a church basement in some tiny town. "The one thing everyone has said who studies death and dying is that when you start facing your own death, you become more philosophical in life," he said. "I have learned to say, 'Hey, to hell with work. Forget it. What matters to me? People matter to me.' I want to do unto others. I would have given anything if someone had done this before me so I wasn't the one who got exposed to AIDS." Nonetheless, people react differently *in extremis*, and the way Darrel confronted the prospect of fatal illness indicated he was made of sterner stuff than many.

That impression was borne out by a conversation I had with a prisoner at the North Dakota State Penitentiary in Bismarck. One evening when we were about to sit down to one of Maurice's sumptuous repasts (I think it was pot roast), the phone rang. On the line was Rob Rippey, who had set fire to the home of his lover's mother eight months before, shortly after he tested HIV-positive. He was serving a four-year sentence for arson. Darrel was trying to get permission to visit him in prison. After asking some questions about the way prison officials were treating him, Darrel handed me the phone.

The story Rob told me went like this. In January, he had moved from Phoenix to Minot, North Dakota's fourth largest city. He and his lover, Jesse Kjelbertson, went to live in the house Jesse's mother owned there. At that time, Rob and Jesse were tested for HIV, with Rob testing positive and Jesse testing negative. Soon after, Rob became ill with pneumonia and was convinced he was dying. He quickly went over the edge. "I was in a state of shock for a couple of weeks after I got my test result," he said. "I don't even remember what happened. I tried to get help but I couldn't." What did happen was that he burned down Jesse's mother's house so his lover could get the insurance money. The mortgage was about to be foreclosed; Rob, in his disturbed state of mind, apparently believed he was doing the family a favor.

Mrs. Kjelbertson didn't think so. She testified against Rob in court. Jesse, his lover, left him and left town. The incident and subsequent trial made the front page of the Minot newspaper and were featured prominently on the local TV news. Rob's life, he said, had been "hell ever since my arrest." In jail, he was segregated from the regular inmates and kept in the orientation area (the cellblock where incoming prisoners are received) because of fear he would spread AIDS. Some of the new prisoners were friendly but many others wouldn't even talk to him. He was forced to eat by himself, off plastic plates, and when he accidentally used the communal silverware, there was an uproar, he said. He felt like a pariah. "People stare at me all the time," he said. "I have no friends here. I worry constantly. I always blended into the crowd. I can't anymore."

Darrel was disturbed because it sounded like Rob believed the misinformation that prison officials were giving him—that sharing silverware could transmit HIV, for example. He feared they were "brainwashing" Rob. To counteract this, Darrel hoped to use his position on the North Dakota AIDS Task Force to get Rob out of jail to attend Coalition and HIV support-group meetings. At least then, he would be armed with more accurate information, which would help him stand up for his rights in prison.

Rob's case underscored the importance of the kind of work Darrel and The Coalition were doing. If Rob had had the benefit of social supports when he first learned he was HIV-positive, he might never have gone berserk and set fire to the house. And if the prison officials were better informed about how HIV was transmitted, they might not have treated Rob as a pariah. In any event, his experience offered a glimpse into the other side of AIDS in North Dakota—and the confusion, ignorance, and fear that accompanied it.

It was in Darrel's basement, too, that I met some of Bismarck's gay men and lesbians. If it could be said that AIDS was having any kind of positive effect in North Dakota, it was that The Coalition was creating a sense of community for the first time in years. There had never been a gay bar in Bismarck, and although there was a gay and lesbian group there in the late seventies and early eighties, it was short-lived. Until The Coalition was formed, Bismarck gay men and lesbians were just a disparate group of people, many of whom had little contact with one another.

Darrel's role in Bismarck paralleled that of individuals in other small cities in the upper Midwest. John Ritter, the Minnesota farmer and writer for *Equal Time,* had told me that in order for a gay community to develop in a small city or town, one person in that community had to be public about being gay. Lenny Tweedon took that leadership role in Fargo; Darrel was doing the same in Bismarck.

So Darrel's basement was an appropriate place to talk to people; it was where The Coalition held its meetings, where the gay library was located, where other Bismarck gays felt comfortable. Maurice brought more coffee and snacks, and members of the town's gay and lesbian community trooped in one by one to say hello.

There I met Phil, a 330-pound teddy bear of a man in his late thirties who had served twelve years in the penitentiary in Colorado for killing a man. He was part American Indian, with jet-black hair and dark eyes. On the outside for a year or so, he had a calm, even demeanor that made me suspect that prison had taken the fight out of him. He had won an international award as a leather designer, a craft he had learned behind bars. Phil's stories of prison life made it sound like one giant gay bathhouse, with orgies in cells and shower rooms. While in jail, he had had a six-year relationship with a "macho Mexican." He made much of having sex in prison with straight men, who under normal circumstances "would have busted you in the head." In prison, though, "a man misses affection and touching and holding," he said.

When he first arrived in the penitentiary, he clashed with the prison guards; then he learned not to let it bother him when they called him "You fucking fag." His size protected him from rape, and his placid manner enabled him to develop a good rapport with the guards, who called him "Ma." The guards left him alone to conduct his sexual liaisons; he rewarded them with gifts of leatherwork. He thought that AIDS had changed everything in prison. It was no longer the sexual funhouse he knew. Now he was living with his mother, spending his days alone in his basement studio bent over his work, dreaming of the easy sex he had in prison and longing for some companionship now that he had finally made it to the outside.

Later, Sandy Jacobson came to dinner. She had lost custody of her two children several years back in the state's most publicized lesbian custody case. Now forty, she worked in the loan department of a bank and lived in a mobile home; the day I met her, she was dressed in her work garb: a ruffled green blouse, dress slacks, and makeup. She and her twenty-six year old lover, Sue, the assistant manager of a fast-food joint, had been together for eight years. "I wish you could meet Sue," she said, her face brightening. "She is a joy and a delight with a wonderful outlook on life."

She described her fourteen-year marriage with her ex-husband, Duane, and their involvement with the fundamentalist Assemblies of God Church in Bismarck. She met Sue when both were working at J.C. Penney's, and her life changed dramatically. When Sandy and Duane separated, a judge gave her custody of the children, then aged two and eight. Her husband appealed to the North Dakota Supreme Court, which overturned the lower-court decision, awarded him custody, and ruled that Sue could not even be in the presence of the kids. Eventually, Sandy was given visitation rights and Sue was allowed to see the children "within reason."

The case made her life and her sexual orientation public. Her name and address appeared in the newspaper and on television. She met other gay people in Bismarck for the first time, even gave a speech on her case to a gay group that existed then. When she began to cry in the middle of her talk, Sue, who was sitting next to her, held her hand. Sandy learned later it was the first time a gay person had ever touched his or her partner at a public meeting in Bismarck.

These days she saw her kids, now sixteen and ten, regularly and was afraid her son, who was very shy, would be accused of being gay. Her children have always known about her homosexuality, which she explained to them as one of many differences in life.

She called Bismarck an "archaic, redneck place," relating a conversation at her office in which her co-workers discussed what they would do if their son came home wearing an earring, which Sandy assumed was code for being gay. One said he would put the earring in his nose and tie him up. (Men wearing earrings seemed to be a subject of continuing controversy in Bismarck.) Sandy didn't think being open about being a lesbian has helped change attitudes towards homosexuals very much. "Our friends say we are just exceptions," she noted. Nonetheless, she had never been happier in her life, she said. The year before, she and Sue got married in a public ceremony at the Unitarian Church in Bismarck, with thirty-five women in attendance. (The Unitarian-Universalist church is the only mainline denomination that recognizes gay unions.) Sue had shown her "life," she said. "When I realized I loved Sue it made me feel complete. I don't think my kids will think badly of me in the future."

The next morning, I went out for a drive with Mike Hartman. Behind the steering wheel of an automobile, he seemed in his natural element; he gripped the wheel as if he were embracing it. With blond hair and a clipped beard, in blue jeans and cowboy boots, Mike looked like every other twenty-two year old in Bismarck. He had come out only a year before and was just getting comfortable with being gay. "A year ago I couldn't be talking to you like this," he said.

He grew up in a town of five hundred people near Bismarck. In high school, he found a gay friend and they would drive around on back country roads and discuss the mysteries of sexuality. Mike was the wild kid who was always partying, who had girlfriends but didn't do anything sexual with them beyond a good-night kiss. "In a town like that, it is hard to grow up not being yourself," he said. "You have to have girlfriends and get married. But I knew what I liked."

Mike couldn't imagine telling the friends he grew up with that he was gay. They would consider him a "faggot" and nothing else would matter, despite their years of being together. He saw himself becoming increasingly distant from his high-school classmates and was genuinely sad about it. "They just wouldn't understand," Mike said mournfully. "No one would understand."

The previous year he had fallen in love with another man, describing it as "heaven, a dream come true." It was his first real relationship. They had lived together for several months; then his lover left to go to school in Minneapolis and had basically ended things with Mike. Mike took it hard. He had been depressed ever since and would start to cry at work for no apparent reason. Only now was he starting to come out of it.

He rhapsodized about his first visit to a gay disco in Minneapolis. He had watched a drag show there and "nearly dropped my johns." It was also the first time he had seen two men dancing close together and touching in public. Mike couldn't believe it. He wanted to stay in Bismarck another year or two to get some job experience, then leave. Meanwhile, he was dreaming of The Cities. "Living in Bismarck is just like the little town where I grew up," Mike said. "You go to work, you go home, you go out once in a while. It is a clean and friendly city. But if you want to do what you want, to be gay or different, it is really hard."

I found Bismarck a harsh environment for gay people. The old stereotypes seemed very much in force. People couldn't seem to grasp that a gay man or lesbian could be "a common, ordinary person," as Darrel put it. A gay medical technologist named Rod Wasem, whose hobby was off-trail biking, related a conversation that a heterosexual friend of his had had about him with another straight man. "I thought your friend Rod was gay," the second man had told Rod's friend. "But after I saw him bicycle for thirty-five miles, I knew it couldn't be true." That kind of thinking "is typical of the attitude around here," Rod said bitterly. "They think every man who is gay crochets all day."

Rod believed that homophobic stereotypes were so entrenched in Bismarck that it didn't matter how much individual gays challenged them. He told me about a gay physician who was very respected until co-workers found out that he was gay. Once it was public knowledge, everything changed. The doctor was viewed as "merely 'a fag,'" Rod said. "He wasn't the able, intelligent physician the way they had thought of him before. He became 'one who likes to suck cock,' as someone at work described him. Just that."

Bismarck seemed a particularly tough place to be gay or lesbian because it lacked some of Fargo's softening influences: three colleges, proximity to the Twin Cities, active feminist organizations, a strongly supportive mayor. If I had doubts about the importance of a gay bar to a small city after visiting Fargo, those doubts vanished after my visit to Bismarck. The town's gay and lesbian community desperately needed a place to congregate. Interestingly, the women I spoke with seemed to do better than the men. They were less discontented, less focused on getting out. One possible reason was that they were in couples, which gave them a sense of stability the men lacked; they were also targets of less day-to-day hostility than the men.

On my last morning in Bismarck, Maurice prepared a lavish breakfast of French toast and bacon, but he was even less talkative than usual. Darrel was engrossed in planning my route to Rapid City, South Dakota. I wanted to travel on a highway that would take me through a couple of Indian reservations; he wanted to send me on the Interstate, in case my car broke down again.

My last image of Darrel was of him standing in front of the house, dressed in black shorts and an "I Love New York" T-shirt. I wondered if I would ever see him again. He had said that you could live for fifteen years with ARC, although I knew that the AIDS epidemic hadn't been around that long, so nobody could really be sure. As I pulled out of the driveway, I felt a sense of helplessness. I wished that somehow I could make it all right for him and for Maurice and for everyone else in Bismarck.

But it was a fleeting thought. I remembered something else Darrel had said, that he believed in reincarnation and was sure he had lived in New York City in another life. "I can go to New York and I never get lost and I've been there thirty or forty times," he told me. "Once I was saying to a friend, 'Around this corner is a house of historical interest.' I had never been on that street before and there was the house! Once we were lost in the Bronx and had no idea where we were and I got us out of it. I have lived there before, that is all I know. Spread my ashes on Broadway!" I figured that Darrel, at least, could take care of himself.

RAPID CITY, SOUTH DAKOTA

(POPULATION 46,492)

I went to see Mount Rushmore at eight o'clock in the morning, as the guidebooks recommended. The day was clear, few other visitors were in evidence, and the Black Hills were green and shadowed and peaceful, with dazzling rock formations. Mount Rushmore itself was disappointing, though. It was impressive that someone had the audacity to carve the massive granite heads of Washington, Lincoln, Jefferson, and Theodore Roosevelt into a Dakota mountainside, but beyond the sheer accomplishment of it, the vista didn't gain much by repeated viewing. I felt sorry for the tourists who saved up retirement pensions or drove thousands of miles in crowded vehicles with squawling babies and bored teenagers for a glimpse of American iconography when a postcard would have produced the same effect.

You can't see Mount Rushmore from Rapid City, twenty-five or so miles away. The town is built on the prairie, and the surrounding hills are rough and empty, with none of the forested covering of the Black Hills themselves. Still, Rapid City exists for Mount Rushmore, for the Black Hills and the Badlands and nearby Deadwood, with its graves of Wild Bill Hickcock and Calamity Jane, and for the tourists they bring. The town is flat and low and modern, with too much sky and wide streets so exposed and open you expect to see tumbleweed blowing down them. Much of the city was destroyed by a flood several years ago, and any intimacy or character appears to have been washed away with it. "Rapid," as the locals call it, was not exactly booming economically. There was tourism, of course, and the South Dakota School of Mines, considered one of the nation's best. Nearby Ellsworth Air Force Base brought some money into the town. But I was told there had been eleven hundred houses on the market the previous spring, and the construction industry had virtually ceased functioning due to overbuilding in anticipation of the basing of the B-1 bomber at Ellsworth.

Rapid, which is located in the far west of South Dakota, near the Wyoming border, was my last stop before I headed on to Denver. I came because I wanted to hike in the Black Hills and also because I wondered what gay life would be like in the shadow of Washington, Lincoln, Jefferson, and Roosevelt, ten hours away from a town of any size or significance. Darrel had planned my route well. The ride from Bismarck had been spectacular, featuring the kind of classic Western scenery I had seen before only in movies. The Badlands, off on my left for about an hour of the drive, seemed to deserve their name: they were eerie and frightening and looked like some uninhabited planet.

But once I arrived in Rapid, I wondered why I had bothered at all. The gay community seemed as lifeless as the rest of the town. There had been a gay bar but it closed because of poor management a year before. The Black Hills Gay Coalition was no longer functioning. The most recent president of the organization had been stationed at Ellsworth Air Force Base; the story I heard was that air force security authorities learned of his identity, brought him in for questioning, and pressured him to hand over a list of names of coalition members for one of the military's periodic anti-gay witch-hunts. One person suggested the former president might have actually been working for military security all the time. But that theory could just as likely have been local paranoia.

My first introduction to the gay community was Carlton, a nervous, reticent fellow in his late thirties who wouldn't tell me where he worked and took me to a deserted, out-of-the-way diner for coffee. A fourth-generation South Dakotan, he seemed sad and isolated and told me very little of his personal life. I suspected he didn't have much of a life of his own. Either that or he expected me to announce that I worked for military intelligence and to insist he give me the names of every gay man and lesbian within a one hundred mile radius.

I did learn some things from him, though. Growing up in South Dakota in the sixties, he said, you were sure you were the only gay person in the world. Everything you ever heard about homosexuality was negative; no one you knew could possibly be "that way." There was no organized gay and lesbian movement in Rapid until 1978, he told me, when the Coalition was formed. Until then, gay male social life seemed to have been centered around pick-ups in the restroom of the Alex Johnson Hotel; many gays at the time were married, and all were in the closet. The bar, which opened in 1985 and lasted a year and a half, attracted mostly younger people and military personnel. Carlton felt out of place there. He thought life was getting better in Rapid for gay people; there was a lively debate in the daily newspaper between the minister of the Liberty Baptist Church and the mother of a lesbian. And he contended that the prevailing ethos of rugged individualism afforded gays some measure of social protection. "You risk ostracism if you are overt," he said. "On the other hand you don't have to be constantly looking over your shoulder." The problem was that Carlton seemed to be doing just that.

I was referred to a woman I'll call Betsy, whom I met for coffee at the Big Boy restaurant downtown. She was in her mid-forties, sold buffalo burgers at arts-and-crafts fairs to make extra money, and was having relationship problems. I couldn't use her name or write anything about her relationship or her job. She had moved to Rapid in the early seventies with her then-husband, who had been in the service, and had two kids, now aged twenty-two and eighteen. She had won custody of them after a court battle and emphasized that "we pretty much have a normal family." Betsy said there was very little going on for gay women in Rapid. You didn't tend to "see" people. For younger lesbians, there was softball, but unless you were part of the "party group," you were out of things. There was a NOW chapter in Rapid, but few lesbians were involved. Most lesbians left town, she said, because of social factors and lack of jobs. She stayed only because of her kids. "To live here you have to accept a four dollar an hour job with no expectations," she said. "People who don't want that or have expectations move away." She was a recovering alcoholic and was eager to start a group for addicted gays and lesbians—"drugs, alcohol, children of alcoholics, dysfunctional families, everything."

Despite this rather depressing introduction to gay life in Rapid City, I persisted. I had written to the Black Hills Gay Coalition before I left Boston, and even though the group existed in name only at that point, a man named Craig Chapman had responded, encouraging me to stop in Rapid. So I went to see Craig and his lover, Jonathan. I hoped they might be more open and just a little more upbeat than the others.

Craig and Jonathan lived in a modest frame bungalow in a Rapid neighborhood that was built in the fifties or sixties but was already beginning to look a little run-down. Craig, who was twenty-nine and appeared even younger, was tall and lanky, with shock of brown hair across his forehead and the air of a precocious adolescent. He made his living as a freelance word processor for local clients, including an ammunition supply company and the local court reporter.

I noticed that Craig was wearing the ever-controversial earring and mentioned all the upset in Bismarck over the issue. In Rapid, Craig told me, no one much cared. "If you don't flaunt it, they don't bother you," he said. "There is an atmosphere of 'live and let live' here." He even walked around town carrying a "purse," which turned out to be an embroidered Greek bag, the sort of thing that members of both sexes toted in Cambridge, Massachusetts, circa 1972. Craig had come to Rapid from Pennsylvania in 1981, after graduating from Bucknell, to work on a master's degree in geology at the South Dakota School of Mines, but he never finished. He was happy living in Rapid; the city was large enough to provide anonymity and social support as well, he said. I suspected he liked it primarily because Rapid was the place where he formed his own identity and learned to function as an adult.

When I arrived, Jonathan, Craig's lover of five and a half years, was huddled over his desk with a book. In keeping with that first impression, he seemed to me rather thoughtful and serious-minded. Balding and a little paunchy (he would be fifty the following month), Jonathan worked as a custodian at a Rapid City hospital. He is a quarter Creek and Cherokee and was married for thirteen years to a Sioux woman. The two had lived on the Rosebud Sioux Reservation near the Nebraska border; his wife and most of the five children still lived there.

Jonathan told me that for the thirteen years of his marriage, he had engaged in a "mental battle" with his sexuality. He had married originally because he was a strong believer in family and thought marriage would "cure" him. "My wife and I clicked but when the uniqueness wears off, you are left with the feelings you want to deny," he said. While married, he had homosexual experiences, which he didn't consider infidelity, just "messing around." After a number of years, the conflict between the two sides of his life became untenable. He attempted suicide and spent eight weeks at a psychiatric hospital in Rapid City. Shortly afterwards, he met Craig, divorced his wife, and moved from the reservation into Rapid. She was hurt and bitter and tried to prevent him from seeing the children. Over time, their relationship had improved, and he now visited his children regularly.

Despite the exhilaration of coming out (he related how wonderful it had been to attend a roller-skating party, his first gay event), the new life did not come easily to Jonathan. Indian cultural values of family and tradition were too central to his world-view to give him much peace. He felt good about being gay and about his relationship with Craig, but he was miserable about having left his wife and children. In an effort to assuage his guilt, he would smoke marijuana every night from the time he came home from work until he went to sleep. Eventually, he checked into a treatment program and overcame his drug dependency. But the conflicts remained.

Jonathan was studying Indian culture and religion under a Sioux medicine man, and this had helped him merge the two parts of his identity. On three different occasions he had gone on a vision quest, in which a medicine man led him—barefoot, with only a blanket around him—to a place in the wilderness where he was left to pray and fast for several days. He received his direction in life from Sioux tradition, prayed every day, and said he could make herbal medicines and perform certain ceremonies.

"Have you read *The Spirit and the Flesh* by Walter Williams?" he asked me. I hadn't, but I was familiar with the book by the UCLA ethnohistorian who examined the tradition of the berdache among Native Americans. The berdache were Indian men who remained unmarried, had sex with other males, often wore women's clothing, and had an accepted—even revered—social status and a special ceremonial role. Jonathan proceeded to tell me about the *winktes*, the berdache of the Lakota Sioux. One role of the *winktes*, he said, was to present male children with sacred names that offered spiritual protection. The naming would take place in a special ceremony, and the *winktes* seem to have functioned as godfathers to the children. They were also believed to have healing powers and sometimes went along on war parties for this purpose. Jonathan became increasingly enthusiastic as he spoke; he was part of a proud and ancient tradition, not just as an American Indian but as a gay American Indian, as well.

Craig's spirituality and his sources of identity and self-esteem were more conventional. He had been on the board of the local Unitarian-Universalist church and was serving as church treasurer. Church members represented his primary support group. The gay community was too party-oriented and cliquish for his tastes, so most of his friends were liberal heterosexuals active in his church, NOW, and the Democratic party. It seemed to mean a lot to him to find acceptance outside the gay community. One woman who had a gay daughter and was president of the congregation functioned as his adopted mother, he told me. She had officiated at the marriage of Craig and Jonathan in a church ceremony a year before, attended by about twenty-five people.

As I was chatting with Craig and Jonathan, two teenage girls wandered in from the rear of the house, picked up the telephone, and ordered a pizza. I thought they lived in a back apartment and had just come to use the phone. In fact, one was Jonathan's oldest daughter and the other was her best friend. Three days later, assuming all went as planned, the teenage daughter was moving in with Jonathan, and Craig was moving out and into his own apartment.

Although Craig and Jonathan insisted they were not breaking up, their relationship was clearly going through some major changes. Jonathan wanted his children to live with him—first his oldest daughter and later on, if possible, the others as well. (The youngest was five years old.) The kids, he explained, had little in the way of educational and other opportunities on the reservation. He wanted them to have the advantages that living in Rapid could bring.

Craig simply did not fit into this evolving family arrangement. He didn't get along with Jonathan's daughter and, as a self-described "quiet home-body," did not want to live in the midst of constant visits from the other children. The fact that the house was small and cramped, with just a living room, Craig's workspace, kitchen, and a couple of bedrooms, made matters worse. Another problem was that Craig ran his word-processing business out of the house. Work would prove difficult if not impossible with the kids around.

It was not an easy situation to resolve. So much about his relationship with Craig was compatible, Jonathan said—their low-key styles, their interests in politics and rock climbing. But he noted that so many remarriages involving children fail, and remarriage was, after all, perhaps the most appropriate way to view his and Craig's relationship. "The pitfalls of kids and remarriage are not unique to heterosexuals," he told me. He said he didn't want their relationship to break up, but at the same time, his kids were his major priority. To make it all work out required "a realigning of space," as he delicately put it.

Although Craig said that his moving out was a decision that had "mutually evolved," he was clearly ambivalent. On the one hand, he said he felt he was increasingly responsible for Jonathan's distance from the kids, and believed Jonathan had a moral and legal obligation to look after them. And he suggested, hopefully, "maybe it will be more romantic this way." On the other hand, he wondered—and worried—if he and Jonathan would ever live together again.

Jonathan was much more optimistic. He saw Craig's departure and his daughter's moving in as representing another stage of the relationship, an accommodation to other realities. "Craig and I each had fantasies of our own and shared fantasies," he said. "Now we have to be realistic about the kids."

Perhaps, all this was a rationalization. Jonathan and Craig might really be nearing the end of their relationship and were trying to find a graceful way of terminating it. But I preferred to take what they said at face value. I saw them struggling with some very contemporary dilemmas—how to balance relationship and family, love and responsibility. They were trying to find a way to keep their relationship going and, at least in Jonathan's case, to solidify ties to children and culture and tradition, too.

What struck me once again was this movement towards a richer, fuller life. Anne, the college teacher in Fargo, had said you couldn't have a one-dimensional existence if you remained in this part of the country. You had to be involved in other things—civic affairs, church, family. Gays who stayed in small towns and rural areas had traditionally had those community ties and involvement. Usually, they had been closeted, often in that deepest closet of all, a heterosexual marriage. Now, many were cautiously trying to combine an allegiance to their roots with some of the openness and community that gays had in big cities. And so many people I met in these smaller towns seemed to have gone through enormous changes within the last six or seven years. There was still fear of exposure, still homophobia, of course. AIDS, while seemingly remote, heightened prejudice and suspicion but also enhanced the possibility of forging links to other gay people, as I had found in Bismarck.

Under the shadow of Mount Rushmore, Craig and Jonathan were struggling with the same issues. In this process of trying to integrate different parts of their lives, they would be exploring the nature of relationships, breaking new ground. Their future together was far from certain. For them, and for everyone I met along the way, there were no pat solutions, not even necessarily happy endings; only tentative moves in difficult directions.

A TIME OF CHANGE

▼ ▼ ▼ ▼ ▼ ▼ ▼ ▼ ▼ ▼ ▼ ▼ ▼

NEWTON, MASSACHUSETTS, AND

MIAMI, FLORIDA

When I returned home to Boston from my trip through small town America, it was as if I was returning to the modern gay world. The gay and lesbian March on Washington was scheduled for the following week; organizers were hoping for a turnout of as many as half a million people. The memorial AIDS quilt—the size of two football fields—was on its way from San Francisco to be unveiled at the march. The film version of *Maurice*, E.M. Forster's novel about homosexuality in Edwardian England, was playing to packed houses in Harvard Square.

In the copy of the *New York Native* that I found in the stack of mail on my desk, the ever-controversial AIDS activist Larry Kramer was blaming the "white middle-class male majority" for the AIDS epidemic—and preaching the gospel of sexual conservatism. "The heterosexual majority has for centuries denied us every possible right of human dignity that the Constitution was framed to provide to all," he argued at a symposium sponsored by the New York Civil Liberties Union. "The right to marry. The right to own property jointly without fear the law would disinherit the surviving partner. The right to hold jobs as an openly gay person. The right to have children. . . .

So rightly or wrongly—wrongly, as it turned out—we decided we would make a virtue of the only thing you didn't have control over: our sexuality. Had we possessed these rights you denied us, had we been allowed to live respectably in a community as equals, there would never have been an AIDS. Had we been allowed to marry, we would not have felt the obligation to be promiscuous."

For its part, *GCN* was proudly publishing photographs of five babies born to Boston-area lesbians earlier in the year.

And Mo was seven and a half months pregnant. Mo and her lover, Ellen, are close friends of my friend Katie. Katie and Ellen grew up in the same Cleveland suburb (they met at Girl Scouts) and went to high school together. I had never met Mo or Ellen but Katie kept me closely apprised of developments in their lives. A couple of years ago, they had moved out of the city to suburban Newton—"For the schools," Katie said. Mo had bought a station wagon. Next, I heard that Mo was attempting to get pregnant through artificial insemination. After twelve months of trying, she was finally going to have a baby.

Katie recounted all these events with a mixture of pride and trepidation. She was excited at the prospect of being an "aunt" but was also concerned that her friends were gradually growing more distant—the move to the suburbs, the station wagon, and finally, of course, the baby. She was worried about being left behind. That was a fear that gay people (and childless heterosexuals) often experienced when married friends started raising children; in the past, you could at least have been sure your gay friends wouldn't abandon you for the suburbs, mothers' support groups, and the PTA.

I was aware that the number of gay people—primarily lesbians, but some gay men, too—choosing to become parents had grown dramatically in the past few years, especially in the large urban centers. In Boston, it seemed as if virtually every lesbian in her thirties was either having a baby or thinking about it. Gay men were becoming sperm donors to lesbian friends for at-home insemination (although fear of AIDS was making most lesbian parents-to-be turn to sperm banks and "unknown" donors); some gay men and lesbians were involved in complicated co-parenting arrangements.

A friend told me about spending the weekend at the home of a lesbian couple in Boston. One of the women in the household was trying to become pregnant; a gay man in Los Angeles was providing the sperm and would play a role (albeit a distant one) in raising the child. My friend, who was sleeping on the fold-out couch in the living room, was awakened early Saturday morning by the doorbell. It was Federal Express delivering a package. My friend signed for it, assuming it was a pair of khakis from L.L. Bean or the latest lesbian detective novel. When her hosts came down for breakfast, she learned the package contained a sperm specimen, packed in dry ice for transcontinental shipment.

As much as people joked about "turkey-baster babies" and the "lesbian baby boom," the decision of increasing numbers of gay people to become parents outside of heterosexual norms marked a major change in gay and lesbian life. Coming out no longer meant forgoing the option of having children, as had been assumed in the past. By the late eighties, with the aging of the gay baby-boom generation, parenting had unexpectedly emerged as the cutting edge of gay and lesbian liberation. It was a new stage in the development of self-affirmation and identity. But to reach that point, a specific gay and lesbian community had to achieve a certain degree of cohesion and comfort. As a result, the new parenting was primarily a phenomenon of large cities and the East and West coasts, where gay people had developed the most extensive support systems and felt the most secure. Lesbians and gay men I visited in smaller towns wouldn't consider the possibility of having children (although many had them from previous heterosexual marriages); it would be too exposing, call too much attention to themselves.

Most lesbians I knew who were having babies were open about their sexuality and were politically active. Mo and Ellen were, to some degree, in the closet; their neighbors and their co-workers were unaware of their relationship. According to Katie, they intended to continue to live discreetly after the baby was born. I thought the fact that these suburban, relatively closeted lesbians were having a child might indicate that the lesbian baby boom was extending to more mainstream women.

One Saturday, six weeks before their baby was due, I went to visit Mo and Ellen. They were waiting for a changing table to arrive from Sears and would be home all morning, they told me when I phoned. I headed for the land of Dutch Colonials and station wagons, of well-dressed parents pushing well-scrubbed children through the park in Aprica strollers, of the comfortable, child-centered middle class. Traditionally a Jewish middle-class suburb, Newton was increasingly drawing Boston-area Yuppies like Mo and Ellen.

I always felt a pang of nostalgia and sadness when I drove to Newton. When I was growing up, my aunt and uncle and my closest cousins lived there. Visiting them was a treat, to be savored weeks in advance. By the time I was in college, my aunt and uncle were in the middle of an acrimonious divorce and my cousins were estranged from them. My relatives had long since moved out of Newton but I couldn't help but think about the breakup of their family every time I went there.

Mo and Ellen's house was a two-story brick fifties-style dwelling located on a main thoroughfare. The interior was decorated with wall-to-wall carpeting, comfortable furniture, and living-room curtains featuring a pattern of ducks; the clock on the mantelpiece was flanked by framed photographs of Mo and Ellen's families. It was friendly, tasteful, undistinctive—the kind of house where most American middle-class suburban kids have grown up in the past three decades.

Mo and Ellen had been together for more than ten years. They met as sorority sisters at Ohio State. No one in their sorority knew they were involved; they were just best friends who spent all their time together and did their best to hide the truth of their relationship. Later, they found out that most of the officers of the sorority were lesbians and that Mo's former roommate had been having an affair with the woman across the hall.

To me, they seemed quite evenly matched—opinionated, good-humored, a little on the boisterous side. Both looked like they should play rugby or lacrosse. Mo was a tall, dark-haired woman of thirty-one who grew up in rural Ohio. She was dressed in a light blue pullover top and matching running pants; her outfit was a cross between sweats and pajamas. "The latest in lesbian maternity apparel," she joked. She worked as a career counselor at a nearby college, but was planning to quit once the baby was born. Ellen, thirty, had long, sandy hair and radiated wholesome good cheer. She was in a management position at a Boston computer company and tended to have a somewhat tough-minded, business-like way of viewing things. Katie told me she thought Ellen had softened and begun to express more of her emotional side since Mo's pregnancy.

Mo had always wanted to have kids but once she came out she assumed it wasn't a possibility. Still, she wouldn't give up on the idea entirely. She asked her gay brother (of five siblings in her family, three were gay) if he might consider offering his sperm so Ellen could get pregnant. He was appalled at the notion, she said; he told Mo, somewhat self-righteously, that she and Ellen should adopt a handicapped child. Mo and Ellen started attending meetings of the Choosing Children Network, a Boston-area group that offered information and support to lesbians considering parenthood. They began to lean towards adopting a child. At about that time, the administration of Governor Michael Dukakis issued the controversial regulations that effectively barred gays and lesbians from becoming licensed as foster parents. This policy was widely interpreted as applying to adoption as well, and adoption agencies were running scared. Mo would call up adoption agencies and ask if they would accept applications from gay couples. "We'll get back to you," they would tell her, but they rarely did.

With possibilities for adoption apparently closed off, Mo and Ellen decided to try artificial insemination (also called AI or alternative insemination, to make it sound less clinical). They began going to a Boston community-health center that performed the procedure. (Under the clinic's policy the identity of donor and recipient remained unknown to each other; donors waived all rights to any child conceived with their sperm.) Mo and Ellen had to wait three months before beginning insemination; in the meantime, they joined a support group of other lesbians who were trying to get pregnant.

The health center permitted them to choose specific characteristics they wanted in a donor—height, hair and eye color, ethnic background, occupation, and the like. But after months of unsuccessful insemination, Mo found herself caring less and less about whether the donor had blue or brown eyes. "After a while," she said, "I was just concerned with getting pregnant. I really didn't care about anything else." In the end, the father turned out to be a six-foot-three Seventh-Day Adventist of Irish extraction from southern California. The health center gave Mo a letter he wrote telling about himself and why he had become a sperm donor; she and Ellen planned to show the note to the child when it got older.

I asked Mo how her parents felt about her pregnancy. She pointed to two large boxes of baby clothes that her mother had sent a few days before, which were still sitting in the front hall. Her parents had known for many years that Mo was a lesbian; that was nothing new. And Mo's baby would be the first grandchild, a fact which made her parents more accepting than they might have been otherwise.

Still, her parents were uncomfortable. Her mother was especially worried about how to explain the pregnancy to her neighbors in the small town where she lived and where the family was quite prominent. Everyone there knew that Mo was unmarried, and her mother had never acknowledged to a soul — not even to her closest friends — that three of her children were gay. But with the baby on the way, her mother had to say something. She began telling neighbors that her daughter was having a child and bringing it up herself. The father, she said, lived in California and would take no part in raising the baby. That was accurate as far as it went. "The disgrace of illegitimacy is better than the truth in her eyes," noted Mo.

Until the couple decided to have a child, Ellen had never told her parents she was gay. But she was seriously thinking about having a baby herself in a couple of years, "to balance things out," as she put it. When Mo began undergoing insemination, Ellen wrote to her parents and revealed the truth of their relationship. Her parents seemed to have responded well. "They offered us a crib," she said. "My mother is buying Christmas ornaments for my sister's child and our child. My father is wondering what he should call the child and how he should talk about it. They are planning to consider it a grandchild."

Mo's mother was preparing to visit after the birth of the baby, and Ellen's parents would follow a couple of weeks later.

That degree of parental support, however qualified, was not typical of the other lesbians (three couples and a single woman) in their childbirth class, they told me. "The other women in the group have parents who are saying, 'This is not our grandchild. We will have nothing to do with this child,'" Mo noted. "We go to these meetings and feel incredibly lucky."

Interestingly, both Mo's and Ellen's parents had become friends, a bond formed before the parents were aware the two young women were lovers. The parents, who lived a few hours' drive from each other, had much in common. Like their daughters, both sets of parents met when they were students at

Ohio State, and were active in their alumni organizations; both were members of the same religious denomination. "If I were a guy or you were a guy, it would be a marriage made in heaven," Mo joked to Ellen. The parents had gone to dinner and the theatre together—without their daughters.

After Mo became pregnant, Ellen's parents invited Mo's mother and father to their home, where they discussed the baby. In fact, Ellen's mother had been helping Mo's mother cope with her worries about the situation. "My mother is less inhibited," Ellen explained. "Mo's parents are very uptight about what people think. Mo has been pregnant all this time but her mother only told her own sister-in-law a couple of weeks ago."

The story Mo's mother was giving out to friends and relatives, that "the baby's father lives in California and won't be involved," was identical to what Mo and Ellen were telling people at their jobs, where both kept their relationship a secret. Mo was convinced that her boss would fire her if he learned she was gay; she was planning to leave anyway once the baby was born. People are "one hundred percent more accepting" of a single, heterosexual woman having a baby than a lesbian mother, she maintained. Ellen said that her co-workers were aware she had a female roommate and that the two owned a house together, but apparently made no assumptions beyond that. She had informed the other employees that Mo was pregnant and that she was going to be the birth coach. "They are telling me, 'You are going to be like a father!'" Ellen said. "I think they understand at some level what is going on, even if it is not a conscious level." Still, Ellen was reluctant to come out at work. Acknowledging her sexuality "wouldn't be good for my career," she insisted.

I asked them how they felt about this misrepresentation of their relationship and of the baby's conception. Mo emphasized that her priority was to protect the child as much as possible. If she had to pretend to be heterosexual for the child to have an easier time, she would do so—to some extent, anyway. "Not to a total extent though," she said. "But I am willing to make some accommodations." What accommodations, I asked. She thought that if her child brought a friend home to stay overnight, there was no reason to make her sexuality known. What about school? About parents of other kids? She just wasn't sure. Of course, they would tell the child about their homosexuality when it was old enough. "Some lesbian mothers are really out," Mo said. "I admire that. But I don't know yet just how open to be. Our big worry is how society will react and how to make it easier for the child. If that means playing a game with people we don't care about, I'll play a game. We're not the most militant people. I think I'll be more middle-of-the-road than most other lesbian mothers. That is how we've lived so far."

I thought that Mo and Ellen might be fooling themselves. I had talked to a number of gay parents who emphasized that a child's comfort with a parent's homosexuality was directly proportional to how relaxed the parent seemed about it. I questioned whether the way Mo and Ellen were planning to handle the issue indicated the necessary degree of ease. How, for example, would the child react to having two mothers in Boston but one mother (and an absent father somewhere in California) when it went to visit its grandmother in Ohio?

In the middle of our talk, the doorbell rang. It was Sears, delivering the changing table. We moved to the front hall, and I thought the deliverymen might assume that, as the only male present, I was the expectant father. But Mo and Ellen immediately took charge, and the men never even looked in my direction. They carried the table upstairs to the guest room, and Mo and Ellen enthusiastically unpacked it. Then, Ellen and I lugged the two boxes of baby clothes from Mo's mother upstairs.

When we sat down again, the conversation shifted. One aspect of child-rearing Mo and Ellen were sure about was that the child would be both of theirs; they were determined to minimize the primacy of the biological mother as much as possible. "I don't want this to be *my* child," Mo said firmly. "It is going to have my last name, and when Ellen has a baby that one will have her last name. But they will be *our* kids and we are going to try to reinforce that in as many ways as we can." They had graduated from college without any money or possessions and had shared everything since then, they said. This would extend to the child. Their biggest problem was what to have the child call them. Most lesbian couples they knew used Mommy and the first name of the co-parent. They rejected this formulation because they felt it reinforced the role of the biological mother as primary parent. But they were unsure what to do instead.

As part of Mo's insistence on downplaying the biological tie, she was determined to bottle-feed the baby. Bottle-feeding would give Ellen an equal role in feeding and prevent her from feeling excluded. The other women in their childbirth class were strong proponents of breast-feeding, however. Mo differed from the rest of the class in still another respect; she was willing to entertain the idea of anesthesia if labor proved too painful, an idea that was totally unacceptable to the other mothers-to-be. In their childbirth class they were "the most mainstream," Mo said. But, always worried about appearing overly conservative, she added, "We are talking about mainstream liberal. Don't get us wrong."

Mainstream liberal or just mainstream, Mo and Ellen were nonetheless pioneers of a sort and they knew it. They emphasized that what they were doing would have been unthinkable ten years ago. As gay people, "We have stopped fighting and started living, really," said Ellen.

Shortly after the first of the year, Katie called me up excitedly. Mo was in the hospital, about to go into labor. For the next day or so, I received up-to-the-minute bulletins: contractions had begun; Ellen was there by her side; the doctors thought they might have to induce labor. Finally, Katie telephoned to announce that Mo had had the baby, a girl named Emma Claire.

In February, I went to Florida for a few days to visit my own parents, who now live there most of the year. During my stay, I spent an evening with six gay women in the living room of a ranch-style home in the Miami suburb of Kendall. All the women but one had been married before. As a result of these marriages, they had eleven children among them.

The house belonged to two women in their early forties—Rexine Pippinger, who managed a Radio Shack franchise, and her lover of seven years, Becky Anderson, a pediatric nurse. (The other women had just come by for the evening.) Rexine's two red-headed, freckle-faced teenage sons wandered in and out, bantering affectionately with their mother. The family dog, a little black spaniel, was about to give birth and was pacing nervously. Despite the cozy "Leave It to Beaver" atmosphere, the women had horror stories to tell. They were examples of gay parenting the traditional way—coming to terms with sexuality *after* marriage and childbearing. And the degree of rage in the suburban living room was sometimes frightening.

Four of the five women who had been married had emerged on the losing end of grueling legal battles with their ex-husbands. Becky, the nurse, had lost her house and custody of her two children (now twenty-one and sixteen) in the late seventies, at the height of Anita Bryant's anti-gay crusade. She wound up taking care of the kids for the next eight years anyway. Her lover, Rexine, initially won custody of her children. Later, her alcoholic ex-husband had sued her for fraud — dragging several of her ex-lovers into court as witnesses. As a result, she lost her children for two years and her house, as well.

Another woman had lost custody and even been denied visitation rights. Her former husband had moved out of state with her two children. Now the ex-husband, his new wife, and the kids had moved back to Miami and she got to see the children. But her oldest daughter was pregnant and unwed; her fourteen year old was having sex with her boyfriend. She got the blame for the kids' actions; everything they were doing was to show *they* were not lesbians, according to their stepmother. "I used to think there was some truth in it until I finally learned to stop laying guilt trips on myself," the woman said.

The one parent who had been spared a custody battle nearly lost her children another way. The previous year, Arlie Brice, a graphic designer in her early thirties, had been living in Jacksonville, Florida, with her lover and her two sons, aged nine and eleven. On the children's school forms, Arlie would scratch out "father" and write "co-parent" instead, putting down her lover's name. Both were members of the PTA and baked brownies for school events. One Saturday when Arlie was at work, she got a call from her lover. An investigator from the State Department of Health and Rehabilitative Services had shown up at their door. Someone had accused them of child abuse. After two weeks of investigation, which proved an "utter terror" for the kids (and their parents), they were cleared of any wrongdoing. Still, once you're reported for child abuse, Arlie noted, "you are on a master computer in Tallahassee, whether the accusation is justified or unjustified. Right now if I wanted to work with kids or be a foster parent, I would be denied."

Their accuser, she found out, was the principal of the public school her children attended. He was a religious fundamentalist. When Arlie confronted him, he admitted he had reported them to state authorities, she said. "I know you love your kids," Arlie quoted the principal as saying. "But you are living a lifestyle that is wrong." Arlie's only recourse would have been to hire an attorney and, as she put it, "make a lot of noise." But in conservative Jacksonville, bringing a court case on such grounds could be "a very dangerous thing to do," she said. "You could lose your job at the drop of a hat." She took her kids out of school immediately; some months later, the family moved to Miami.

After listening to these stories, I turned to the one woman in the group who hadn't been married, a twenty-six year old Cuban-American named Sonia Fandino. Sonia lived at home with her parents and managed a gas station. I asked her facetiously if she ever planned to get married. "No," she laughed. "But I am planning to have a child soon." How did she plan to become pregnant? I asked. "Artificial insemination," she replied, and everyone in the room broke into laughter.

I thought back to that glimpse of old-style gay parenting when I returned to Newton to visit Mo and Ellen two months after Emma Claire was born. Ellen led me upstairs to the baby's room, where Mo was giving Emma Claire a bath. There, on the changing table that had arrived during my previous visit, was a squawling little baby with big blue eyes. The room was now furnished with two cribs — a large one filled with stuffed animals, and a second, smaller one for Emma Claire. Mo dried the baby, put her in a flannel nightgown, and laid her down in the crib. Ellen and I headed downstairs to the living room, now equipped with a baby's swing chair and decorated with a mobile depicting various animals.

Once Emma Claire had fallen asleep, Mo joined us. The two filled me in on events since I had last seen them. Childbirth was the toughest thing she had ever done in her life, Mo said. In the middle of the contractions Mo shouted to Ellen, who was holding Mo's legs as she worked to push the baby out, "This is really going to be hard for you when it's your turn!"

In general, the hospital staff had been at ease with them, they said. By coincidence, another lesbian who had become pregnant through AI was in the next room. When Mo mentioned to one nurse that they knew the woman next door, the nurse apparently assumed Mo was a lesbian. She began barraging her with questions: How did she get pregnant? What was AI, anyway? Did she know the baby's father?

According to the hospital rules, only husbands could spend all day in the room with the woman during and after labor, but Ellen remained and no one objected. Another regulation said no visitors except husbands could bring a baby from the nursery to the mother's room. Ellen went in and asked to take Emma Claire. The nurse balked. "I'm a partner," she insisted. The nurse relented, eyeing her suspiciously as she walked out the door with the baby.

Mo's mother came up from Ohio for the birth and stayed for two weeks. Mo had lost a lot of blood during childbirth and was too weak and exhausted to be very enthusiastic about holding Emma Claire. Her mother tried to get her to bond with the baby. But she went to such lengths that Ellen felt she was deliberately trying to freeze her out of any role. Mo's mother was constantly sending Ellen out of the house on errands. She would call Mo "Mommy" in the baby's presence, something Mo and Ellen had agreed not to do. At one point, the grandmother grabbed the baby right out of Ellen's arms and gave her to Mo to hold. Ellen became increasingly convinced that the mother's intention was to make it clear that the baby was Mo's, not Mo *and* Ellen's.

Caught between her mother and her lover, Mo was trying not to take sides. Her mother would come around, she was convinced; she just had to get used to the situation. And she had been helpful during the two weeks after the birth of the baby. The following weekend, Mo and Ellen were planning to bring the baby to visit Mo's parents. But if her mother persisted in trying to demonstrate that Emma Claire was Mo's and Mo's alone, her daughter was ready to insist she "cut the 'Mommy' crap."

Our mutual friend Katie, a social worker by profession, suspected that Mo's relations with her parents were about to undergo a major change. Mo, in her view, had always been the family mediator, listening patiently as her mother complained about the travails of having three gay children. Now, with the birth of Mo's baby, Katie thought that Mo would have to become more outspoken in defending the child and affirming her own relationship.

Meanwhile, Ellen reported that people at work were bringing her gifts for her "roommate's" baby. One co-worker gave her a bib; another bought a suit for Emma Claire. Everyone was asking her how the baby was doing. "I've been getting some weird questions," she said. "One of my co-workers asked me, 'Is your roommate being a surrogate mother?' But generally, people seem to go along with it and understand that I come home after work and help take care of the baby." In fact, a male co-worker had called earlier that week to ask Ellen out on a date. "I'm involved," she told him.

A month after the baby was born, a disquieting incident occurred. Ellen's brother-in-law, who held a highly sensitive post in the navy, had been called into his superior's office. "Do you know your sister-in-law is a lesbian?" he was asked. Of course, he knew, he replied. "Just as long as you are aware of it," his superior told him. Apparently, the navy was afraid of a potential blackmail situation.

Ellen's sister had called her up and told her about what had happened. She and Mo were upset and angry. They were puzzled about how the navy could have known about their relationship. Both their names appeared on the home mortgage, they noted. They were also on the mailing lists of the *Gay Community News* and a gay hiking club. Was the military spying on gay organizations? "It could have ruined our lives if we weren't 'out' to our families," said Ellen. Added Mo, her middle-of-the-road approach veering towards militance, "I'd like to know how national security is compromised by my love life!" Ironically, the same week, a federal court of appeals panel in San Francisco had struck down the army's ban on homosexuals.

At the time the United States Navy was questioning Ellen's brother-in-law, rumours were flying in the small Ohio town where Mo's parents live. Mo received a letter of congratulations from a high-school friend; in the letter, the woman noted that her grandmother had heard about the baby at her bridge club. She added that the grandmother had heard that Mo had gotten pregnant through "artificial whatever," a fact that Mo's mother had never revealed. Mo had no idea how the woman could have known. "I was floored," she said. "Information about our personal lives seemed to be sweeping the land. The government was spying on us, and everyone in Ohio was talking about us!"

Despite these minor but dramatic incidents, the new gay parenting as exemplified by Mo and Ellen was still worlds apart from the horrors related by the lesbian mothers in Miami. In Mo and Ellen's case, there would be no ugly custody battles, no ex-husbands exacting revenge, and (one assumed) in liberal Newton, no over-zealous school principals alleging child abuse. But clearly the future would not be easy. The tension between how open or discreet to be about their sexuality and the difficulties of dealing with parents, schools, and society in general were something that Mo and Ellen would have to face squarely.

So far, most of these challenges lay in the future. Parents and baby were doing reasonably well. Ellen's mother and father had been up to visit; some of the neighbors had come by to see Emma Claire. Ellen was still quite determined to have another baby within the next year or two; the sleepless nights since Emma Claire's arrival had not dampened her enthusiasm. On the Friday night after my visit, six lesbian couples, all with babies, were coming by for a potluck.

Still, I couldn't help but speculate on how Emma Claire and all the children of these unusual parenting arrangements would turn out. Would they feel embarrassed about their parents? Protective? Proud? How important would the "absent (and unknown) father" issue be for them as they got older? Would they perceive themselves as different from the other kids? Or would growing up in a community like Newton, where divorced and single-parent families were commonplace, help them feel accepted? Would they be rebellious adolescents trying to prove *they* weren't gay? No one knew. The only studies of children of gay and lesbian parents had been done about traditional gay parenting (after heterosexual marriage), with its complicating factors of divorce and late coming out. Those studies had all been quite positive, but there was no doubt that psychologists and sociologists would have an interesting future studying the children of the lesbian baby boom.

BOSTON

had first come upon the issue of gay and lesbian parenting in the spring of 1985 when "the foster-care case" emerged as front-page news in Boston. The Massachusetts Department of Social Services (DSS) had placed two brothers—aged twenty-two months and three and a half years—in the foster care of a gay male couple. When the *Boston Globe* published an article about the placement ("Some Oppose Foster Placement with Gay Couple"), the agency panicked. Within twenty-four hours, it ordered the two boys removed from the household.

Governor Michael Dukakis, until then viewed at least as a lukewarm supporter of gay rights and the gay community, strongly defended the removal of the boys. Indeed, many believed that the governor had ordered the removal himself, although his office denied this. Two weeks later, the state's Human Services secretary issued a new directive on foster-care placement. Previously, placements had been decided by social workers on a case-by-case basis. Now, a hierarchy of desirable foster homes was established. Under the new guidelines, only in "exceptional circumstances" would children be placed in nontraditional settings—that is, with single parents or unmarried couples. The latter placements could be made only with permission of the DSS commissioner. Although the new policy did not explicitly bar gays and lesbians from becoming foster parents, the Human Services secretary indicated that such a placement would be highly unlikely.

The result was a major controversy that galvanized Boston's gay community like no other event of the eighties except the AIDS epidemic. Gay and lesbian activists dogged the governor, picketing his appearances all over the state. The national gay press reported the story, tarnishing Dukakis's reputation as he tried to garner the support of gay and lesbian voters in the 1988 presidential primaries. Although the governor attempted to mollify the gay community by pushing hard for legislative approval of a gay-rights bill and by vetoing legislation that would have absolutely barred gays from becoming foster parents, the rift was deep.

The Dukakis foster-care policy was couched in relatively enlightened language about role models and the desirability of having two parents of opposite sexes. Nonetheless, it seemed to inscribe as state policy the old canard that loving someone of your own sex meant you were somehow unfit to raise children, that you would molest them, "convert" them (to homosexuality), or at the very best provide a bad example. To many, it smacked of Anita Bryant's "Save Our Children" campaign of the seventies. And by telling gays they weren't fit to be parents (or at least not *as* fit as heterosexuals), the liberal governor found himself in collision with the evolution of gay self-acceptance and community, with the march of homosexual history.

At the time the foster-care case broke, I was a staff writer at the *Boston Phoenix*. Along with Scot Lehigh, the paper's state house reporter, I was assigned to cover the story. My task was to find out if the *Boston Globe* article about the neighborhood "controversy" that had triggered the removal of the two children was accurate; I was also supposed to gauge the reaction of the gay community. Scot's job was to see how high up in the Dukakis administration the order to remove the two boys had originated.

In my research, I found that two of the three individuals in the neighborhood whom the *Globe* had quoted as opposing the placement had clearly never even known about it until they were asked their opinion by the reporter writing the story. One even apologized to the foster parents after the article came out. The third person quoted was a local activist who, according to our sources, had been attempting to stir up the neighbors on the issue for several days with little response. He and the *Globe* reporter had apparently created a dubious story of a neighborhood up in arms, and the Dukakis administration had fallen for it without bothering to do its own investigation.

As much as Scot tried, he could never quite prove that the decision to remove the children was made by Michael Dukakis himself. There were rumors of a lesbian "Deep Throat" who had overheard a telephone call to that effect, between the governor and Philip Johnston, the cabinet-level state Human Services secretary. But if this "Deep Throat" was a real person, we never found her. Scot did get Johnston to admit that the lower-ranking commissioner of the Department of Social Services had consulted with him throughout the decision-making process; he also gained an admission from someone close to the governor that Dukakis's office had been conferring with a Johnston aide, at least about media coverage of the issue.

In the end, it didn't much matter whether the *Globe* story had been concocted or whether it was Michael Dukakis himself or one of his subordinates who had broken up the foster family. The damage had been done. And it was not just gays and lesbians who were outraged. Scot, who is heterosexual, wrote in our article, "Through the incompetence and cowardice of the administration, the controversy exploded into a national news story in which the administration's capitulation to homophobia ended up aiding and abetting the gay-baiting of the Jerry Falwells and Jesse Helmses of the world."

The new state foster-care guidelines were in place, which required that applicants for a foster-parent license be asked about their sexual preference for the first time in the history of Massachusetts. Gay men, in particular, found their options for parenting restricted by the new state policy. They couldn't have children through artificial insemination, of course. Beyond co-parenting arrangements with lesbian friends, foster care and adoption had been the only ways gay men could become parents. Now, in view of the new state policy, adoption agencies were more reluctant than ever to approve gays as adoptive parents.

A couple of years after these events, I went to see Don Babets and David Jean, the two men who were at the center of the case. The couple lived in a modest home in the Fort Hill section of Boston, overlooking the Metropolitan Bay Transit Authority yards where buses and trolleys were stored. It was a neighborhood of run-down turn-of-the-century dwellings, of craters covered with vegetation where other houses had been burned down (Fort Hill had been the site of widespread arson). The area was predominantly black, but there were a number of white gay residents; in the seventies, a gay commune called the Fort Hill Faggots for Freedom had been established there. Although the commune had long since disbanded, some of former communards remained. Other white gays, like Don and David, gravitated to the decaying inner-city neighborhood where houses were still relatively affordable and some sense of community existed.

Don and David had been in the neighborhood for four years and together for eight when they applied to be foster parents. They hoped to establish a track record as parents and then apply to adopt a child. It was a try-out, designed to give them a "taste of parenting," as David put it, to see if they wanted to make a long-term commitment.

Don in particular had strong reasons for wishing to be a foster parent. His mother and father had both been adopted, and he had been legally adopted by his stepfather. A major influence in his life had been a Lutheran minister, who had seven adopted children of a variety of racial and national backgrounds. Don remembered going to the minister's house as a young man and being "really impressed." There were all the kids—black and brown and Asian—and pictures of Martin Luther King, Jr., and Malcolm X on the wall. "I thought, this is how it is supposed to be," said Don. And Don noted that "the other side of being adopted" was being abandoned. "When you have had that abandonment more or less healed through adoption," he said, "you have an obligation to pass that on."

At thirty-six, Don Babets was a tall, balding man who worked as an investigator for the Boston Fair Housing Agency. A sense of outrage smouldered just beneath his relaxed and friendly demeanor; he was someone, after all, who placed his trust in the promises and good will of the system and now felt betrayed. Don, who grew up in Cleveland, spent several years in the military in the seventies, during which time he was an active alcoholic. Eventually he got sober, left the military, and went to college. He worked as an alcoholism counsellor and later as a legislative aide to a Massachusetts state senator. While he was stationed at Fort Devens, just west of Boston, he met David Jean. David, thirty-two, was shy and unassuming. Unlike Don, who was a self-described "political type," David was an unlikely person to be at the center of a public flap and has never seemed comfortable in the role. Trained as a nutritionist, he had worked as a cook and dietitian; he was currently an administrator at a women's health center. The evening I visited, he made a shepherd's pie for dinner, using a recipe out of George Bernard Shaw's vegetarian cookbook.

David admitted that he never had a "burning desire" to have or adopt children. He had assumed that the possibility of becoming a parent was something he would forgo when he first accepted his gay identity. But, as time passed, he began to question why he couldn't be as capable a parent as any of his heterosexual counterparts. He, too, could provide "a stable home, a loving home. I did some thinking about what was important to a child," he said. "And I came to believe that what was important wasn't necessarily two parents of different sexes. What a child needs is love, understanding, acceptance. I can make brownies, too."

Don and David became the first openly gay couple to go through the Massachusetts Department of Social Services screening process to be licensed as foster parents. They attended the required six-week training program. They filled out an extensive forty-page questionnaire. A social worker spent three half-days with them doing a "home study." "We were treated just as a straight couple would have been," said David. Finally, it was the associate DSS commissioner himself who approved their application.

They let friends, co-workers, and neighbors know what they were doing. Don, who is Catholic and was teaching Sunday school at his church, told the parents of his students. David informed the pastor at the neighborhood Unitarian-Universalist church that he attended regularly. They let their families know, too. Only Don's stepfather was critical. "You are just taking in someone else's trouble," he warned.

The couple were licensed as foster parents and prepared a child's bedroom for when the Department of Social Services called. But the DSS was hesitating. When the agency finally did contact them a full year later, Don and David were asked if they could take not one child but two. They agreed.

On the day they arrived, the two little boys, Michael and Paul, were hysterical, Don and David remembered. They were also bruised and battered. Michael, three and a half, had "a little imprint, a black-and-blue mark right in the middle of his backbone," said Don. "It was clear that he had been kicked. You could see the impression of the place between the sole and the upper shoe." Don and David had a rabbit that distracted the kids.

David did not exactly recall that first week with nostalgia. "I wasn't ready for it, I'll tell you," he said. "The kids would wake up every couple of hours. They kept throwing up in the night. And we were always washing clothes. The washer and dryer were going every night."

Don said that the first night the boys arrived, Michael threw a potato peeler at him. Don yelled at him. Then the boy threw a glass of water. Don took a step in his direction, and Michael immediately ducked. Don said it took a week to break him of that response. "I promised I would never hit him, and he pushed me a couple of times to see if it was true," said Don. "I didn't hit him and trust started to be built."

After the first week, things began to calm down. The men took Michael and Paul for a haircut and then to a lumber yard to buy material to build a rabbit hutch. The following day, they took the kids to Mass and to the aquarium. The boys called them "Daddy Don" and "Daddy Dave." Meanwhile, David was learning new culinary approaches. "I always swore when I had my own kitchen I would never allow instant mashed potatoes," he said. "That was the first vow to go."

While Don and David were absorbed in washing clothes and building rabbit hutches, a neighbor named Ben Haith was making trouble. Haith was a black community activist who had been instrumental in organizing the neighborhood against arson. He had forged close links with the gay community, winning the endorsement of the Boston Lesbian and Gay Political Alliance in his unsuccessful race for a city-council seat a couple of years before. Haith and Don Babets were also friends. Don had helped Haith gain the gay political group's support. According to Don, Haith had had dinner at his and David's home; Don had babysat for Haith's kids.

It was unclear why Ben Haith was determined to make such a fuss over the new arrivals at the household down the street. Some people in the neighborhood suggested he felt his stature in the community was waning; he needed a cause to recapture his preeminent position. Others thought he was planning another city-council bid and was trying to use the issue to gain support among conservative black voters. When I interviewed him for the *Phoenix*, Haith seemed most upset that DSS officials had not consulted him first about the placement. He assailed the "dumping" of two children in the community as an extension of the abuse the neighborhood had taken on a host of other issues. "They expect us to go along with anything, and that angers the hell out of me," he said. "They are not looking at us as people but as some kind of guinea pigs."

Ironically, David first found out something was amiss after a conversation with Haith's wife, to whom he gave a ride home a couple of weeks after the kids arrived. As they drove, he related how the presence of two young children had completely altered their lives. "That's great," David recalled her saying. "But you have to be careful. There are some people who don't approve of this."

A few days later, the *Boston Globe* ran its story. That morning, Don received a call from the Department of Social Services. Agency officials told him that the boys' mother would have to sign a statement that she was aware that Don and David were gay and that she didn't object. Don met with her. "We took the boys to Mass for the first time in months on Sunday," he told her. She signed. But by then, Don said, the order to remove the kids had already been issued. The only reason that the DSS made the mother sign that document, Don said bitterly, was to protect the agency from a lawsuit.

And so late on a May afternoon, the social workers and the television cameras arrived on Don and David's front steps. David had already packed the kids' bags. Little Michael was asking, "Is Mommy all better now?" a reference to the mother's drinking problem. Don told him, "Mommy is still sick. But they are taking you to another place where there will be other boys and girls to play with." Don and David loaded the kids into the car. Paul, the youngest, screamed, "Where are we going?" and that was the last Don and David ever saw of them. The children had been in their household for just seventeen days.

For Don and David, the period after the boys' departure was difficult. They had to confront their own feelings about the loss of the kids — and their own guilt about what happened. For Don, the outspoken one who tended to see things in political terms, talking to the media provided an outlet; so did railing against the governor whom he increasingly saw as the villain of the piece; so did a suit to overturn the state's policy, which was filed by the Civil Liberties Union of Massachusetts and the Gay and Lesbian Advocates and Defenders (GLAD), the New England public-interest law firm. David, on the other hand, kept most of it inside. "I remember initially feeling like I had done something wrong by attempting to become a foster parent in the first place," he said. "It took a lot of working on myself to see that was ridiculous. But they were the first kids that we had. It was their first foster home and I wanted it to be good."

There were other problems to cope with. Rocks and bottles were thrown at their house. Teenagers drove by yelling epithets. Don and David appeared on national TV news a week before Don was to attend a family wedding in Cleveland. As a result, he felt compelled to call his aunts and uncles, all of whom would be at the ceremony, and tell them he was gay. Don and David's relationship went through some rough periods, as well. "It was a combination of trying to deal with our families, the media, the court case, mourning the losses, dealing with the guy down the street [Ben Haith]," said

Don. "It was like taking a pair of glasses and suddenly seeing people in a new light."

If there was a bright spot, it was the response of the Boston gay community. "I couldn't get over *that*," Don said. First, there was the rally held at Boston City Hall Plaza, which drew close to eight thousand people. Speakers included openly gay city councillor David Scondras, irate social workers, and the young son of a gay father. An organization called the Gay and Lesbian Defense Committee (GLDC) was formed. Out of the GLDC emerged the Dukewatch, a direct-action protest group that immediately began to target Governor Michael Dukakis. "Everyone was passing the buck and saying 'This is the governor's policy,'" recalled Sue Hyde, one of the founders of the Dukewatch and current director of the Privacy Project at the National Gay and Lesbian Task Force in Washington, D.C. "So we ended up focusing on Dukakis. This gave us immediate media interest and credibility."

Dukewatch activists, mostly lesbians, sat-in outside the governor's office, marched on his home on Father's Day, and generally kept the issue alive far longer than anyone would have expected. From May 1985 to the fall of 1987 when Dukakis launched his presidential campaign, the Dukewatch picketed the governor thirty-five times, Hyde estimated.

The issue continued into Dukakis's presidential campaign. The Defense Committee was determined to prevent Dukakis from running a national campaign without the foster-care issue gaining high visibility among gay and lesbian voters. Activists unsuccessfully tried to unfurl a huge "Foster Equality" banner at the Boston rally where the governor announced his presidential candidacy; he was picketed in Des Moines before the Iowa caucuses and faced an angry gay audience in Los Angeles during the California primary campaign. In a televised debate a few days before the California vote, the Reverend Jesse Jackson, Dukakis's only remaining rival, sharply criticized the foster-care policy.

During the primary season, Dukakis did not fare well with gay voters. According to ABC News exit poll data, in the New York State Democratic primary Jackson defeated Dukakis among self-identified gays and lesbians by a margin of fifty-one to thirty-seven. In California, Jackson's margin was even greater: sixty-two to twenty-nine. For Jackson, white gays provided a significant inroad into the white vote. How much these margins reflected

Jackson's strong support for gay and lesbian issues (he had addressed the gay and lesbian March on Washington in the fall of 1987), and how much it had to do with Dukakis's image problem among gays stemming from the foster-care issue, is unclear. No network exit polls attempted to identify gay and lesbian voters during the November general election. But a *Washington Blade* survey of fifty precincts in ten cities with large gay populations found that Dukakis won seventy-four percent of the vote. By November, it appeared, anger over the Reagan administration's slow response to the AIDS crisis and concerns about the composition of a Bush-appointed Supreme Court swayed gay and lesbian voters more than did the foster-care issue.

Whatever their effect on the 1988 presidential campaign, parenting and family issues had clearly moved towards the forefront of the gay political agenda. In the rhetoric of the gay movement, the definition of family widened to include lover relationships (and sometimes close friends), whether or not there were children present in the household. AIDS heightened this development. For example, as more and more gay men became ill, recognized ties became important to prevent a dying man's assets and possessions from reverting to his parents or other members of his "family of origin." The highly publicized case of Sharon Kowalski in St. Cloud, Minnesota, was more proof that recognition of alternative family structures was crucial. Kowalski had become a quadriplegic and suffered brain damage as the result of an automobile accident. Her family prevented her lover of four years from having any contact with her. As Sue Hyde noted, parenting and family issues were "nowhere to be found" ten years ago on the laundry list of issues important to lesbians and gays. By the late eighties, she asserted, these concerns had become "the leading edge of the gay and lesbian revolution."

At least when I talked to them, Don Babets and David Jean hadn't given up their attempt to become a family in the more conventional sense. They still wanted to adopt a child. In fact, David had been in the office of an adoption agency that very week looking through files. A picture of Michael and Paul sat on an end table in the living room. Even though the traumatic removal of the children had taken place two years before, they said they still missed the kids, who had been in four foster homes since and were now back with their mother. (The Boston media had reported that the boys had been sexually abused in one of the homes they were sent to after being taken away from Don and David.) "There was a way that Paul [the youngest] would say 'bye, bye,'" Don said. "Sometimes when I am in a store or someplace and I hear a kid say it that way, I will turn around, thinking it might be Paul."

I didn't run into Don and David at the 1988 Gay and Lesbian Pride March in Boston. But as I stood at the intersection of Beacon and Charles streets and viewed the parade, I did see a contingent of twenty or thirty lesbian mothers pushing their babies in strollers in the hot June sun. Among them were Mo and Ellen. They waved, and Ellen left the parade for a moment to tell me some good news. She had just enrolled in the program for women who wanted to get pregnant at the health center Mo had gone to. Because they wanted to create a genetic bond between the children, she planned to use semen from the same donor Mo had used. The women had bought "a year's supply," which was frozen in a sperm bank in Los Angeles. In September, Ellen would begin insemination.

She rejoined Mo and Emma Claire (now six months old), and I stood and watched the parade for a while longer. Marchers from the Lesbianas Latinas and Am Tikva, the organization of gay Jews, passed; so did the William and Mary Gay and Lesbian Alumni and the Patsy Cline Fan Club. There was a gigantic float, representing Cleopatra's barge, advertising a local bar, and a lively women's percussion group called the Batucada Belles. In the midst of all the high spirits, a group of marchers from ACT UP/Boston, the organization that does AIDS demonstrations and "zaps," rounded the corner. They were all clad in black, holding black balloons. Their "float" was a coffin.

BOSTON; DOTHAN, ALABAMA; AND

NEW YORK CITY

A friend who writes obituaries for the gay press was teaching me how to read the death notices in the *New York Times*. It was a way of getting a sense of the toll of the AIDS epidemic, he said. More often than not, the paid notices didn't mention AIDS as cause of death; you had to do some detective work. "I'll tell you an easy way to find the AIDS deaths," he said. "First, weed out the older folks. If it says 'Miami,' move on. If there are repeats—different organizations and benevolent associations—skip those, too. But don't go past someone just because it says 'beloved husband of.' You'd be surprised how many of those say 'Contributions to GMHC [Gay Men's Health Crisis, the New York AIDS services organization].' Look for certain professions—especially the arts. And look at anyone under fifty."

I was following his advice. Each morning, at breakfast, I was finding one or two deaths likely to have been the result of AIDS. There was one that went "Thirty-eight years old. Producer of off-Broadway plays. After a long and difficult illness." And another: "Thirty-five years old. From Fort Wayne, Indiana. Worked for the New York Parks and Recreation Department. Memorial contributions to GMHC and the PWA [People with AIDS] Coalition." The most moving one I came across was a notice addressed to one man from another: "My brave and beloved friend and life partner of more than six years struggled gallantly against a long and trying illness. Finally succumbed in peace and dignity at the tender age of thirty-two. His passion, sensitivity, creativity, and bright-eyed loving smile will be sorely and dearly missed . . . Your loving friend always . . ."

After weeks of this, I was forced to confront the epidemic in a way that I hadn't before. I began to sense its terrible dailiness. And I was starting to feel a little bit haunted. I would speculate on what these men were like, imagine their lives, their families in Fort Wayne, their "bright-eyed, loving smiles."

AIDS had come relatively late to Boston, and I had been fortunate compared to many of my friends, who had suffered great losses. While I knew a number of people who had been diagnosed with or who had died of the disease, none of those closest to me had yet become sick. Sometimes, I felt guilty that I had gotten off so easily—at least so far.

Then, a little more than a month after I had returned home from my cross-country trip, on Friday, November 13, Tim Grant was diagnosed with AIDS. Tim, a thirty-five year old professional photographer and co-owner of a small business that designs art postcards, is the lover of a close friend of mine. I had first met him years ago when we were both working at the *Gay Community News*. Tim had just been hired as the advertising manager when I was finishing up my stint as editor. When I talked to Tim on the phone after his diagnosis, he sounded characteristically cheerful. He had not developed any symptoms yet, except for skin lesions, and felt fine. I was optimistic. Tim had Kaposi's sarcoma, a tumor involving the connective tissues that leads to a diagnosis of AIDS. I had recently read an article that reported that virtually all of the people with AIDS who had survived three years or more had been diagnosed with Kaposi's sarcoma. Within three years, surely, some effective antiviral drug would come along, I thought.

When I met Tim's lover, Jim Marko, for coffee, the reality of it all became clear, however. I had been romantically involved with Jim many years ago and we had remained friends, usually meeting for lunch or coffee every week or two to discuss politics or books or developments in our personal lives. On this particular occasion, Jim sketched a dark picture: of journeys in and out of hospital rooms, caring for Tim through a myriad of bizarre illnesses, of eventually watching him waste away. "That is what life holds for both of us," he said. Jim himself had tested negative a few months before.

In early March, a few months after he first became ill, I met Tim for lunch at a restaurant in Harvard Square. An attractive man with dark, shaggy hair and an impish, lopsided grin, Tim looked much the same as ever—except that his face was covered by what appeared to be dark ink spots, the lesions that characterize Kaposi's sarcoma. He told me he was treating his cancer topically with something similar to a photographic chemical; he was applying the substance himself and it was supposed to focus his immune response directly on the lesions. The treatment was very experimental; if it worked, he wouldn't see any results until summer. "In the meantime, all I need is a good makeup job and I'll be set," he deadpanned.

Still, the change in his physical appearance bothered him. The previous evening, he had gone out to a record store near his apartment. The gay owner, whom he barely knew, approached him. "I see you have AIDS," he said. He then launched into an exposition of the theory that AIDS was really an advanced form of syphilis. Tim was so taken aback that he left the store without saying a word.

Tim has always been a very reserved person who spent much of his spare time in the darkroom. He stood in the shadow of Jim, who was opinionated and intellectual and entertained himself reading obscure South American and Eastern European novels. Yet when Tim talked now about his illness, he spoke with quiet dignity and self-assurance. Ironically and tragically, he seemed, finally, to have come into his own.

He said that having AIDS had become real to him only when he went to tell his parents he had been diagnosed. Until then, he had been able to convince himself it wasn't happening. Tim's parents lived in a small town in northern Maine, where his father worked in a paper mill. They had known he was gay for several years. It was Christmas, a month and a half after his diagnosis, when Tim visited. He stood with his back to his parents and told them he had had a biopsy that indicated he had cancer. Their gasp "seared my mind," he said. He told them he wasn't through yet: He had AIDS. They were speechless.

In that manner, he began the process of accepting his illness, of telling himself, "I know I've got it and this is how I am going to deal with my life from now on." He began to live "for today" and today only. "That came as a revelation because in the past I had thought I had always done that," he said.

Jim began to change as well. The two had been together for almost ten years and I often thought that Jim took Tim for granted. Now he became extremely solicitous, to the point that a mutual friend described him as "transformed." Tim scoffed at that description. He pointed out that a close friend had recently died of AIDS, and that Jim had observed how people rallied around the dying man's lover. "Jim is going to have to go through that at some point," Tim said. "He can't be a difficult person and expect that people will want to be with him. So it is partially a matter of self-interest." I preferred to believe that Jim really loved Tim, and that AIDS made him realize it. In any event, they were much closer now, Tim said. In the past when Tim had wanted to go somewhere or do something, he usually planned it on his own. Now he and Jim did everything together. "If I hurt, I tell him I hurt," he said. "That is something I would never have done before."

The following weekend, Tim was going to Maine to visit his parents. He was worried about them. They had no one to talk to about his illness; his mother had been sick herself over the past couple of months. The seriousness of his condition was eating her up inside, he was sure. His parents had never experienced death of any kind. All four of their parents (his grandparents) were still alive. His mother had eleven siblings and his father had nine; Tim himself was one of seven brothers and sisters. No one in the family had ever been seriously ill. In the small factory town where they lived, AIDS was a taboo subject. Tim was hoping to put his parents in touch with some people from the Maine AIDS service organization who might be able to help them. "I can't make them talk to each other or tell their friends, if they don't want to," he said. "But I want to make them realize what they are doing to themselves."

A week before our lunch meeting, Tim's close friend Bob, whom I also knew well, had died of AIDS. Seeing Bob in the last days of his life had been extremely painful for Tim. It was also a glimpse into what was most likely to be his own future. If there was anyone he wanted to emulate in dealing with AIDS, it was Bob. They had been able to talk a few times before the end. "The thing about Bob," Tim said, "was that in the few weeks before he died, he was feeling that everyone was encouraging him to live. But Bob wanted his friends to be able to say, when it got to be too much, 'Bob, it is OK to die.'" This made a big impression on Tim.

At this point, he was far from that stage. He was still working long hours at the struggling postcard business that he and a friend had established a couple of years before and that wasn't yet turning a profit. Shortly after he had been diagnosed, he and Jim had gone off to London for a week. But Tim said, "I am perfectly well aware that there isn't going to be a miracle cure that will save me because I am Tim Grant." For the moment, he was reluctant to undergo chemotherapy to treat his Kaposi's sarcoma. "When I put that kind of thing into my body is when I will go downhill the fastest," he said.

Tim's story is probably not too different from that of many other gay men with AIDS. In many respects, he was fortunate; he had a lover, a supportive family, friends who cared. He even had a role model, someone whose way of facing illness and mortality he could emulate. I tell his story primarily because I am fond of him and of Jim and admired his gallantry in the face of what was apparently fatal illness.

As of this writing, gay men made up close to seventy percent of the AIDS cases in the United States. By 1993, if the estimates are correct, more than a quarter of a million gay men will have been diagnosed with AIDS. Fifty to sixty percent of gay men in some studies conducted in New York City and San Francisco were shown to have been infected with HIV; more than half of those infected will eventually go on to develop full-blown AIDS, according to current projections. The numbers are staggering. The men who survive will likely find their worlds wrenched, impoverished; so many of their friends will be dead. Of all the challenges that gay men have faced over the years— isolation, rejection by family and friends, struggles with personal acceptance and self-esteem—AIDS represented by far the greatest challenge.

In my travels across the country, I found that, instead of causing division and despair, the epidemic was creating a new basis for community among gay men. Unlike in the past, it was not a community based on the search for a lover or a sexual partner or even on the desire for political and social change; it was a community founded on caring. And AIDS was bringing individuals into organized gay life who had never been involved before. Frequently, the door to involvement was through the large AIDS social-service organizations that emerged out of the big-city gay communities—Gay Men's Health Crisis in New York, the AIDS Action Committee in Boston, AIDS Project Los Angeles, and many others. As the epidemic wore on, many became involved with activist groups, such as ACT UP in New York City, whose members performed civil disobedience to focus attention on the slowness of governmental response to the epidemic. But the new breed of AIDS activists were not only to be found in New York and Boston and San Francisco. They were also in small towns and mid-size cities and among gays of color. Darrel Hildebrant and The Coalition in far-off Bismarck, North Dakota, was just one of many examples.

In Dothan, Alabama, a New South town in the middle of peanut-growing country, I met Mike Fain, a twenty-five year old man who worked at the Dairy

Queen and who looked like the prototypical "good ol' boy." ("I am a football fanatic," he told me. "I would rather have my arm cut off than see Auburn beat Alabama.") Mike and a friend organized an AIDS benefit at the local bar, featuring performances by twenty-two female impersonators and a question-and-answer session with a local health official. For years, they had been trying to bring gay people in Dothan together for a barbecue, to start a softball team, anything. No one was willing. But AIDS was beginning to change those attitudes. In Dothan, gay men had been going out of town to have sex, to Birmingham and Atlanta, to the beaches of the "Redneck Riviera" near Pensacola. They were worried. As one of Mike's high-school teachers had told him, "Alabama may be the end of the earth, but that doesn't mean it isn't connected to it."

In Washington, D.C., I met a black man who, with his goatee, dress shirt, and red suspenders, looked half community organizer and half investment banker. There were three categories of black gay men, he told me: "openly gay, socially gay, and socially gay but not out." He had always fit into the last category. His participation in organized gay life had been limited to membership in one of Washington's twenty or so social clubs (with names like the Gents, the Commodores, and the Razzle Dazzle) that provided the social framework of the city's black gay male community. Until AIDS, "that monster," came along. Now, he was forming an organization to provide education and money for blacks who he feared weren't being reached by the city's large AIDS service organization. Many blacks who had sex with other men didn't see themselves as gay, he said; consequently they didn't feel they had to practice safe sex. How to reach them? He was trying to play down any connections with the white gay community and to get his buddies in the social clubs to raise some money. "There comes a point when you have to take a stand," he said.

And in places like Jackson, Mississippi, where most gay men were fearful of becoming involved in AIDS organizing (out of concern that they might be perceived as having the disease), lesbians were picking up the slack. There, I found Sheila Espey, a large, down-to-earth, gregarious woman who worked at a hospital switchboard and whose phone number spelled D-Y-K-E. Six years ago she told her parents she was a lesbian. Since then, they had had almost no contact. She knew what rejection was all about. Sheila and some other women (and a few gay men, too) were turning the Greek Revival house where General Sherman stayed when he burned Jackson into a residence for AIDS patients. The number of men who returned home to Jackson from the big cities after they were diagnosed with AIDS whose families couldn't or wouldn't take care of them was growing. So the Mississippi Gay and Lesbian Alliance had bought the fine old house, just a few blocks from the state capitol. Sheila and her friends had spent four months sanding floors, fixing the roof, sheet-rocking it, plastering. Now it was bright and shiny, ready to go.

But the upsurge in AIDS activism involved more than rallying the previously apathetic. Often, it was accompanied by an intense personal evolution, particularly for men whose gay identity and sense of community had revolved around sex with large numbers of partners. For them, AIDS forced a reevaluation of how they lived and what they considered important. It made them rethink what it meant to be gay.

I was referred to a man named Frank, the thirty-three year old founder of a small but quite successful Boston-area company that produced computer software. I had expected a blue-suited Ivy League type (Frank had graduated from Harvard Business School). But the computer industry doesn't fit the corporate mold, and Frank was casual, dressed in a rugby shirt and khakis. We met at a Cambridge restaurant that was the closest thing in town to a New York deli. Frank told me it was his favorite spot. He had grown up on a farm in Kentucky and had worked as a grain trader in the South and Midwest. "When I saw Iowa in my future, I knew I had to get out of grain trading," he said. He went to the Harvard Business School and, after graduation, stayed in Boston and started his own company.

Until AIDS came along, Frank had led a comfortable life. He was able to say, as few small businessmen could, "My main rival is IBM, and we are cheaper and better." He didn't have a lover, but he and his closest friend spent many an evening at the Bird Sanctuary in Cambridge, along the Charles River, where anonymous sex with other men was easily available.

Frank was cut off from the gay movement and organized gay activities. He was convinced that gay organizations were filled with leftover sixties radicals who would revile him for his business-school background and his politically conservative views. "I hate people making assumptions about me," he said.

"And the assumption often is that if you are gay you are into the Third World and into black feminist poetry. That you are against the contras, wanting to disarm, and to increase welfare. And I am not in favor of those things." As a kid, he had cut his "political teeth" on the Barry Goldwater presidential campaign, and he still claimed that Goldwater had "the best stands of any presidential candidate since I've been alive." In 1980, he voted for the Libertarian party candidate for president; in 1984, he supported Ronald Reagan. "I have been a Republican all my life," he said.

Within a period of a few months, his two closest friends—one a lawyer at a prestigious downtown firm, the other a college teacher with whom he used to cruise the parks—were both diagnosed with AIDS and died. From then on, Frank couldn't lead his life as before.

He stopped frequenting his outdoor cruising haunts. He had been going less frequently, anyway, he said; he was getting older. In retrospect, he felt there had been a "schizophrenia" about his sexual patterns. "You had close friends but you had sex with strangers," he said. "There was a kind of incest taboo, I guess." He began to conclude that the real reason that he couldn't form stable relationships was because of difficulties with intimacy. He was "afraid to be close, doing things to avoid being close. It was a vicious cycle." Eventually, Frank became involved in a relationship that seemed to satisfy his needs for both intimacy and independence. He and his lover lived in the same building in Cambridge but had separate apartments. "It is a wonderful compromise," Frank said. "We come up and down in our slippers. But we have our own bathrooms, our own places."

Frank was now spending his Sunday evenings playing on a team in the gay volleyball league. Gay volleyball, he joked, wasn't that much different from the Bird Sanctuary. "You get together for physical activity," he said, "see people you don't see otherwise, and spend two or three hours together on a Sunday night."

But the deaths of his friends had a greater impact on his life than merely leading him to substitute team sports for group sex. Before AIDS, he said, "the future was always bright. Things were always looking up." That just didn't seem true anymore. He had always been very goal-oriented, he said, but now he was asking the eternal question, "How should a man live?" Frank wondered, "Do I push to build up my company? Do I enjoy myself? Do I lead a relaxed life? Is that what it's all about? We are not going to have kids, so what do we do? Do we create something to leave behind? Institutions, organizations?" If AIDS hadn't come on the scene, he would never have asked those questions, he said. He would have continued to lead the unexamined life, putting his energies into expanding his business and making money. "I saw two close friends cut down in the prime of their lives, doing exactly that," he said. "You look back and you think, did these men make the right decisions?"

In the midst of all this reevaluation, he started volunteering at the AIDS Action Committee (AAC), Boston's social-service and educational organization. Frank became a member of the finance committee. The AIDS Action Committee "fit my politics," Frank said. "It is a perfect example of Reagan's volunteerism, of private initiative. The gay community came together. We are taking care of ourselves." It marked the first time he had gotten involved in any kind of gay community organization. He even found himself marching in the Lesbian and Gay Pride Parade, side by side with the same political types he had once been so determined to avoid.

But as much as volunteering for the AAC had given his life direction and meaning, he was now somewhat disillusioned. A "nice entrepreneurial organization" had become "bureaucratized," he felt. Volunteers were playing a less crucial role. Frank's finance committee had started out overseeing the budget; now, with the budget approaching the six million dollar mark, that function had been taken away and handed over to paid professionals. The committee was relegated to supervising the handling of assets. The AIDS Action Committee was becoming less and less a gay community organization (publicly, it claimed it wasn't a gay organization at all, although it had been founded by gay and lesbian activists, and the majority of its volunteers and many of its paid staff were gay men and lesbians). And he thought that the AAC was also becoming an extension of the government, with state and city funding accounting for about half its budget. That reliance on government money put its independence into question and certainly didn't fit Frank's entrepreneurial, libertarian politics.

Whatever his feelings about the AIDS Action Committee, the foundation of his life had been changed. For people his age, Frank noted, "Sex was such a big part of our identity. You really have to redefine things. I had a fairly comfortable self-image and lifestyle that has been radically altered. As it turns out, the things I have changed to are a lot more enjoyable." Still, he said, "I am in mourning. Those days seem fun in retrospect. I am not so sure they actually were. But I hate having things taken away from me."

That sense of having something taken away, of being in mourning had a flavor that was distinctly generational. It was the experience of many men in their thirties and forties, the post-Stonewall generation. I wanted to see how AIDS was affecting the younger, college-age men, the generation that was just coming out. They were growing up in a more sexually conservative era, one in which AIDS was a given, a fact of life right from the beginning of their sexual awakenings, not some ugly surprise dropped from the sky in mid-passage. So I contacted the gay student group at Boston University (BU). Jeff Nickel answered the phone.

Jeff was a nineteen year old freshman majoring in business and psychology; he was also treasurer of the BU gay group. He had never engaged in anything other than safe sex, he told me. He was also a firm believer in sexual exclusivity. "AIDS," he said, "has given me the excuse to be the way I want to be."

Tall and sandy-haired, Jeff had one of those open, trusting undergraduate faces. He lived off-campus in an apartment he shared with two other gay students. The walls were decorated with posters of movies with gay themes— *Another Country, Parting Glances*. We sat on his roof deck, from which you could see up and down Beacon Street—lined with brick townhouses and treetops to Kenmore Square (with its famous neon CITGO sign) and the beginnings of the BU campus.

Jeff grew up in a suburb of Albany, New York. By age fifteen, a year after after he realized he was gay, he had read everything about AIDS he could get his hands on. "I knew intuitively that AIDS was something I would have to worry about, especially as far as my parents went," he said. "The more I knew about it the easier it would be for me to deal with my parents' doubts about my being gay." (He came out to his mother when she found a suitcase containing thirty-five books on gay subjects.)

And Jeff decided he wouldn't be sexually active until he knew for sure what was safe and what wasn't. At that time, the theory of safe sex was well developed, he said, although there was some controversy about whether the virus might possibly be carried by saliva. (In the end, it was determined that saliva was not a mode of transmission.) "Even then I made up my mind that kissing wasn't risky," said Jeff. "Maybe that was a rationalization. But people have to decide what is safe for them. I know people who decided to be celibate. That would drive me crazy. Different people choose different degrees of safety."

While in high school, he started going to the gay community center in Albany, even to some gay bars. At seventeen, he had sex with another man for the first time, after dating for two and a half months. Soon after, he began to go out with someone else; again, he waited a month before going to bed with him. "I am sort of unusual in that when I first came out I wanted to get to know the person first," said Jeff. "I had no sexual explosion, no sleazy period, and I guess I never will."

When it came time to apply to college, he wrote letters to the gay groups at the schools he was considering. It finally came down to a choice between Boston University and Tufts. The BU gay students invited him for a weekend; he spent four days getting to know them. That visit and the fact that BU offered a more challenging environment for gay students than Tufts (Boston University's controversial president, John Silber, is well-known for his anti-gay views) convinced him to go there. "I didn't want things to be too easy," Jeff said. "I didn't want to be in this quiet gay group in which thirty people had tea every week. I need some enemies and I need something that is not given to me on a platter."

At BU, he continued the same pattern of serially monogamous relationships that he had begun in high school, although he was relenting a little. "I used to be very strict and say only when you're in love should you have sex," he noted. "I've gone away from that but I think I am coming back to it. I'm at the point now where I think there should be at least a possibility of a relationship before you have sex."

That attitude was typical of his friends but still rather unusual overall, he admitted. He said he knew a lot of people who still "fooled around," but did so safely. That was fine from a health point of view, but it wasn't how he wanted to live. "To be honest, I don't happen to think that is right," he said. "Maybe it is right for them but not for me."

Jeff noted that older gays would tell him tales about the "good old days" of uninhibited sexuality. But to Jeff, such reminiscences had little appeal. "I can sort of step back and look at it and say it was liberating in a way to fool around with anyone you wanted," he said. "But to me, being liberated is accepting being gay and being able to be open about it. To me, a liberation that is from high sexual activity is sort of false. That is judgmental on my part, I know." Jeff noted that the men he knew who were sexually active with a large number of partners tended to be the ones who were the least open about being gay.

To Jeff, the sexual act was "such a small part" of being gay. More important was "dating someone special, falling in love. God, that's best!" he said. In fact, Jeff's view of gay identity seemed a curious combination of Hollywood romanticism and political militance. "I dream of living by the ocean with someone I love, of going on vacation, walking through the park holding his hand," he said. "That is what defines being gay for me. And being honest with myself and others and not compromising."

For him, AIDS was not *the* issue. He was more concerned with gay people becoming part of society, he said—for gay couples to achieve the same recognition as married couples, to have the right to express their sexuality, to create their own institutions. Those were the subjects on which he became impassioned. "You never see gay people walking down the street holding hands, except on Christopher Street," he said. "We have the right to do it. It is not fair to ask us to repress our sexuality. Some say, 'We'll accept it, just don't shove it in our faces.' People have to understand that straights are shoving it in our faces twenty-four hours a day!"

It would be wrong to give the impression that every gay man was seeking the relative safety of a monogamous relationship or shared Jeff's old-fashioned views on coupling and romance. I talked to my friend Michael Bronski, cultural critic for the *Gay Community News* and author of the book *Culture Clash: The Making of a Gay Sensibility* (South End Press). Throughout the AIDS epidemic, Michael has tried to promote a positive view of sexuality among gay men. In our conversation, he argued that many younger gay men he knew were actually quite envious of the fact that they didn't have the sexual options of the previous generation. "What I hear more and more," he said, "is young men feeling that they had missed something and are angry and frustrated about it." He strongly criticized the notion that AIDS was suddenly causing gay men to discover the joys of being in a couple. He himself had been in a relationship for fourteen years. "When I came out in 1968 I wanted a boyfriend and so did everyone else," he said. "The same was true in the seventies and it is true today. To imply that there was only wholesale sexual license in the seventies and that now, wholesale coupling is the correct, healthier response is ridiculous. There is just as much desire for sexual freedom now as there was fifteen years ago."

Michael suggested that I talk to a friend of his named Christopher Wittke, a twenty-seven year old typesetter at the *Gay Community News* who had written an article on jerk-off parties for the newspaper. Chris had been involved in a relationship for two and a half years, and neither he nor his lover wanted to be monogamous. In that sense, they were not very different from many gay men in the more sexually uninhibited seventies. But they had also adapted to the new realities.

Chris told me that he and his lover had gone to a J. O. party for the first time a few months before in a private home in Cambridge. The men who organized it called themselves The Full Moon Jerks; that evening, indeed, there was a full moon outside, giving a New Age gloss to the event. About forty men were in attendance. The party had specific rules — "no sucking, no fucking" — in keeping with safe-sex guidelines to prevent transmission of HIV. Pieces of black cloth divided the room into smaller spaces for privacy, and the hosts had tacked up humorous signs like, "Keep your jizz to yourself." There were paper towels and lubricant wherever you turned. "People were nervous at first," Chris admitted. "Then the host walked through the living room naked and said, 'Let's get going.'" And so they did, for an evening that at one point took on the character of the proverbial eighth-grade "circle jerk." Chris emphasized that everyone followed safe-sex guidelines. "There was peer pressure to be very careful," he said. "And there was a real sense of sponta- neity and of camaraderie. Everyone was there for exactly the same purpose."

Chris was delighted. It had "all of the mess, none of the worry" of an outside sexual encounter. He went to two more parties of The Full Moon Jerks, and, when he and his lover went to New York City on a vacation, they went to a commercial J. O. establishment in the city's meat-packing district.

The club was similar to the Boston party, with about fifty men present. The PA system blared "No Unsafe Sex, No Drugs," and someone walked around unobtrusively making sure people obeyed the rules. (A warning sign read, "Lips Above the Hips or Else.") Chris's impression was that you could get thrown out for doing anything unsafe. He found the commercial establishments a creative development after the first few years of the AIDS epidemic "when people were freaking out and didn't know what to do." In his view, the J.O. clubs offered the message: "OK, they've shut down the baths. So we'll stay within the law and have as much fun anyway!"

On that same trip to New York, he and his lover attended an event that was billed as a safe-sex party but that made them uneasy, nonetheless. It was a private gathering in a huge loft, sponsored by the people who had been associated with the Mineshaft, the well-known gay sex club that had been shut down by the authorities. The organizers of this party deemed oral sex without a condom to be safe. (In fact, there is no absolute agreement on what constitutes safe sex for men. While anal sex without a condom is believed to provide the highest risk for HIV transmission, there is still some dispute as to whether the virus can be spread through unprotected oral sex.) Chris had thought this gathering would be like the J.O. parties in Boston. Instead, it was a "sucking party," as he put it, whose theme seemed to be, "Let's see what we can get away with." Chris conceded he was tempted, but he and his lover were determined to abide by the established safe-sex guidelines. It wasn't worth the risk.

Another adventuresome approach to safe sex that Chris had taken up was telephone sex. These days, the pages of the gay press were filled with phone-sex ads, and the advertisements seemed to keep some publications in business. (One issue of the *New York Native* in the fall of 1988 had twenty-three full pages of phone-sex ads, urging readers to call phone numbers like 550-HUGG and 990-DUDE.) For Chris, phone sex was an opportunity to be verbally creative. "It is so much faster," he noted humorously. "You don't have to worry about how you are presenting yourself. All that is missing is actual human contact." He ridiculed the idea that, for the gay men who were so disposed, a disembodied voice on the phone provided any substitute for real human warmth and affection. He didn't think its popularity had much to do with AIDS either; phone sex was catching on before the epidemic arrived.

"It is a techno thing," he said. "You wouldn't want it to be your exclusive way of relating to people. It is a supplemental thing."

As adventuresome as Chris was trying to be in his own sex life, he was dismayed at what he perceived to be the general trend. Gay men just weren't being creative about safe sex. "They are sad about losing things but are not being very experimental," he said. At the bars he frequented, he found a neighborhoody atmosphere but little sexual energy. People tried to put forward a nonsexual image, he said. Chris thought they were still having sex but weren't admitting it. But the fact that sex was something people felt compelled to pretend they weren't doing was in marked contrast to just a few years ago.

Meanwhile, Chris fantasized about moving to New York City, where he could go to the commercial J.O. clubs any time he wanted and not just wait until a full moon. "I am very frustrated that there are no places for sexual choice that I can take advantage of on a daily basis," he said.

Despite Chris's more uninhibited view of sexuality, he wasn't much different from the more conservative Frank and Jeff in one respect. All of them were struggling with developing new norms, with finding ways of expressing their sexual and emotional needs in a world transformed by AIDS.

On a visit to New York City, I talked with a psychotherapist in his late thirties named Michael Shernoff. Michael worked in Manhattan's Chelsea neighborhood, at the epicenter of the epidemic, and his clientele is almost entirely gay. I figured that he had a unique window for observing the way AIDS was affecting the lives of gay men. In addition, Michael was trying to create new norms for gay men on a community-wide scale, through workshops he had helped design for Gay Men's Health Crisis. He himself was HIV-positive.

As was the case of so many in New York's gay community, Michael was living in the midst of what he called "bereavement overload." He knew fifty or sixty people who had died of AIDS, including thirteen of his patients. His brother had died from the disease, and Michael had taken him in and cared for him during his last fourteen months, even though they had never really gotten along very well. Normally when someone died, he said, working through feelings of grief took two to three years. But in the current atmosphere, he said, "You mourn one person who died and the same week you may hear of two more people you know who have been diagnosed." He had lost more friends and acquaintances than his parents, who were in their late seventies. The result was a sadness, a depression, but also "a triumph, a real sense of triumph about life." There was nothing somber about Michael. He was brash, full of energy, wearing a flamboyantly patterned shirt. Perhaps he was one of the triumphant—at least so far.

In his practice, he was seeing the whole spectrum of personal responses to the epidemic. It was impossible to make any assumptions about how people reacted, he said. On the one hand, there were some men who refused to enter into relationships at all. They feared a potential lover might develop AIDS, demand months or years of care, and die; some were afraid they might develop AIDS themselves and didn't want to put other people in the position of being forced to take care of them. Those anxieties, he said, could provide "a new rationalization for avoiding relationships." On the other hand, he said, he had seen two persons with AIDS fall in love and become involved, as well as several very healthy men who had formed relationships with men already diagnosed with AIDS.

Some longstanding couples who had previously had a good deal of sex outside of their relationship were now trying to be sexually exclusive. "There are many men who were used to using outside sexual encounters as a way of diffusing intimacy, intensity, and anger," he noted. "Now, they frequently come into therapy seeking help in trying to re-eroticize and re-romanticize their own relationships." That wasn't easy, he said. And he was concerned that some were remaining in relationships they ought to get out of, for fear of returning to the "sexual marketplace."

If there was an increasing desire among gay men to be part of a couple, Michael didn't attribute it entirely to AIDS. "Don't forget," he said, "most of us are in our mid-thirties and forties. There is a maturing in our community. Many of us became sexually active in a way that involved defining our sexual orientation by what we were doing sexually. Having sex with a lot of men, going to the baths had to do with identity formation. I am not saying it is bad, but you do outgrow it because it is a natural adolescent phase."

More and more people, he stressed, wanted "more than just a genital experience." This was not a uniquely gay issue. "What happened was that the sexual revolution didn't prepare anyone—heterosexual or homosexual—

for the experience that we were going to have a lot of feelings, no matter what we did with our bodies. You learned how to be a sexual performer. That was the seventies. But often such behaviors left us more alone and more distant from other people than we wished to be. So a lot of people reaching their thirties and forties wanted to be connected."

This change was happening simultaneously with the advent of AIDS. At the same time, urban gay communities were developing stronger institutions. New York City, for example, had its own gay and lesbian community center in a former maritime cooking school in the West Village, where more than 180 different gay groups met. "We learned we didn't have to fuck in order to define ourselves," he said. "We found we could define ourselves in the variety of ways any human being defines himself."

Still, he saw a danger in the growing emphasis on the desirability of coupling. "We may be creating a class society where people who are in a couple are viewed as more valued, more intact, and having better mental health than people who are not coupled," he cautioned. "That is social and sexual fascism, and we are beginning to see a little of that within the gay community."

Out of this desire for connection, Michael found many gay men struggling with the concept of dating. For the previous fifteen years, going out on a date meant "getting laid," he said. Now, dating meant genuinely getting to know someone, and a lot of people's skills were rusty. Michael, along with two other men at Gay Men's Health Crisis, developed a dating workshop specifically aimed at gay men. He would start each workshop by having people tell three lies about how they felt on a date. The three he related were always the same: "I am never anxious on a date; I don't care if I get laid on a date; and dating always makes me feel fabulous." The workshops offered a series of role-playing exercises ranging from "First lines" to "How do you tell someone in a nice way that you are not interested in them sexually" to "How to tell someone that you are seropositive or have AIDS."

The dating workshop wasn't the first that Michael had developed. He had also helped create one called "Eroticizing Safer Sex," which had been widely imitated throughout the country. This workshop emphasized the use of condoms as well as the more playful aspects of sex. "What people say they love about safer sex is that foreplay goes on forever," said Michael. "That they are making love for a longer period of time. That they aren't focused on the orgasm. It has taken a lot of men out of the competitive sexuality that a lot of gay male couples can get into and making it more playful."

The safe sex workshops didn't impose any kind of sexual morality on the participants. They emphasized that individuals could have sex with as many partners as they wished as long as they did it safely. As Michael put it, "You can go to a dirty movie and have sex with twelve people and it doesn't matter, as long as you do it safely. It is more dangerous to have anal sex with one person without a condom than to be at a jerk-off party with two hundred people." Still, he was finding that a lot of people wanted something more than a no-risk ticket back to old sexual free-for-all. They wanted sex with emotional continuity.

Clearly, mores were in flux. In his book of nonfiction, *States of Desire*, published in 1980, before AIDS, the novelist Edmund White wrote of gay New York City, "Sex is casual, romance short-lived; the real continuity in many people's lives comes from their friends." If Michael was right, that wasn't the way most gay men wished to live their lives anymore. At the same time, it seemed to me a pity if the sexual freedom, the ability to form the less restrictive relationship configurations of the period before AIDS was to die out in an era of sexual retreat. If things had gone too much to one extreme in the past—with too little stress on the positive aspects of commitment and long-term relationships—it was important today, I felt, for the pendulum not to swing back too far in the direction of a stifling new conventionality. Michael himself was trying to find an approach to sex and relationships that left room for commitment and variety. "I believe in sexual libertarianism," he said, "if you practice safe sex."

That kind of creative adaptation was an opportunity that AIDS offered gay men, Michael felt. There was another opportunity, as well. In early middle age or youth, gay men were learning to value life. "We are observing people close to us struggle with this final stage in their lives in their twenties, thirties, and forties," he noted. "No one is taking anything for granted. No one is assuming there is enough time." Referring to his own positive antibody status, he added, "I don't put off a trip to South America for five years. I will take it this year. I wanted to go to Egypt; I did it. I tell my friends whom I love that I love them. I don't let them assume it. Should I spend my money, run my credit cards up to the limit, or save for my old age? How do you balance it? That balance is an art. That is where the real triumph is, living with this."

A few days before I was to leave for San Francisco in May, Tim Grant's lover, Jim, called me on the phone. Tim's partner in his postcard business, another gay man, had given Tim thirty days to sever his connection with the firm. His partner claimed that Tim's ability to work was impaired, even though Tim was working ten-hour days. Tim and Jim were going to get a lawyer. That wasn't all Jim had to tell me. Tim's head was becoming slightly enlarged; his glasses didn't quite fit anymore. They were doing tests, Jim said. It looked like he might begin chemotherapy the following week.

SAN FRANCISCO, PART 1

ventually, of course, I had to go to San Francisco. To tell the truth, I delayed my trip as long as possible. I was afraid it would be too depressing. In my mind, the city had become synonymous with AIDS. It was true that New York City had a greater number of AIDS cases. But San Francisco was a much smaller city, a small town really, as everyone there was to tell me. Its gay community was much more geographically concentrated than New York's. I feared that arriving in San Francisco would be much like coming upon London in the middle of the Blitz, the city devastated, its inhabitants being picked off by a few well-placed bombs each evening. So I temporized, spending my time in small towns and obscure places where the bombs hadn't yet begun to fall and perhaps never would.

When I did arrive, one of the first people I called on was Armistead Maupin, the witty chronicler of San Francisco mores, gay and straight, who had turned his columns in the *San Francisco Chronicle* into a series of highly popular novels. Armistead lived just off the Castro in a tiny cottage with a breathtaking view but about as much space as a Manhattan studio apartment. I climbed one of those steep San Francisco streets that makes you feel like you are defying the law of gravity and, once I reached his gate, was faced with yet another formidable climb to the house itself. "Don't give up. You're almost there," a voice with a warm North Carolina twang hailed from somewhere above. I climbed a few more steps and Armistead came into view, standing on his front deck cradling a little poodle in his arms.

Armistead is an amiable, auburn-haired man who dressed that day as he might have when he was an undergraduate at Chapel Hill almost twenty-five years before—blue oxford dress shirt, khaki pants, pink socks, and saddle shoes. Over a cup of Red Zinger tea, he told me that since the advent of AIDS, journalists sought him out expecting him to confirm a preconceived notion— that gay San Francisco was "a ruined ghost town," that "Sodom has fallen." In fact, he was convinced that the Castro, the predominately gay area, was more "habitable" than it had been in the heyday of sexual liberation. The neighborhood was "richer and less ghettoized," he said; there were a lot more women in evidence, for one thing. There were now three gay and lesbian bookstores on Castro Street (one of which his lover managed). "The bars are being replaced by bookstores," he said, an observation that I chalked up to a novelist's fantasy. As for himself, he was "cocooning," he said—staying home and watching television and cooking dinner for friends. "A lot of us are reaching middle age at the same time," he noted. "I am forty-four, and it is difficult to separate the effects of the AIDS crisis from the effects of middle age."

Still, wasn't it depressing in San Francisco? I asked, returning to the "ruined ghost town" mode of interrogatory that he so deplored. He insisted it wasn't so. "This city feels like the last safe place on earth," he said. "The population is civilized about gays and AIDS. You can walk down the street holding hands with your lover." He contended the city's gay community had managed to assimilate AIDS because it had been very well-organized when the disease first appeared. The central trauma for San Francisco, he said, was not the AIDS crisis but the assassination of Harvey Milk, the gay city supervisor, in November 1978. "That is when the party ended for us," he said. "So by the time AIDS hit we were a little tougher than the rest of the country. We had already had the experience of a collective trauma and we were able to mobilize." Gay community institutions for people with AIDS in

San Francisco had become so refined, he said, that there was even an organization to care for the pets of those who were too ill to do so. Members of the group, called PAWS (Pets Are Wonderful Support), would walk your dog, take him to the vet, and feed him his morning meal if necessary. If a pet owner died, they would find a home for the animal.

One consequence of AIDS, Armistead maintained, was that his friends were "working as they had never worked before." That was especially the case if they had tested positive for antibodies to HIV. "There has been a tremendous creative outpouring," he said.

I wondered if Armistead wasn't putting a brave face on what was really a tragic and hopeless situation. But as I spoke to gay San Franciscans, I found an entire community living with a presumably fatal illness with a matter-of-factness that was startling. In fact, the most exact resemblance to wartime London was the "stiff upper lip." Typical was the attitude of an old friend whom I met for a drink in a smoky bar just off the Castro. His lover was battling with cancer (not related to AIDS). His two best friends had been diagnosed with ARC. His brother had just had an artificial bladder inserted; his mother was in and out of the hospital with serious heart problems. "You have to understand that this is nothing new for me," he said, matter-of-factly. "I have been living with terminal illness around me since I was two years old. And the one thing I have learned is that terminal can mean forever."

In San Francisco, virtually every gay man I met seemed to know his HIV antibody status. All the antibody positive men were taking one drug or another—sometimes the government-sanctioned AZT, more often untested underground treatments—whether they were showing symptoms or not. In Boston, on the other hand, many gay activists contended that there was no need to take the HIV test—only to practice safe sex on the assumption that you and anyone you might have intimate relations with was positive, too. The Boston view was that confidentiality issues were still worrisome (you could potentially lose health- and life-insurance coverage if your antibody status became known) and that treatments hadn't reached the point to make testing worthwhile. But such hesitations did not seem to exist in San Francisco, perhaps because gay men felt so secure there.

Often decisions to begin taking one drug or another were traumatic ones, forcing individuals to face up to the fact that their future was, at the very least, uncertain. I stopped by to visit Winston, a man whom I had known in New York and who had moved to San Francisco eight years before. Winston worked doing word-processing for a large law firm, the kind of dead-end job so many overeducated gay men wound up trapped in years after they had migrated to San Francisco for the views, the weather, and the atmosphere of sexual freedom. In New York, Winston was famous for his flamboyant style; I mostly remember him reading Edna Ferber novels, listening to Nina Simone on the stereo, and wearing two or three brightly colored scarves whenever he left the house, even at the height of summer.

These days, he had other things on his mind. Winston had tested positive for antibodies to HIV. His T-helper lymphocyte count (a key indicator of the functioning of the immune system) was fluctuating. Although he had no noticeable symptoms of AIDS-related illness, he was already taking an underground antiviral drug called AL-721. He was also considering taking Antabuse, a drug usually prescribed for recovering alcoholics. (It causes you to throw up if you drink alcohol.) In Europe, he told me, research had shown that Antabuse increased T-cell levels. The problem with Antabuse was that once he started taking it, Winston would have to give up drinking completely. Not that he drank much alcohol anyway (he preferred coffee, which he drank nonstop). But taking a drug that restricted his normal activity in any way, even an activity that he claimed to do infrequently, was frightening. It meant he had to face up to the future. So he continued to delay taking the drug, telling me, "I am *almost* ready to start taking Antabuse."

Meanwhile, he was working prodigiously. He was a painter, and his apartment was crammed with huge abstract canvases—swirls of dark blues and purples. He would return each day after work and paint long past the dinner hour. I had never considered Winston a particularly disciplined person; now, he seemed to be working as if against a deadline.

I had asked Armistead Maupin about San Francisco's lesbian community. I speculated that given the toll AIDS was taking among gay men, the women might be assuming a higher profile. First, he told me a story. Several years back, he said, he had emceed a fund-raiser at the Castro Theatre, in which female impersonator Charles Pierce shared the bill with the Lesbian Chorus.

When Pierce got up to perform, he immediately launched into his customary impersonations of Tallulah Bankhead and other film stars. The women in the audience were offended and began walking out in droves. Armistead tried to "calm" the audience by putting on a clip of the earthquake scene from the movie *San Francisco*. That seemed to sum up the situation perfectly.

As that incident demonstrated, connections between the gay male and lesbian communities had been problematic over the years, although individual relationships flourished. A major cultural gap existed. By and large, the men saw the women as sexually conservative and possessing an exaggerated and intolerant sense of "political correctness"; the women saw the men as overly preoccupied with sex and lacking in social commitment.

So although community events were supposed to be cosexual, Armistead noted that neither the men nor the women really felt the necessary bond. Now, he argued, the bond was becoming a genuine one. "Lesbians are fighting for and caring for men with AIDS," he said. "Men are looking for friendship." He and his lover had spent a month the previous fall on the Greek island of Lesbos, enjoying the sun and searching for their Sapphic roots.

Armistead's comments put me in mind of Roberta Achtenberg's campaign for the California state assembly the month before. As an open lesbian, Roberta had run a surprisingly strong race against the choice of the entrenched Democratic party machine. Was this an example of women taking a more visible role in the community?

I climbed still another steep hill and went to call on Roberta. At thirty-eight, she was a former law school dean and currently an attorney with the Lesbian Rights Project, a San Francisco–based civil rights organization that deals primarily with family and custody issues. Her lover, Mary Morgan, was also quite well known. She was a San Francisco Municipal Court justice, the first openly lesbian judge appointed in the United States. Roberta and Mary were attractive and energetic and gave the impression of being professional, but in a friendly, unpretentious way. They lived in a Victorian house high above the Castro, with spacious rooms in which the furniture seemed to get a little lost; banks of windows and French doors led out to decks offering panoramic views in all directions. When I arrived shortly after dinner, their blond, talkative three year old son, Benjy, was lying in bed, watching a sci-fi movie on television.

"First lesbian in the state, first lesbian in the country, first lesbian in the universe!" was the euphoric phrase on the chalkboard at a party given by San Francisco's Gay and Lesbian Bar Association. The year was 1981, and the event was held in honor of Mary's appointment to the bench by then-governor Jerry Brown. (Altogether, Brown appointed five openly gay judges in the state, with Mary the only woman among them.) Since then, in line with the California system in which judges, appointed by the governor, have to go before the voters after an alloted time, Mary had been reelected without opposition. She was up for another term in 1990, which she expected to win easily.

Mary was an earnest and dignified woman who measured her words in lawyerlike fashion. The job of municipal court judge was hardly a very glamorous one, she assured me. She handled "misdemeanors, run-of-the-mill crimes, shoplifting, prostitution, and street brawls," she said. "We also hear the first stages of all serious crimes, called preliminary hearings. And we hear civil cases up to $25,000." She told me that she had had "nothing but the most polite reception" from her colleagues since her appointment. In fact, she had just finished a year as the presiding judge of the San Francisco Municipal Court. "Quite frankly, I am a well-respected judge," she said, and I didn't doubt it.

She was actively involved in judicial education and had coordinated some of the first training programs in the nation to sensitize judges to gay issues. Although, as a municipal court judge, she didn't rule on the constitutionality of laws that affected gays and lesbians, Mary believed she was making an important contribution by breaking down stereotypes. "There have been instances," she maintained, "when I know that my colleagues have made different decisions than they might about certain issues, particularly in regard to lesbian mothers and gay fathers, because they know me and Roberta and our son Benjy."

The previous year, she had been chosen Trial Judge of the Year by the San Francisco Trial Lawyers' Association. The organization gives out an award to a superior court justice and a municipal court justice at an annual dinner dance, and Mary and Roberta attended the event together. When the superior court judge rose to accept his honor, he closed his remarks by thanking his wife. Not to be outdone, Mary concluded by expressing her gratitude to "my partner Roberta." "And I have to tell you," Mary informed me, "there was just as much applause for me as for him."

Mary had no illusions about what it meant to be the first openly lesbian judge. Her appointment signaled some progress, she thought, but it hardly represented "the be-all and end-all." "I am not naive," she said. "Just because I am a judge does not mean there aren't people beaten up on Castro Street. Visibility is extremely important but it can give a false sense of security to people, too."

I asked how lawyers and clients who appeared before her in court tended to react to the fact she was gay. As soon as the words were out of my mouth, I realized it was a silly question. "She's the judge!" Roberta broke in.

If Mary was serious and dignified and could seem a bit formal, Roberta was warm and outgoing, with a no-nonsense charm. When Art Agnos was elected to succeed Dianne Feinstein as mayor of San Francisco in December 1987, his state-assembly seat became vacant. City supervisor Harry Britt and other gay and lesbian politicos declined to run for the seat (which includes the Castro and whose constituents are estimated to be twenty or thirty percent gay). No one thought they could win. So Roberta tossed her hat in the ring. A political novice, unknown outside the gay community and the National Lawyer's Guild, she found herself facing John Burton, brother of the late congressman Philip Burton and last of the line of a prominent political family. A former congressman himself, John Burton had resigned from Congress in 1982 to enter a rehabilitation program for cocaine addiction. Burton had raised $750,000 and had strong name recognition, as well as the support of the Democratic power structure and the influential State Assembly Speaker Willie Brown. Burton's substance-abuse problems did represent a liability, one that Roberta referred to obliquely in the course of the campaign by pointing out Burton's poor attendance record while in Congress.

Still, the race remained, in Roberta's words, "a David and Goliath" contest. At the beginning of the campaign, she met with the political reporters in town. "I told them when they referred to my opponent as a former congressperson, they should describe me as a civil rights lawyer or attorney," she said. "They could call me lesbian all they wanted. But for them to write an article headlined "Achtenberg Gives a Speech on Daycare," there was no reason for them to refer to me as a lesbian activist right off." She wanted the newspaper readers to get to the heart of what she had to say without being influenced by a label that might be stigmatizing. "I felt it was a victory if they didn't call me a lesbian until the seventh paragraph," she noted. "And the media was better about it than they had ever been."

In the end, the thirty-eight percent of the vote she received (and the $300,000 she raised, mostly from San Francisco's gay community but also from gays and lesbians nationwide) wasn't a bad showing for the young David. The election had taken place a month before and she was pleased about the campaign. "I didn't just win the Castro," she said. "I won the Noe Valley and the Mission and the Potrero Hill section. I put together for the first time in a long time progressive issues, renters' issues, daycare, gay and lesbian issues. I resolidified an alliance with the progressive Chinese community."

Roberta's campaign for the state assembly was the most visible race a lesbian candidate had ever contested in San Francisco (black lesbian activist Pat Norman had run twice for city supervisor and was planning a third try). Roberta had raised $300,000, she told me, a "war chest" that represented more money than any other openly lesbian candidate for public office in this country had ever raised. Perhaps most importantly, Roberta's campaign signaled the emergence of the lesbian community as a political force in a city where gay in politics largely tended to mean gay men. Although in the past many lesbians had tended to dismiss electoral politics as patriarchal and not worthy of their attention, the presence of an openly lesbian challenger in such an important race rallied large numbers of women. "Because lesbians have traditionally been so invisible, the women just flipped," said Roberta. And even though she had lost, Roberta would be at the head of the line of potential gay and lesbian candidates the next time a legislative or congressional seat opened up.

As we talked about gay politics in San Francisco, Benjy tired of his movie and came downstairs to visit the adults. He immediately fell asleep in Roberta's arms. Although Mary was his biological mother (he had been conceived through artificial insemination), Mary and Roberta were raising him as co-parents. "Having a child is the best thing I have ever done," said Roberta.

Roberta told me that she and Mary were members of the local gay and lesbian synagogue, called Sha'ar Zahav. (The synagogue had its own building and was affiliated with the Union of American Hebrew Congregations, the Reform wing of Judaism.) As many as thirty families in the congregation had children. Some of the kids, like Benjy, had been conceived through artificial insemination; others were adopted or foster children or were the result of previous heterosexual unions. But all were now part of some lesbian and gay family configuration. Given these demographics, the congregation had just voted to start its own religious school. Roberta and Mary were thrilled. The school would give Benjy an automatic peer group of children of like backgrounds. "Our children will have a sense that they come from somewhere and they belong to a whole group of people beyond their parents," said Roberta.

Roberta felt that because of the AIDS crisis, lesbians and gay men having babies acquired a particular importance. The presence of Benjy and other children of gay parents showed there was life in the community, she said; the kids were a source of regeneration. Fear of HIV transmission had cut down the number of gay men who were available as sperm donors, it was true. But Roberta said that many lesbians still wanted their gay male friends to participate in their children's lives, whether the men were the actual donors or not. Benjy's two "main men," she observed, were their gay friends Steve and Sherman. "They want to be his uncles more than life and he just looks up to them," she said. "Benjy knows how to pee standing up on account of Uncle Sherm taught him how and that is cool."

And Roberta observed that the majority of lesbians she knew who had babies through artificial insemination gave birth to boys. Scientifically speaking, she said, a woman was more likely to have a boy when a child was conceived through AI. Regarding the lesbian and gay community, she offered a more mystical interpretation. "In wartime, when there is a tremendous amount of death and devastation, you will find historically that the character of the birth rate changes," she said. "Women are twice as likely to have male children as female. I think we are compensating for the loss that is going on due to AIDS by having all these boys." She paused for a moment, laughed, and returned to being the no-nonsense community activist. "Now, remember. That is just Roberta," she said, referring to herself by name. "That is just Roberta's cockamamie theory!"

A few days later, I went to visit a lesbian couple named Trinity Ordoña and Desiree Thompson. I had been given their names by a woman in San Antonio who had met Trinity at a conference of gay people of color in Los Angeles. Trinity and Desiree are of Asian/Pacific descent (this term includes people from the Pacific Islands, as well as East and Southeast Asia). I had expected we would talk about being Asian in the predominately white gay and lesbian community. Instead, they told me a story of love and marriage.

The story began in July 1985, when Trinity, who manages an academic department at the University of California at San Francisco, went on a two-week visit to her sister in Honolulu. A few days before she was scheduled to return home, she met Desiree and fell in love with her "in about twenty minutes." The only trouble was that Desiree was involved with another woman and that Trinity lived three thousand miles across the Pacific.

They met through a mutual friend at a Honolulu women's bar. Trinity, thirty-seven, was the sixth of thirteen children of Filipino immigrants who came to the United States in 1946 and settled in San Diego. She had gone to Berkeley and had been active in politics, ranging from the anti-Marcos movement to the Jesse Jackson campaign. Desiree, thirty-two, was an indigenous Hawaiian who came out while working at the women's studies department at the University of Hawaii. Today, she works as a mail carrier.

At that first meeting, Trinity asked Des to dinner and gave her her phone number. But on their date (a showing of the documentary film, *The Times of Harvey Milk*), Des broke the news that she was involved with someone else. Trinity was unfazed. She spent her remaining few days in Hawaii writing poems in her diary and love letters that she never mailed. The night before Trinity was to return to San Francisco, she was given a farewell party. Des was there. A mutual friend took her aside and told her of Trinity's feelings. Trinity telephoned Des at three in the morning to say good-bye. Des was still awake—she was writing Trinity a letter.

Trinity left as planned, and they began corresponding. After three weeks, Des's lover demanded a halt. Des gave in.

The two had had no contact for a year and a half when Trinity returned to Honolulu for a Christmas visit to friends. She and Des met at a party but hardly spoke. It so happened that Des's lover was going away for a few days. And it was also the case that Des's feelings for Trinity had remained constant all that time. Now was her opportunity. "I had to try," Des said. "How often do you get a second chance?"

At that point in her life, Des said she usually became involved in relationships because the other person was interested in her, not the other way around. This time it was different. There may have been other factors, too. In Honolulu, Des had come out into a lesbian community where there was little interaction between local gays and lesbians, usually of Asian/Pacific descent, and *haole* gays (whites). Most of the openly gay community was composed of *haoles*, many of whom were in the military; the majority of the gays and lesbians born and raised in Hawaii were in the closet. The close-knit nature of the local population made it virtually impossible for them to come out. Although that kind of community clearly offered a sense of security, its constrictions also may have made Des yearn for a larger world. She found it in Trinity.

In any event, Des broke up with her lover during that second visit, and she and Trinity spent three weeks together in Honolulu. Soon after, Des flew to San Francisco to test it out. In May, five months after their Christmas reunion, she moved in with Trinity and got a job as a mail carrier in suburban Daly City.

It was a year later when I visited them in their apartment overlooking Mission Dolores Park, a few blocks from the Castro. The place had a tropical flavor—a canary singing away in its cage in the living room, a Gauguin painting over the couch depicting two women in a South Seas landscape. From the window, there was an expansive view of the park, the Spanish-looking Mission High School, and the hills beyond. One wall was lined with family portraits—Trinity's mother and father, her twelve siblings, Des's parents and brother. Trinity and Desiree were cordial and relaxed, dressed in sweats and sneakers.

They were going to be married a month later, they told me, on the day before the annual Gay Freedom Day Parade. And the main reason they had decided to marry was because they wanted to have children. When they had initially talked about having kids, Trinity said flatly, "We'll have to get married first." Des was reluctant. She didn't believe in marriage and was opposed to imitating what she viewed as the heterosexual model. "I had the women's studies point of view," she noted. But gradually Trinity convinced her that marriage simply represented an expression of love and commitment that was neither intrinsically heterosexual or homosexual.

Trinity and Desiree became engaged the previous December, exchanging rings and informing their friends. A few months before I visited, they had gone to San Diego to tell Trinity's parents. Her parents had known Trinity was a lesbian for years, but Trinity wanted to know where they stood on the subject of Desiree. She asked her mother, who is a seamstress, if she would be willing to make her a traditional Filipino wedding gown. Trinity has seven sisters, all of whom had married, but she was the only one who had requested a traditional costume. Her mother obliged. In fact, she also offered to make a traditional Hawaiian gown for Desiree.

The women showed me the full-length white gowns—Trinity's with short, embroidered sleeves, Desiree's characterized by a high collar and long sleeves. (The more formal Hawaiian style was influenced by the missionaries, Desiree said.) To Trinity, her mother's decision to make the gowns was very significant. "My parents are traditional Filipino immigrants with traditional Filipino values," she said. "So this was a big step forward."

Trinity and Desiree related an earlier incident in which they went with Trinity's parents to the wedding of a niece near Lake Tahoe, Nevada. The Ordoñas drove the two young women back to San Francisco. On the ride home, Trinity dozed in the back seat while Des sat in the front with Trinity's mother. At the urging of Mrs. Ordoña, mother and future daughter-in-law had their first heart-to-heart talk. "How *is* Trinity?" asked her mother. After Des gave some vague reply, Mrs. Ordoña cautioned that Trinity was a perfectionist and that she could be difficult to live with. "Mother-in-law advice," concluded Des. Then Mrs. Ordoña asked her, "Why did you leave your girlfriend?" Des told her the whole story.

Trinity and Desiree showed me their *Bridal Wedding Planner* (with a handsome white man and glowing white woman on the cover, of course). Inside, there were sections for the guest list, gifts, flowers (in this case, heliconia and anthurium), and the like. On the living room mantelpiece, I noticed shoe boxes filled with origami birds. According to Japanese-Hawaiian wedding tradition, Des explained, the bride-to-be makes a thousand origami cranes from gold paper for good luck. They had folded some five hundred so far and planned to string up the full thousand at the wedding reception. Each crane took about five minutes to make; whenever their friends came by to visit, they were handed paper and put to work.

The wedding was to be held at Golden Gate Park, with the reception at a Thai restaurant. A hundred or so guests would be present, including Trinity's parents, many of her twelve siblings, and her boss and co-workers. Her brother and his band were coming from San Diego to play. Des's brother was flying in, and several friends were coming from Hawaii, bringing leis and flowers. The mutual friend who had played matchmaker would officiate at the wedding ceremony and perform a Hawaiian wedding chant. She was a spiritual person, Desiree said, "steeped in the Hawaiian renaissance," who had dropped her Americanized name for her Hawaiian one and performed traditional hulas. Another friend's three year old daughter—conceived through artificial insemination—would be the flower girl.

The only missing ingredient would be Desiree's parents. Desiree had never told them directly that she was a lesbian, let alone that she was marrying another woman. But her brother had discovered love letters that Desiree had written to Trinity on their home computer. When Desiree told him about the wedding, brother and sister discussed the subject, and he volunteered to tell their parents. But her mother and father had taken the news badly, agonizing about what they might have done "wrong."

For Trinity and Des, the planned wedding was more than just a public expression of commitment to each other. It represented an opportunity to reconcile two different aspects of their identities—the ancient Filipino and Hawaiian cultural heritages with the more modern concept of gay and lesbian identity. That was why the traditional aspects—the gowns, the Hawaiian wedding chant, the leis and flowers, those one thousand cranes—meant so much to them.

Attempting to integrate the different parts of themselves went beyond the wedding ceremony, though. Trinity had put together a slide show about the role of gays in Asian/Pacific culture, which she showed before different gay audiences. She had been quoted by name in an issue of *Philippine News*, the newspaper of the West Coast Filipino-American community. The newspaper had featured an article about a retreat held by Asian/Pacific lesbians, which Trinity had helped organize. She was trying to be strongly Asian-identified in the gay and lesbian community and strongly gay-identified in the Asian/Pacific community. "I want to be myself all the time," Trinity said.

Part of being herself included having children. Like many a "just-married" couple, they planned to wait a few years first, to enjoy themselves a little. When they were ready, Des, the younger of the two, would probably bear the child. It would be conceived through artificial insemination. Unlike other women I interviewed, they ideally wanted a man they knew to be the sperm donor and hoped he would have some involvement with the child. They also wanted the donor to be Asian; Des in particular hoped he would be gay. "We think it is unfair for a child not to know his father," said Trinity. "And we want to be sure he is a good person."

In the meantime, they had more immediate concerns, planning the wedding and the honeymoon. They still weren't sure where they would go on their wedding trip. They were thinking about Mexico's Yucatán Peninsula, but admitted they might settle for the nearby Russian River, a resort popular with San Francisco's gay community, instead.

It was time for me to leave. I had planned to go to Friday night services at the gay and lesbian synagogue, Sha'ar Zahav, and was already late. I retraced my steps to the other side of Castro Street. It was foggy and cold and drizzling and I had only a vague idea where I was going. I wandered down narrow streets with gloomy Victorian houses and a few souls huddled under umbrellas. Then I turned a corner and there was Sha'ar Zahav, all lit up and welcoming, in an old wooden building that looked like it had once been a church.

I took my seat as the lighting of the Sabbath candles was taking place. The cantor played a plaintive tune on a clarinet. The place was packed. About eighty people were present; many of the men wore yarmulkes. There were a number of Hebrew prayers and melodies, most of which I didn't recognize from the Americanized synagogue I had attended while growing up. For a moment, I imagined I was in an Eastern European synagogue in the last century. Perhaps the feeling was caused by the smallness of the sanctuary with its dark wooden benches or the seriousness with which the worshippers seemed to approach everything. Or maybe it was just the sense of disorientation caused by my hurried walk through unfamiliar, fogbound streets.

I had never been to a gay synagogue before; the only time I had attended synagogue at all in recent years was on the High Holy Days (Rosh Hashana and Yom Kippur) with my parents at the synagogue I had grown up in. The worshippers here were doing what Trinity and Des were trying to do several blocks away—combining two identities, two cultures. Yet in a way, I had felt more at home with Trinity and Des than with my fellow Jews. Maybe it is when you expect to be a natural part of things and you aren't, that you feel the most out of place.

As the service progressed and I began to feel a little less alienated, something totally unexpected took place. The rabbi called two women up to the pulpit. A few others—apparently their friends—followed. The women, Dana and Prudence, were going to be married the following week, the rabbi announced. Tonight was their *aufruf*, the traditional prenuptial blessing. The rabbi removed his prayer shawl. He and the other people on the pulpit held it over the couple, much like a *hoopa* at a Jewish wedding. Dana and Prudence beamed. The congregation began clapping their hands rhythmically and chanting, "Mazel tov vah sim-tov," the traditional good luck phrase. Then, as if prearranged, members of the audience began to throw chocolate candy kisses at the couple. Dana and Prudence caught a few kisses; most fell on the floor of the pulpit. The couple kissed passionately and returned to their seats. The rabbi continued with the rest of the service.

I didn't stay for the *oneg shabbat,* the post-worship refreshments. I needed to sit alone for a moment and sort things out. Here was AIDS, and a community trying to deal with disease and death as best it could (during the service at Sha'ar Zahav, the rabbi had asked members of the congregation to call out names of people who were suffering from AIDS in order to pray for them, and many did). But here were also love stories, marriage and babies, gold paper cranes and chocolate candy kisses. It wasn't just a question of life going on in the midst of crisis. There was more to it. I felt as if I was witnessing the formation of a new culture—one of gay and lesbian families, gay marriages, gay religious schools, of ancient traditions merging with a long-stigmatized sexual identity.

I headed back to the Castro. It was still raining, and few people were on the streets. I found a Mexican restaurant that was open. Gay San Francisco wasn't at all what I expected. It was full of surprises. Then, something else came into my mind. I was in the capital of the sexual revolution. But what had ever happened to sex? Armistead Maupin had said to me, "The women can do anything the men *can't.*" Maybe the women could provide the key.

SAN FRANCISCO, PART 2

A
sk me anything!" offered Susie Bright, the thirty year old high-spirited editor of the lesbian sex magazine *On Our Backs*, and adult-film reviewer for *Penthouse Forum*.

The subject was lesbian sex, and I wasn't quite sure where to start. Before I had a chance to phrase a question, though, Susie was off and running. "Oral sex is supposed to be what lesbians do, what we are experts at," she began. "But I have a different idea about that. Since the oral sex revolution in the sixties, straight people are just as good at oral sex as gay people. What lesbians know about that straights don't know is fucking."

"Oh," I said nervously. "Really?"

"For the heterosexual couple," she maintained, "fucking consists of penis-vagina intercourse in one, two, or three positions. For lesbians it can take a number of forms. For us, it is something you do with fingers, your entire hand, or [sex] toys. In the way you can explore a woman and create different sensations, there are a lot more things that can happen in lesbian fucking than in straight fucking. You get to feel a lot of things you wouldn't feel in the missionary position. I didn't like fucking until I was into lesbian sex. Why do you think the group who wrote the G-spot book thanked a group of Miami lesbians for help in their book? Because lesbian fucking involves much more G-spot stimulation than straight fucking!"

Susie loves to talk and she loves, above all, to be provocative. Later she admitted, "My put-downs of oral sex certainly don't mean that millions of lesbians don't love it." But for the moment, her main interest lay in demolishing preconceptions. She charged ahead: "I'm saying this about lesbians and penetration like it is a big secret, but it is one of those secrets that everybody does but nobody talks about. It is our invisibility as lesbians that covers it up. I tell people I edit a lesbian sex magazine and they say, 'Is that a joke? Isn't that a contradiction in terms?' or 'I thought lesbians don't have sex.'"

A revolution in lesbian sexuality has been taking place since the early eighties, and Susie Bright and the lively and irreverent magazine (circulation, ten thousand) she edits have been at the heart of it. As the flamboyant evangelist of lesbian sexual exploration and experimentation, Susie's goal is to once and for all destroy the image of lesbians as "eunuchs," as "loving but sexless companions." Once dubbed the "X-rated intellectual" by a *San Francisco Chronicle* columnist, she looked the part almost exactly. The intellectual Susie is reflected in the pointy, old-fashioned eyeglasses, the brownish hair she wore pulled back in a bun. The X-rating derives from the skin-tight flowered slacks, the red high heels, and (in the epitome of lesbian "political incorrectness") the heavy application of rouge and lipstick. That is the Susie Bright who was an extra in the safe-sex porno film, *Behind the Green Door II.*

I met her at the offices of *On Our Backs* in the center of the Castro. It was an office much like that of any other small and struggling publication—desks and chairs and computer terminals, glossy mounted covers of the magazine's back issues adorning the walls, a coffee pot bubbling in the kitchenette. Above Susie's desk was a watercolor that read "Flamboyant Vibrator." Off to one side, a couple of women were huddled around a videocassette machine. They were editing lesbian porno videos. In addition to publishing four issues of *On Our Backs* each year, Blush Entertainment, the magazine's corporate entity, has produced a number of thirty-minute hard-core videos, as well as a full-length soft-core feature of a lesbian burlesque show.

I observed that lesbian burlesque was a phenomenon that hadn't yet reached Boston, as far as I was aware.

"You never heard about it?" marvelled Susie, her tone suggesting I must have spent the last several years on a desert island. "We did a burlesque show every week for two years," she explained. "It started because we needed money to print our first issue. Debi, our publisher, is a stripper. She suggested that we put on a show and charge admission. People went bananas. They had favorites and regulars and it was like a major scene. After a while, it was imitated and audiences fell off." When you write about sex, she noted, "you don't get bank loans or grants. We are not considered educational. None of us has a trust fund or private capital. Just a lot of imagination and determination."

To appreciate how radical, how heretical all this was (and, to a large extent, still is), one has to understand something about lesbian attitudes towards sex and sexuality. While many gay men spent the seventies and early eighties testing the outer limits of sexual taboos, lesbians were exploring the joys (and pitfalls) of conventional domesticity. Most were coupled off in monogamous relationships. Sex was something that was not discussed; when it was, it was mentioned primarily in terms of its role in the victimization of women, rather than in terms of its potential for self-expression and self-enhancement. The butch-femme culture that had characterized prefeminist lesbian life had virtually disappeared, at least among middle-class white women.

And sex was something the majority of lesbian couples weren't having very often. In their book *American Couples*, published in 1983 and still considered the definitive work on the subject, University of Washington psychologists Pepper Schwartz and Philip Blumstein found that the 788 lesbian couples they surveyed had sex far less often than heterosexual or gay male couples. Among lesbian couples who had been together for between two to ten years, thirty-seven percent had sex once a week or more, compared to seventy-three percent for similar gay male couples and married heterosexuals. The researchers found that when sexual frequency fell off, lesbians did not compensate by having sex outside their relationships, as gay men did.

Susie Bright came out in seventies Los Angeles, in an atmosphere of social and sexual conformity. All the women she met wore their hair short, dressed in work shirts and Levi's. It was "a Maoist look, definitely not sexy," she recalled. "When I came out, I didn't even get that you were a lesbian for sexual reasons. It was almost like it was just another political challenge." She admitted that for the first several years after she came out, she had "lousy sex." She knew she could have better sex with a man because, in a heterosexual encounter, she didn't have to abide by the rules of politically correct sex. "I could be uninhibited with a man, do fifty different things," she said. "But with a woman I couldn't touch her breast. That would be objectifying her. I couldn't fuck her. That would be male-penetration oriented. I couldn't spend more time on her or more time on me. That would be unequal."

In retrospect, Susie saw the mores of that period as traditional female sexual repression under a different guise. "Even though I had a radical rhetoric in my head to explain why I couldn't do X, Y, and Z, it was really just old-fashioned good-girl inhibitions with a new label," she said.

In the early eighties, after graduating from the University of California at

Santa Cruz, Susie moved to San Francisco. There, things were beginning to change. The lesbian community was alive with discussions about sex and sexual politics, about butch-femme and S and M. She began working at Good Vibrations, a shop that sold vibrators. Women customers were constantly confiding their problems about sex. Often, they told her they had never had an orgasm in their entire lives. "I never once had a man come in and tell me he had never had an orgasm," she noted. "But that is the most common thing a woman will reveal about herself. What does that say? You don't know how to rouse yourself and a reach a climax! That is pretty repressed. To me, it is like the fifty-nine cents on the dollar routine [the economic gap between women and men]. It is shocking."

She began to conclude that in order to become full human beings, it was essential for women, especially lesbians, to free themselves from the sexual "yoke." When you had two women socialized to be ignorant about their bodies, the result was "devastating in terms of sexuality," she felt. For lesbians, this was compounded by what Susie called *The Well of Loneliness* tradition (from the Radclyffe Hall novel of the twenties): "The lesbian as the noble soul will always put her principles above her sexuality." She and her lover started to experiment with butch-femme roles, then with sex toys. Exploring sex was akin to women breaking into a nontraditional job, she thought. "There is the sense of confidence, the sense of accomplishment, of power."

While Susie Bright was starting to achieve a new sense of herself as a sexual being and San Francisco lesbians were talking nonstop about sex and sexuality, a similar ferment was taking place on the East Coast. On April 24, 1982, Barnard College in New York City hosted a landmark conference called "Towards a Politics of Sexuality" that brought divisions on the subject to the forefront. Instead of discoursing on women as victims of sex and sexual violence, conference participants read papers that portrayed many kinds of sex as enjoyable and affirming. (A collection of papers delivered at the conference was titled *Pleasure and Danger*, reflecting the split in feminist thinking about sex.) Participants addressed many of the same issues the women in San Francisco were talking about—butch-femme, S and M, and the like. As a result, the conference was picketed by activists of the organization Women Against Pornography (WAP), whose flyers denounced several speakers as perverts. Amy Hoffman, then an editor at *GCN*, recalled how shocking it was at the time for feminists to call other feminists "perverts." "Everyone at the conference was tarred with the brush of S and M," she said.

The lines were hardening. But the sex debates, as they were called, continued. Two years later, in Boston, Amy Hoffman and Cindy Patton, also an editor at *GCN*, founded a lesbian sex magazine called *Bad Attitude*. It offered a combination of essays, fiction, graphics, and photographs, in an effort to "provide an ongoing place where some of these issues could be explored," according to Cindy Patton. A number of other publications sprang up, as well. In the Boston area, two lesbian S and M publications emerged, *Outrageous Women* and *Idos*. (Much of the inspiration for these publications came from women's experiences, of course, but the influence of the more sexually adventuresome gay men was also crucial. As a result, cities where lesbians and gay men tended to work together politically, notably Boston and San Francisco, emerged as centers of lesbian sexual radicalism.)

On the West Coast, Susie Bright heard that some women were starting a lesbian erotic magazine called *On Our Backs* and wanted to publish one of her poems. Intrigued (and charmed by the magazine's name, a play on the name of the sexually conservative feminist publication, *off our backs*), she became a volunteer. She started by selling ads, which turned out to be a major challenge. "You were selling the idea of a lesbian market, that a lesbian audience existed and that it was sexual," she recalled. "I felt like I was in the sixties talking to advertisers about the black community. Here was a large group of people that no one notices." Selling ads taught Susie that invisibility was "the lesbian trademark, our burden."

Because she worked at Good Vibrations, Susie had contacts for recruiting potential advertisers. The magazine's first issue in the summer of 1984 largely featured ads from shops that sold "sensuous accessories" or from companies that offered mail-order sex products. A glance at the June 1988 issue showed a wider range of goods and services advertised. There was a full-page ad from a San Francisco gay and lesbian bookstore, another full page from a company that taught "defense techniques for nonviolent persons" (defensive handguns and kubotan), ads from two bed-and-breakfast establishments, psychotherapists, and masseuses from as far away as Chicago, plus the usual sex-shop and mail-order ads. There was also a two-page section of classified personals. One went: "ATTRACTIVE BROWN SKIN TOP. That's me. I'm also stern, understanding, safe, androgynous, and into army fatigues, leather, latex, and attractive femmes and faggy butch bottoms who need a drill sergeant, big brother or sister, or Daddy." And another: "THREE SEXY COLLEGE LESBIANS. Help! We're trapped in a small Midwest town in an isolated college community. We're in desperate need of inspiring wall decorations. Please, anyone, send us photos—singles, couples, groups, naked, clothed—whatever. We'll worship you forever."

That first issue of *On Our Backs* featured a parody of a *Playboy* centerfold, called "Bulldagger of the Season." (Bulldagger is a term for a butch woman.) The bulldagger was none other than Susie's lover Honey Lee Cotrell, pictured in a rather severe-looking pose with her breasts showing. There were also smaller snapshots of Honey Lee getting her first permanent at six years old and as a twenty-six year old hippie. The "Dagger Data Sheet" that accompanied the photos included her measurements, turn-ons ("my wooden dildo, my pocket pepper mill, motorcycles, tattoos"), and secret fantasy ("the back seat of a Rolls Royce on fur-lined seats after a picnic"). Honey Lee's "ideal woman" was "tall, smart, talkative, pretty." As it turned out, that was a pretty good description of Susie Bright.

The humorous Bulldagger of the Season centerfolds did not become a regular feature of *On Our Backs*. While straight and gay male porn offered ideas and material to parody, the magazine wanted to develop a lesbian erotic aesthetic all its own. Part of that aesthetic was diversity—*On Our Backs* was determined to expound the view that many different kinds of women were sexy and appealing. That was different from men's porn, said Susie, where there was one look defined as attractive—the *Penthouse* "pet" or the *Blueboy* man. "Compared to them [male porn], we are all over the map," she insisted.

The same aesthetic of diversity extended to the erotic fiction the magazine published, which Susie characterized as ranging from "soft-core to hardcore, from kinky to romantic to melancholy." What she was aiming for, she said, was "to get you a little turned-on; you learn something about a sexual point of view you have never known before; you get offended by something." She conceded that that kind of variety, the "shotgun effect," as she described it, partly had an economic motive. It pulled in a lot of different readers in a market that was relatively small. "If the magazine only had the girl-next-door type of lesbian I don't think we could sell enough to survive," she said. "And," she added, "I like it this way. We are able to enlarge the scope of what is out there, of what sexual fantasy consists of."

Recently, the magazine featured an article by Susie about safe sex for lesbians. Although many people (including many lesbians) tended to disparage the idea that gay women should be worried about contracting AIDS, given the handful of cases documented among lesbians at the time, Susie wasn't convinced. The official AIDS statistics, compiled by the Centers for Disease Control, didn't subdivide women into straight, gay, or bisexual categories, as they did men, she noted. And the medical experts "don't know anything about our practices," she maintained. For those reasons, and because AIDS was a life-and-death issue, lesbians had to "get on the ball. It is up to us." Even if individual lesbians were in a low-risk situation, her view was, "Why not experiment with this stuff so if you are in a position where you are more vulnerable, you're not going to be sitting there like a schoolgirl who has never been kissed!"

Just what did safe sex for lesbians mean anyway? I asked. Susie walked to the back of the office and produced a lesbian safe-sex kit available by mail from a company in Macon, Georgia. It was attractively packaged and came in a red and white box with a design that looked like gift-wrapping paper. The contents included a mint-green dental dam, a piece of latex that could be put over the vaginal or rectal opening. You could feel heat and wetness through it, Susie said. There was a beige piece of latex, a finger cot, to be used for penetration. The kit also contained condoms and lubricant.

Susie said that she was interested in fetishizing safe sex as a way of increasing women's erotic options. If the threat of AIDS ended today, she said, she would continue to use condoms on her dildos because she hated to wash them. "I will continue using rubber gloves when I fist women because they don't scratch. Using dental dams for rimming makes that activity much more appealing," she said.

She admitted that most lesbians did not take the threat of AIDS seriously and were not using safe-sex techniques. Susie had written in *On Our Backs*, "When I bring up safe sex to most lesbians, they make a face like someone just pushed a bowl of cold spinach in front of them." But as the editor of a national lesbian periodical, she emphasized that ten years from now, she didn't want to be the one who had said "nothing to worry about."

Of all the aspects of lesbian sex and relationships, Susie thought that monogamy was the arena where change had been slowest. Sexual fidelity remained the dominant pattern of lesbian relationships; when one partner started having sex outside the relationship, that usually signalled the beginning of the uncoupling process. "Sometimes, I feel I was the only kid who grew up in the sixties," Susie said. "All my peers are so caught up in monogamy." She noted that lesbians were not "monogamous with a capital M," but they were serially monogamous. Lesbians' "dirty little secret," she said, "was yes, we're monogamous but it only lasted two years." The most tragic cliché about lesbians, she said, was "marry the first girl you have an orgasm with. Isn't that the feminine, romantic thing to do!"

Susie thought it made perfect sense that monogamy would be the last of the lesbian sexual patterns to go, if it ever did. Going out and buying a sex toy was pretty nonthreatening, she noted, compared to the insecurity and self-esteem issues that would likely arise if one or both partners were having sex outside a relationship. For that reason, she thought, being adventurous within one's own relationship didn't necessarily translate to being adventurous outside it.

Bad Attitude magazine co-founder Cindy Patton noted another factor. For middle-class lesbians at least, she said, couple relationships have been the traditional building blocks of community. That was why it was so traumatic when long-term lesbian couples broke up. And nonmonogamy, more than anything, was a threat to the stability of that structure. "Heterosexual life revolves around institutions that create structure—churches, schools, traditional families," she said. "Gay male and lesbian working-class culture developed around bars. But middle-class lesbians, by and large, haven't had these institutions. We only have relationships."

It was difficult to measure just how much an impact the sexual revolution had made on lesbians. Amy Hoffman took a somewhat cautious view. "The change may have only been in being able to talk about what you were doing," she said. "I don't even know if there was a change in what people were actually doing. But lesbians could be more open about sex and talk about it with their friends and their therapist. That was a significant change."

For the always-optimistic Susie Bright, the revolution had reached what she called the lesbian silent majority. The letters to the editor of *On Our Backs* offered evidence that interest in the subject had a wide geographic range at least; one issue included correspondence from Ward Cove, Alaska, "northern Alabama," and Sydney, Australia. Susie said she was prepared to go on a talk show and relate all kinds of case histories of people who were "trying something new with their partner in their sex life, in their fantasy life, who were daring to do something new."

She was convinced that among the new, postfeminist generation of lesbians, sexuality was "in." For many younger women, "expressing yourself as a lesbian is cool," she said. The attitude was something akin to "watch out, here we are, we're bad!" That, she thought, was "an incredible sensation to be riding on. Instead of the old nerds for the revolution." She added, "I am still really a nerd, but I am out of the closet about my sex stuff at least."

BOSTON AND NEW YORK CITY

On a blissful Sunday afternoon in early June, I went to a forum that would have delighted Susie Bright, if only because of its name. It was called "Lesbian Smut." The panel discussion, part of the events of Boston's annual Lesbian and Gay Pride Week, was sponsored by *Bad Attitude*, the East Coast counterpart of *On Our Backs*. Some seventy or eighty women decided to forgo the beautiful summer day to sit on rickety wooden chairs under the fluorescent lights of a university lecture hall. There was only one other man in the audience.

Amy Hoffman, one of the founders of *Bad Attitude*, started off the proceedings with an analysis of the early lesbian feminist opposition to talking about sex (attributing such reluctance to a "fear of revealing differences" that might undermine the idea of sisterhood). Then she shared some of her musings about lesbian porn. Was *Bad Attitude* just "jerk-off material"? she wondered. Was it too funny to be jerk-off material? Did it pass the "wet panties test"? By creating new lesbian erotic scenarios—the gymnasium, the masseuse—were publications like *Bad Attitude* and *On Our Backs* opening the imagination or merely limiting it?

The most dramatic presence on the panel was that of New York writer Joan Nestle. Describing herself as "a feminist femme" and a "big-assed Jewish woman from the Bronx," she had a mass of black hair, dangling earrings, and seemed to be wearing nothing but a black slip. Perhaps the high point of the afternoon came when she asked the women in the crowd who labelled themselves femmes to raise their hands. About a dozen hands went up.

I reacted to the large number of self-identified femmes in the audience the same way I did when Susie Bright informed me that lesbians were "experts" at penetration. Penetration? Femmes? Butches? What was going on here? The echoes of heterosexual sex and the butch-femme lesbian couples of the fifties seemed curiously out of keeping with one of the most enlightened, politically conscious lesbian communities in the country.

A few months later I was sitting at Joan Nestle's dining-room table in her apartment on Manhattan's Upper West Side. That evening, she had traded her theatrical black slip for a more conventional turquoise sweater and grey slacks (plus silver earrings and nail polish). She was telling me about her coming out in a working-class Greenwich Village bar in the fifties, when the norm for lesbians was a stereotypically masculine or feminine appearance, butch or femme.

"We knew ourselves by our passion," she was saying. "In order to live this passion, we wore it. We dressed it. If I wanted to meet a butch woman, I had to announce my need of her and my interest in her by how I dressed. History both trapped us and gave us power. We had no other choices, didn't know we had other choices. We came out of a long butch-femme tradition that was also an empowering tradition."

There is a poetic intensity about Joan Nestle. When she speaks, her voice is suffused with deep feeling. She is a survivor, the woman who has come through. The same qualities are in evidence in her writing—in her recollections of prefeminist lesbian culture, of her lovers and her mother, even in her political essays and pornographic stories. More than any other individual, Joan Nestle has been the catalyst for the butch-femme revival in the lesbian community. To her, the butch-femme tradition was an honorable one—the basis of the lesbian erotic heritage. But it was not just a relic of the past. It was also something to be lived out today, representing a sexual identity that was a still a viable option for lesbians.

Now nearing fifty, Joan came from a very different generation than Susie Bright. Her life as an open lesbian has spanned more than three decades—the prefeminist and pre-gay liberation fifties and sixties when butch-femme culture flourished; the politically conscious seventies when the feminist movement offered lesbians a cloak of respect and respectability; and the eighties with the lesbian sexual revolution in which Joan Nestle has been such an influential figure.

History is everywhere in Joan's apartment. It starts at the front door, which bears the inscription, "Women are History: Past and Present." (Under it, someone had scrawled, "All There (sic) good for is hump and dump and the dishes," which Joan hadn't bothered to erase.) The past spills from the rows of filing cabinets and the bookshelves, looks out from the photographs and posters of lesbian heroines like Gertrude Stein and Mabel Hampton. For Joan's apartment is also the home of the Lesbian Herstory Archives, a collection of historical documents and memorabilia, including complete sets of lesbian newspapers and periodicals, that attracts a thousand visitors a year. In fact, Joan appeared to have no private space outside of the archives, which says as much about her as anything else.

Joan grew up in a working-class Jewish family in the Bronx. She never knew her father; her mother raised her and her brother as best she could. At thirteen, she took her first job, selling dollar dresses part-time in the bargain basement of S. Klein, the Union Square department store. Her mother wanted her to leave school and work full-time. Joan refused. "I knew that if I quit school none of my life would happen," she said years later. So she moved out of her mother's house to live with her aunt. "It was a tremendous act of self-assertion," she maintained. When people dismissed femmes like herself as parodies of traditional women, she often recalled that moment of adolescent determination. "I have never met a passive femme," she said.

She came of age sexually in the fifties, not a good time to be gay or lesbian. Her mother was convinced that Joan was a member of the "third sex." She took her daughter to doctors, one of whom pronounced her hormonally imbalanced because she had facial hair.

Beginning with her coming out as a femme in 1958 and continuing throughout the sixties, the butch-femme bars provided the center of her life. In the "lesbian air" of the Sea Colony bar in Greenwich Village, she could "breathe the life we could not anywhere else, those of us who wanted to see women dance, make love, wear shirts and pants," she wrote in *A Restricted Country* (Firebrand Books), her collection of essays, memories, and fiction. But if the Sea Colony was a refuge, it was a humiliating one. To go to the bathroom, she wrote, you had to stand in an endless line that often wound past the bar and the front-room tables. The line was presided over by a butch woman "whose job it was to twist around her hand our allotted amount of toilet paper." Because they were considered "deviants," only one woman at a time was allowed in the bathroom. To Nestle, the bathroom line symbolized that "we were a criminal people," she told me. "We had a very hard life, surrounded by the police and insecurities and the sense of being a freak."

With the advent of feminism and gay and lesbian liberation in the late sixties and seventies, her world changed dramatically. Butch-femme culture—the core of Joan's sense of self and community for so many years—was dismissed as politically retrograde, as a replication of male-female coupling, a sign that you "had a prick in your head." Femmes, in particular, became objects of scorn. "At gatherings of the seventies, if a woman walked in wearing makeup, lipstick, nail polish, even heels, she would not be spoken to, or asked to leave," Joan recalled. "She was viewed as the enemy." The result was the "exclusion of a whole community of women," she said. Some of the old butches and femmes faded from sight, went underground; others, like Joan, adapted.

Perhaps because she was politically minded (she had registered black voters in Alabama and taken part in Dr. King's march from Selma to Montgomery), Joan adapted more easily than many. In her lesbian-feminist consciousness-raising group, she learned very quickly there were some things you could talk about and others you could not. "I learned to be silent about what I called 'old lesbian ways,'" she said. "For instance, liking penetration. In the new world of lesbian feminism, lesbians were not supposed to like penetration. I learned to 'pass,' to be as good a lesbian feminist as anyone."

To a large extent, her life had stabilized. She was in the midst of an eleven-year relationship with another woman, with whom she co-founded the Lesbian Archives. For a number of years she had been teaching immigrant students at the SEEK program at Queens College. Her sense of "freakishness" had faded. But increasingly, she was convinced there was "a missing voice in everything we were doing" in the lesbian-feminist movement. The new world had cut itself off from its butch-femme roots. She wanted to express her thank-yous to the old lesbian culture. In 1981, she published an essay called *Butch-Femme Relationships: Sexual Courage in the 1950s.* In it she wrote, "Although I have been a Lesbian for over twenty years and I embrace feminism as a world view, I can spot a butch thirty feet away and still feel the thrill of her power." Butch-femme relationships and culture, she argued, represented "a radical, sexual political statement" and "a conspicuous flag of rebellion." Predictably, she said, "all hell broke loose."

That essay made Joan a controversial figure in the lesbian community. Many were grateful, of course. But for others, merely acknowledging the past represented a threat to the new-found sense of respectability that feminism had given them. What Joan has called the "second McCarthy period in my life" began. According to her account, a member of Women Against Pornography (WAP) went to Queens College, where Joan worked, and warned students and faculty about her; the woman accused her of being a lesbian, being into S and M, and engaging in "unequal patriarchal power sex." At the Barnard conference the following year, Joan was among the speakers labelled "sexual deviants" by WAP protesters. During the conference, she was confronted by one of the antiporn crusaders who told her it was acceptable to write about butch-femme relationships in the past. But, the woman warned, if she persisted in advocating butch-femme as a way to live in the present, she would find herself on the "enemies list."

Over the years, Joan said, most of the criticism she has received from other women has been more the result of her writing erotica rather than her coming out as a femme. She didn't get attacked for being a femme very often these days, she said, "because that is me, my life. Given the rhetoric of respect in the lesbian movement for individual women's lives, it is hard for people to attack me for that." And as much as she was infuriated by the demands for conformity within the lesbian community, she understood them to some extent. They were rooted in the sexual victimization of women. "Just like we saw back in the old bars, the stronger the push is from the outside, the more cohesive the internal group has to be," she said. "We saw it with black nationalism and Zionism." But within her own community, she was still determined to fight for acceptance of and respect for diversity.

And so largely thanks to Joan Nestle, butch-femme—that discredited identity from the prefeminist past—met the lesbian sexual revolution of the eighties. It did not, of course, become the cultural norm, the mandatory code of dress and behavior that it had been in its heyday when lesbians first coming out were pressured to take one role or the other. It became part of the mix, one of many sexual styles open to women.

For many, like Joan and Susie Bright (who also called herself a femme), the butch-femme dynamic provided a sense of tension and conflict that enhanced sexual pleasure. "I find it the most erotic way to be," Joan told me, "because it is a kind of wonderful conflict of tensions, of women tensions. The misconception about butch-femme for so long has been that someone is the man and someone is the woman. But it is always two women—one of whom will perhaps play with or put on what seems to be male attire, or a cock that can be taken off and put on." It was the "difference among sameness" that provided what she called the great erotic potential of butch-femme sex. She noted that she had recently read that the definition of a good lesbian relationship was one where women were mirror images of one other. "That would drive me absolutely crazy," said Joan. "No wonder women stop making love."

I asked her if the butch-femme dynamic was confined to the sexual act or if it extended to other aspects of one's relationship as well. Joan said you couldn't make such distinctions. Butch-femme was a "world view, a way of cherishing," she maintained. "A butch woman, to me, is a very special kind of woman who moves in the world in a very special way. I like to encourage, I like to cook for my lovers. Butch women take a lot more shit on the street and part of how I love is to give them a home in many kinds of ways. A home that both encourages their butch self and also gives them a vacation from it."

Nonetheless, she insisted, she had never moved in with any of her lovers; they had always moved in with her. She was the homemaker, but she had also been working since she was thirteen. No one had ever supported her financially. "I am a powerful woman of the world," she said. "Being a femme has nothing to do with passivity, with giving up freedoms, it has to do with two very different styles, with cherishing."

Susie Bright, who came out as a femme more than two decades after Joan, saw butch-femme in a narrower sense. Susie was baffled that anyone might think that because she identified as a femme that meant she had to do the dishes or do what her girlfriend said. She couldn't believe that someone might think she lived "something really dumb—a Fred Flintstone and Wilma lifestyle." She was a consciously liberated femme who saw butch-femme as "first and foremost a sexual statement." It was reflected to some degree in one's appearance, like her makeup. But it just wasn't taken as seriously as in the old days; it wasn't a lifestyle.

Joan had no desire to return to the fifties; she wasn't romanticizing the past. The progress, the security provided by feminism and gay liberation were things she was unwilling to give up. She even admitted that with the new lesbian sexual revolution, she was more erotically adventuresome than she had been in the butch-femme days of her youth. She wanted to integrate the virtues of the past with those of the present. She had a younger lover now, she said, who had come out at women's music festivals. "She is tattooed with unicorns," she said. "She works in a warehouse. She is a wonderful mixture of things. She wears dildos when she feels like it. She is totally open to sexual exploration and gives me the right. And in my experience this was not possible in the fifties. We have the best of all possible worlds today."

Although roles had certainly played a part in gay male culture in the past, for men there was no equivalent butch-femme revival. Relationships between men certainly became more egalitarian as a result of gay liberation, but the men had always had more erotic options, had never felt they had to repress their sexual possibilities. They had never disowned their erotic past the way lesbians had. With the arrival of AIDS, that was beginning to change. Now, as lesbians moved towards a more openly sexual stance, many men, facing AIDS, were retreating towards the very sexual patterns lesbians were questioning or abandoning. Despite attempts to find new kinds of sexual pleasure within the guidelines of safe sex (which, after all, was just another erotic exploration), the general watchword was caution for more and more men.

To Joan, who had battled so hard for her own sexual freedom, even within her own community, it was very poignant to see gay men taking the "safe ground" of monogamy. She feared that the same thing that happened to lesbians could happen to gay men, that sex could "become almost a kind of drudgery." She hoped that lesbians might be able to "keep a certain flame of sexual experimentation alive while men are dying. If we give up sexuality to death, we will lose hundreds of years of progress."

Once again I received a glimpse into that curious relationship between gay men and gay women. Gay men were confronting issues of mortality, and lesbians were having babies. Many gay men seemed to be turning away from sexual experimentation; after years of repression, many lesbians were increasingly open to it. The men, identified in the seventies with fun and frivolity, were asking "How should a man live?"; lesbians, once viewed as earnest and dogmatic, were taking themselves less seriously. Two communities so often at odds seemed to be complementing each other in unexpected ways. Eventually, perhaps, the men and the women would meet at some point in the middle—where stable relationships and sexual exploration and freedom would coexist in that "best of all possible worlds." The role of sexual pioneers played by homosexuals in the past was continuing into the uncertain future in ways no one would have imagined ten or fifteen years ago.

RACE AND CULTURE

▼　▼　▼　▼　▼　▼　▼　▼　▼　▼　▼　▼　▼

MEMPHIS, TENNESSEE

We were in the car on our way to the chili dinner sponsored by the Memphis chapter of Black and White Men Together (BWMT), the multiracial gay organization. Ed and I were having a friendly argument. Ed, who is black, was telling me that he used to think that being black and gay were mutually exclusive. If you were one, you simply couldn't be the other. The two terms black and gay were identities created by each group, he said. And the gay community, as he perceived it at the time, was white. Although he had changed his mind long ago, lots of black men still thought that way, he maintained. For them, gay sex was just "messing around"; gay identity was a white concept that had no relevance to them. These days, he said, with no effort to hide his bitterness, he sometimes wondered if they were right.

But why can't you have two identities, I asked him? "I'm Jewish and I'm also gay and I never felt they were mutually exclusive." Have you ever been discriminated against within the gay community for being Jewish? Ed demanded. "Well, no," I admitted.

Ask Ed a question and he will discourse for fifteen minutes or half an hour. He will analyze an issue from all sides, construct a theory about it. His lover, Mike, told me Ed possessed an IQ of 210. I wasn't sure that anyone had an IQ that high. (I had read somewhere that John Stuart Mill, nineteenth-century prodigy and philosopher, had an IQ of 190. I thought that was as smart as you could get.)

Still, I didn't doubt Ed's superior intelligence. When I first met him, he was in his backyard weeding his begonia patch, surrounded by a pile of books about ancient Egypt; he was studying for an Egyptology exam. A trim, handsome man in his thirties, he was a little distant, preoccupied; perhaps he was just lost in the farthest depths of the Nineteenth Dynasty. ("How is Rameses?" someone asked him later that evening. "It's Rameses's mother that I am interested in," corrected Ed.)

It was a warm April night and Ed's lover Mike was behind the wheel. Mike was concentrating on the road as we sped past Overton Park, down the broad avenues of Memphis into parts of town I hadn't become acquainted with during my brief visit. Mike knew enough to let Ed do most of the talking, but he was always ready to cut him off when he felt Ed was going on too long, taking the listener off into arcane realms. Mike, who is white, looked like a football tackle. He was six feet, five inches tall, broad-shouldered, and balding at thirty-six. About eight months before, he had moved to Memphis from Marion, Indiana, to live with Ed. They had met through mutual friends in BWMT. In Indiana, Mike worked for the RCA Corporation; in Memphis, he was still looking for a job. Mike was sexually attracted to black men, almost exclusively it would seem. He helped found the Indianapolis chapter of BWMT in order to meet blacks. In the process, he became sensitized to black concerns, emerging as an enthusiast of black culture. That evening he was wearing a red, green, and white dashiki.

Mike was dynamic—somewhat of a firebrand, in fact. At the national BWMT conference held in Milwaukee, Wisconsin, the year before, a prominent black gay writer gave a speech in which he intimated that the primary reason white gays were interested in black men was to exploit them sexually. Mike was furious and confronted the speaker after he had finished. People nearby were afraid they would come to blows. At the upcoming convention, Mike was running for co-chair of the national organization. (He was eventually elected to the post.)

Although BWMT was not a major force on the national gay political scene, it was one of the most important and visible gay organizations in Memphis. In a city almost fifty percent black, it was the only gay group whose major focus was black-white issues. There was no exclusively black gay organization of any consequence in Memphis; the major gay groups in Memphis—were overwhelmingly white. All the gay bars in town were predominately white as well, except for the Apartment Club, which was almost exclusively black.

One Memphis white gay politico told me that most of the men in BWMT were closeted, but the organization seemed quite active. The Memphis chapter had produced an AIDS brochure aimed specifically at the black gay population; the group supplied the Apartment Club with condoms to give away to patrons. Two chapter brothers, including Ed, were members of the state task force on AIDS. BWMT-Memphis put out a monthly sixteen-page newsletter; the issue I saw featured a report on racial discrimination in the city's gay bars. The organization also sponsored discussion groups three times a month. According to the BWMT calendar, upcoming topics included "Gay Bashing—Is It Worse in the 1980s?" "How Do You Meet the Gay Man Who Is Independent, Busy, and Productive?" and "Black and White Expressions of Anger."

We stopped to pick up a man named Charlie who lived with his parents in a working-class black neighborhood of two-story brick apartment buildings. Charlie was a big man, with his hair carefully molded into a flattop; he was uneducated and fond of street slang, much of which I didn't understand. He declined to reveal his age and claimed that no one in BWMT knew it. I thought he was in his late thirties, but he could have been older—or younger. As we drove, Charlie told me his parents had never given him any trouble about being gay, although he had never told them directly. "They always knew I was different because I spend two hours getting ready in the morning!" he said. I had a hard time imagining Charlie primping in front of the mirror.

The dinner was held at an apartment in an older section of the city. As soon as we entered, I was cornered by Irwin, a fortyish, heavy-set white man from Brooklyn who worked at a hospital and was studying for his MBA. He gave me the Memphis public-relations pitch. With the U.S. population gravitating to the Sunbelt, the sprawling metropolis on the Mississippi River was emerging as a major distribution center, he said. It wasn't just a cotton-trading town anymore. He ticked off the number of companies that had started in Memphis or moved their corporate headquarters there: Federal Express, Holiday Inns, International Paper. "Transportation, communications, health care, all the leading growth industries are here," he said. "Do I sound like the Chamber of Commerce?" Irwin was the voice of the new Memphis—with a Brooklyn accent. When dinner was served, he declined the chili and cornbread, substituting a Diet Coke instead. He was on a liquid diet, had lost eighty pounds, and was trying to lose more.

The diversity of the evening's group was impressive. Ed and Irwin were the resident intellectuals, prepared to debate any topic at the slightest provocation. Mike, perhaps assisted by his football player–like frame, was the conciliator. There were two preppy black men in their early to mid-twenties who constituted the younger generation. They were lovers and wore matching designer polo shirts; one of them was in the navy. Charlie and a man who arrived midway through dinner were older and from black working-class backgrounds. There were two other middle-class white men (one was the host); they cooked the food and remained on the fringes for much of the evening.

After dinner, as we sat around the living room, Ed brought up the question we had been discussing in the car on the way over. Did anyone think when growing up that he couldn't be both black and gay? Lauren, one of the preppy men, nodded his head. As a teenager in a small Georgia town, he thought being gay was "a white thing." That assumption had made it harder for him to come to terms with his sexuality. "It took a long time," he said. Ed turned to me with a look of triumph on his face: "You see!"

The conversation shifted to the treatment of blacks in Memphis gay bars. The Apartment Club, the lone black gay bar in town, had been established a couple of years ago largely because Memphis black gays felt uncomfortable in the predominately white gay clubs, Ed said. He described how white bars still frequently harassed blacks by demanding several forms of identification from them and switching from black to white music when management felt there were too many blacks there. Some white bars did not serve malt liquor, a favorite of Memphis blacks, apparently in an effort to limit black patronage.

Lauren said he felt that waiters and bartenders in the white clubs ignored him, in spite of his very middle-class appearance (he worked as a customer-service representative at a local company). He would only go to white bars "for something different," he said, preferring the Apartment Club even though it attracted "a more deprived group of people." Charlie, the man whom we had picked up on the way over, disagreed. He had never felt any discrimination in white clubs. "Maybe that's because you're such a big guy," someone suggested. "No one wants to mess with you."

Then the men in the room counted the number of black bartenders employed in the white gay bars in town. They could only come up with two. (The BWMT chapter in Atlanta had made the hiring of black bartenders in the city's gay bars a major priority.)

Black gay bars, Ed insisted, didn't try to keep out whites. Blacks were sensitive to others because of their own experiences with discrimination, he contended. Then Irwin jumped in. Did members of one oppressed group automatically empathize with others in similar situations? Irwin, who is Jewish, didn't think so. People compartmentalize experiences, he said; he felt that blacks could be unaware of what Jews or white gays went through, and vice versa.

But Ed argued that you couldn't make those distinctions if you truly felt discriminated against. The problem with white gay men was that they weren't sure whether they were oppressed or not. On the one hand, he said, they saw themselves as victims of discrimination; on the other, most could pass as straight and enjoy the privileges of white heterosexual men. Because of this basic confusion, white gay men had trouble sympathizing with others. In the final analysis, he contended, that was why white gay bars carded blacks and changed the music and no one (except BWMT) much cared.

Everyone in the room was listening politely to the conversation. They were evidently used to Ed and Irwin's circuitous discourse. Still, I could see Mike becoming restless, preparing to change the subject. Then a black man named Larry arrived. He was dressed in formal clothes. Larry was an organist by profession (he mostly played in black Pentecostal churches) and had just been performing at a banquet. He removed his tuxedo jacket and bow tie and straightened out the ruffles on his white shirt. "I love my white friends," he announced, with a wide grin. "They call me an oreo cookie."

Larry quickly turned the conversation back to the subject of the bars. He said he found the Apartment Club "scary"; the security there was lax, he claimed. He had never experienced any problems at white bars, he said, and preferred to go to them.

Larry insisted he never noticed skin color, just the person—a claim that seemed to conflict with his professed preference for white men. Lauren, the preppy, wouldn't go along with that. You are always aware of race, he said; that is what you notice first. Mike, always the politician, moved in and tried to strike a compromise position. "It is a question of emphasis," he said. "Of course, you notice race. But it depends on how much stress you give it."

How did black gays in general feel about interracial relationships? I asked. Jeff, the naval officer, had had a white boyfriend before he became involved with Lauren. He felt that his early relationship had been frowned upon by other blacks. He described the time he and his white lover had gone to a black bar in Los Angeles; someone had shouted abuse at them. While involved in that relationship, he avoided being around other black gays. "They would try and dissect you all the time," he said. "They were always trying to figure out why you were going out with a white guy."

For his part, Ed related running into a black friend at the Memphis airport, someone he hadn't seen since he and Mike had become lovers. "How is life with the oppressor?" his friend asked. "It is great," Ed replied. "Mike has just gone to get my bags."

Many white gays viewed the black community as quite homophobic, and I asked if the men in the room shared that impression. "The black community will accept it as long as you don't make waves," said Jeff, the naval officer. Irwin was the only one to challenge him. "That's not acceptance," he maintained. Significantly, none of the blacks in the group had told his family he was gay. Lauren said he would acknowledge it if his mother put the question to him. Larry, the organist, said his mother had once asked him and he had said "No." Charlie was sure his parents knew. His brothers and sisters would call him a "sissie"; once he had a boyfriend who would pick him up at his house each day. His siblings would say, "Your boyfriend is out there." But his parents never confronted him. "I don't have to say anything to my mother," he said. "She just knows."

Larry, the church organist, said that his parents' view was "If you're gay, you're wrong," and that was that. His father was a Pentecostal minister. Charlie, who had first met Larry when they were in a church choir together, said that if it was known that Larry was gay, he wouldn't be able to get jobs as an organist in black Pentecostal churches. "I thought to get a job as an organist in a black church you had to be gay," someone said. Everybody laughed.

It was time for dessert—a sweet-potato pie that Jeff had made. Jeff had joined the navy right after college, where he had been in NROTC. He had been an officer for three years now. Even though the navy officially bars homosexuals from its ranks, and anti-gay purges sometimes occur, Jeff claimed he felt relatively secure. When he was stationed in Maine, there had been several gay men and lesbians in his squadron. "It was known and not talked about and nothing was done," he said. He doubted you were in any danger of getting in trouble unless some "hard-core, anti-gay officer" reported you. "Lots of gays think the Naval Investigative Service is just around the corner," he said. "That just hasn't been my experience."

Still, Jeff said he wouldn't become sexually involved with another man who was in the navy. It was too risky: if that person was caught, he could potentially be forced to give your name. Jeff kept himself aloof from people he worked with and lived off-base in an apartment in Memphis. He had never told anyone in the military he was gay. "I had a close friend in Maine who I was sure would understand," he said. "But I still didn't tell him." Sometimes navy people—mostly the younger or the older guys—made anti-gay comments. But Jeff kept quiet. "You can't be too sympathizing," he said, or you could give yourself away.

Jeff said he had thought of marrying a woman as a "cover." Lots of gay guys in the navy married, he said. It was easy to do, especially if you and your wife could arrange to be stationed in separate places, he said.

At that point the host, a muscular young white man who had been quietly attending to his kitchen for most of the evening, perked up. A few years before, he had married a lesbian friend in the navy who was being investigated by Naval Intelligence. It was strictly a marriage of convenience designed to protect his friend. But he soon began to worry about his financial obligations towards her—her name was on his life insurance, he was about to buy a house. They were divorced six months later. As far as he knew, the ruse had worked; she was still in the military. His story created a stir. "We never knew anything about this!" everyone exclaimed. "Why didn't you tell us this before!"

I felt that the men at the chili dinner were trying to do something about racial divisions in the gay community, at the very least providing a social setting where whites and blacks could mingle. The origins of BWMT, it was true, lay in sexual attraction, specifically attraction to men of another race. (Some in the national organization wanted to change the name to "People of All Colors Together" to expand the membership and overcome the group's reputation as a glorified sex club.) Mike had gotten involved with the organization back in Indiana because he wanted to meet black men; Larry, the organist in his ruffled shirt and tuxedo pants, loved his white men. Out of it all came sex, I assumed. But there was also a dialogue, an attempt at mutual understanding, an effort to address some of the issues facing black gay men in the community.

It harked back to the earliest days of gay liberation when gay theoreticians touted sex as way of overcoming barriers of race, class, and culture. I recalled an essay by the sociologist and poet Paul Goodman, and I looked it up when I got home. In the 1969 essay called "The Politics of Being Queer," Goodman wrote, "I have cruised rich, poor, middle class, and petit bourgeois; black, white, yellow, and brown; scholars, jocks, Gentlemanly Cs, and dropouts; farmers, seamen, railroad men, heavy industry, light manufacturing, communications, business, and finance; civilians, soldiers and sailors, and once or twice cops." He contended that "queer life" can be "profoundly democratizing, throwing together every class and group." It was the old gay-liberation ideal, lost in the waning of gay male sexual radicalism, the rise of the gay middle class, and the scourge of AIDS, but it lingered in the warm spring air that evening in Memphis.

The dinner was breaking up. Mike and Charlie had promised to take me to the Apartment Club. Ed had already gone home; he needed to get a good night's sleep in order to study for his exam, Mike said. And besides, Ed didn't really enjoy the bar very much. "I think it is his intelligence," Mike confided. "There is just not enough to stimulate him there."

As I got into the car, Mike gave me one last chance to back out. "Are you sure you really want to go?" he asked. "We could go to another place where you might be more comfortable." I assured him that if I felt ill at ease, I could always leave. We stopped to buy some malt liquor (the Apartment Club is the only bar I have ever been to where you could bring your own booze) and then headed downtown. The lights of the bridge across the Mississippi River to the Arkansas shore blazed just ahead of us; Beale Street, once the vibrant heart of black Memphis, now spruced up for the tourists, was off to the left.

I was glad to have Mike and Charlie as my guides. The Apartment Club was not exactly easy to find, and that, in part, may be intentional. The bar was located in a warehouse district on the fringe of downtown, under a highway viaduct. We parked the car in an adjoining lot and walked down an alley and through an unmarked door. As soon as we paid our four dollar admission fee, we were frisked by a security guard.

The bar was huge, low-ceilinged, and somewhat disorienting. The music was loud and pulsating; lights flashed from two artificial trees in the middle of the room and from a strobe over the dance floor. In the front of the club was a stage (with a Miss Apartment '88 banner) where a female impersonator was lip-synching a disco tune. During breaks between shows, people would climb on stage and dance. The actual dance area was off to one side. In the lounge, people played pool, reclined on couches, and watched videos; one group was huddled around a table playing cards. A huge crepe-paper heart decorated one wall, a holdover from a Valentine's Day party, I suspected.

The place was packed with hundreds of people, and seemed to be divided evenly between men and women. The patrons milled around greeting one another—a woman in a white fur hat, men in drag, student types with glasses and serious demeanors. Most people were casually dressed. It was hard to figure out social distinctions, but it seemed to be a class and cultural mix you would never find at most white gay bars. From what I could observe, Mike and I were the only whites there. And Mike was the only person wearing a dashiki.

By day, I suspected the Apartment Club was probably shabby and run-down. But in the evening, with its flashing lights and the alcohol- and music-induced euphoria, it had a certain glamour. I couldn't believe so much was going on at one in the morning in this otherwise deserted corner of Memphis.

Charlie went off to greet some friends and Mike and I sat at one of the long tables that surrounded the stage. "A lot of people here know me and they know I like black men," he said over the music. "I wonder what they will think when they see me sitting with a white guy." Shortly after, he asked me, "Have you ever been involved with a black man?" I answered, "No." "Would you be open to it?" "Sure, why not?" was my reply. It didn't seem that he was trying to fix me up; he was just endlessly fascinated by the subject of black-white relations—and relationships.

Then a female impersonator named Ta Ta Star came on stage, and Mike dropped the subject. The show had begun. Dressed in a long white dress and imitation pearls, Ta Ta lip-synched and danced to an Anita Baker song called "No One in the World." She was in total command, and her fans lined up in front of the stage to tip her as she performed. "She is the favorite here," Mike said. He had been among the judges of a drag contest at the bar earlier in the year; Ta Ta had been the winner. She had also been helpful with AIDS education, he told me; BWMT had held a forum on AIDS at the Apartment Club, and Ta Ta had put in an appearance.

A lesbian performer came next, mouthing the words to a disco tune I didn't recognize. She wasn't trying to imitate a woman or a man. She was just herself—small and cute and chunky, wearing a black hat, a silver vinyl suit that resembled space garb, and big sneakers. It was striking to see a lesbian performer in the middle of a drag show. Lesbian feminists have traditionally been critical of drag; they felt that it made fun of women. Here, a lesbian in androgynous clothing lip-synched to the same music as the "queens" and no one gave it a second glance. The women in the crowd stood waiting to tip her, as if she were the great Ta Ta Star herself.

Charlie returned. He had spotted another white person, he said. With Mike and me, that made three. I asked Mike why more whites didn't come to the bar. "They are intimidated," he said.

We watched more of the show, then took another walk around the bar. Charlie and Mike greeted friends. They introduced me to a few people, but the music was too loud to say much. Another impersonator came out on stage in a sequined gown and danced holding her wig in her hands. "Miss Sweets," Charlie informed me. I was getting sleepy, even though the action would go on for another two hours here; bars in Memphis closed at four A.M.

I took one last look around and said my good-byes to Mike and Charlie. The place seemed as full of life and music and conviviality as ever. "Write in your book that Charlie is in love with a guy named Delano." Charlie said to me. "Will you promise to write that?" I said I would and headed out.

MINNEAPOLIS, MINNESOTA

was following the advice of my friends in Rapid City and reading Walter L. Williams's *The Spirit and the Flesh*, the study of gay American Indians and the berdache tradition. Writing about the Chippewa (Ojibwa) of the western Great Lakes region, Williams quoted an early nineteenth-century explorer: "I have known several instances of some of their men who, by virtue of some extraordinary dream, had been affected to such a degree as to abandon every custom characteristic of their sex and adopt the dress and manners of the women. They are never ridiculed or despised by the men on account of their new costumes but are, on the contrary, respected as saints or beings in some degree inspired."

In Minneapolis, long after the berdache had almost vanished, victims of the white man and the inculcation of Christian values and prejudices in the Indians, I met some gay Chippewa. "I've only been sober for two years," Lee Staples was explaining. "I'm just beginning to think about these things." For Lee, the operative word was recovery—ongoing recovery from alcoholism, which had dominated most of his adult life; recovery of the American Indian spiritual tradition. For his friend, Sharon Day, who was sitting next to him, the operative word was discovery—in her case, of her sexuality.

We were in Lee's office at American Indian Services, a twenty-bed Minneapolis halfway house for Native Americans, where Lee served as acting director. The office door was wide open, and Indian men wandered up and down the halls as we talked. Lee's secretary, whom he had met at Indian AA, was typing and answering the phone. American Indian Services had an unfortunate location for a halfway house. It was right down the street from a park where Indian men hung out and drank, which seemed appropriate. But it was also next door to a liquor store.

Minneapolis–St. Paul has one of the highest concentrations of American Indians of any city in the country, and Sharon told me that alcoholism and drug abuse were the community's biggest problems. Sharon had more than just a passing acquaintance with those subjects. She was Director of Chemical Dependency Services for Minnesota's Indian population, administering an annual budget of more than two million dollars for programs of prevention, continuing care, and aftercare. That position made her the highest-ranking American Indian in Minnesota state government. It also made her one of the highest-ranking out-of-the-closet lesbians in the state. She was not afraid to come out, she told me, because Minnesota Governor Rudy Perpich had issued an executive order banning discrimination in state employment on the basis of sexual orientation.

In a light blue jacket and jeans, Sharon, thirty-six, didn't much look like an important official, although when dignitaries from Washington came to visit her tribe, Sharon was often the one to greet them. She was a self-confident woman with big glasses and an appealingly round face. Her car's bumper sticker read, "Love a Mother." Sharon had two daughters, aged fifteen and eighteen, who lived with her. She grew up on a Chippewa reservation sixty miles south of International Falls, in the far north of the state.

Married at nineteen and divorced soon afterwards, Sharon lived for years convinced she was heterosexual but that there was just no man who interested her. Only after she became involved in women's issues and started working politically with lesbians (in the reelection campaign of State Representative Karen Clark, an open lesbian) did she finally recognize she was gay. She had a coming out party that featured women's rituals and an Indian tobacco ceremony. But she viewed her new identity in an emotional and political sense only. "I was going to be this celibate lesbian," she said, amused by her own naïveté. It wasn't until two years later that she met her current lover and began "practicing." Earlier this year, she and Lee had established a support group for Indian gays and lesbians, the first in the Twin Cities.

Sharon noted that lesbian women of color tended to marry more often than white lesbians. The reason, she thought, was related to an absence of role models, but in an odd way. "In my family," she said, "the women were always very self-sufficient. They took care of themselves and the family. I had aunts who had their own salt lick and hunted deer. Growing up, I thought that was the way to be." Among whites, she thought—speaking in rather broad stereotypes—such self-sufficiency might indicate a woman was gay. But among Indians, distinctions weren't so clear-cut. That made it harder for Indian lesbians to recognize others—and lacking a context, to recognize themselves.

What about sexual attraction, what about romance? I asked her. But Sharon didn't respond directly. "I never heard anyone on the reservation described as a lesbian," she said. "I never saw a lesbian couple until I was a waitress in a restaurant when I was seventeen." For Sharon, sex and romance just didn't seem to enter into it. The key was identity, a framework to make feelings comprehensible; without that, the other things just didn't matter.

"Indian women certainly are butch!" Lee broke in with a laugh. Lee, forty-two, had a handlebar mustache and a nervous, tentative quality. He grew up on a reservation one hundred miles north of the Twin Cities. Beginning at age twenty-one, he spent a lot of time in gay bars. "I tried to assimilate into white society in a real bad way—drinking and the bar scene," he said. Now he was sober—clearly the central fact of his adult life—and he approached everything with the sense of wonder of the reborn.

I asked him if the prevalence of alcoholism among gay Indian men had to do with conflicts over assimilation. "Good God, yes!" he said. Indians, gay or straight, were caught between two worlds, he felt; their belief systems had been shattered. Alcohol was the answer for many. Indian gays—with a whole additional layer of difficulties—often left the Indian community for the white gay bar scene. That was why joining Lee and Sharon's support group was such a major step for many men. "For a lot of them, it means going back to a community they left some time ago," Lee said. At the group's most recent meeting, there were eighteen people in attendance; for the first time, the majority were men.

Sharon suggested that Indian gay men and lesbians assimilated into white society in very different ways, mirroring the overall experiences of Native American men and women. "When the whites came, it was the men who were sent out to school," she noted. "The whites wanted to assimilate the Indian men first; the women would follow. But the women went underground and continued transmitting the traditions. Indian women in general maintain more cultural ways than the men." As Indian gay men moved from the reservation to assimilation (and often into the white bars), most of the Indian lesbians Sharon knew remained strongly tied to their culture. They practiced tribal spirituality, did things "the Ojibwa way." Even when Native American lesbians became involved in relationships with white women, it was the whites who became culturally Indian, not the other way around, she asserted.

With the resurgence of cultural pride in the recent generation of Native Americans and with new ethnological research into the role of gays in the various tribal traditions, Indian gays and lesbians had an opportunity to be accepted. Both Sharon and Lee were very aware of this. Sharon talked proudly about "ceremonial dykes who lived apart." However, as Lee noted, for men, the berdache were rather archaic cultural models. They more resembled drag queens or transvestites than average contemporary gay men. The idea of two "masculine" men having a socially sanctioned relationship didn't fit into the American Indian tradition any more than it did into white culture.

Lee blamed the Roman Catholic church for inculcating anti-gay attitudes in the tribes and encouraging the abolition of special gay ceremonial roles. "There was a such a push for the Indian community to be more white," he maintained. "Without even knowing it, we adopted their attitudes. Homophobia is a part of this. Now, the big thing among the younger generation is to be traditional. I hope that such people remember how gay men were accepted in the Indian community way back." That recognition, he added, "would be my true test of being traditional."

Cultural pride can cut two ways, though, and Sharon was worried about a backlash. She was afraid that some of the new traditionalists might accuse the support group she and Lee had formed of being culturally assimilated and contend they had "caught the white man and white woman's disease [homosexuality]." She recalled an Indian woman asking her for historical data on whether Indian gays and lesbians actually existed. Sharon loaned her Jonathan Katz's book, *Gay American History*. The woman returned the copy, unimpressed. "This was written by whites," she sneered.

Nonetheless, lesbian and gay Native Americans had an advantage over their black, Latino, and Asian counterparts. They could cite a recognized, even revered, role for gays in their culture and tradition, something that was harder for most of the other groups. In other respects, the experience of gay Indians was similar to that of other minority groups within the gay community. Sharon said to me, "I used to wake up in the morning and ask myself 'Who am I going to be today?' Do I go to the gay and lesbian community to educate them about my identity or do I go to my own community but not acknowledge my sexuality?" I could hear Ed's voice describing his identity conflicts at the Memphis BWMT meeting.

The attitude that homosexuality was "the white man's disease" worried Sharon. It was exactly the same line that right-wing nationalists used against black gays. The difficulties in coming out to family that I found among black men in Memphis were shared by Sharon and Lee. Sharon had never acknowledged her sexuality to her mother, even though her mother knew that she and her lover slept in the same bed. Her mother had even been present at a social occasion in which Sharon's lover had stated publicly that she was a lesbian. And Lee was reluctant to discuss his homosexuality with the aunt and uncle who had raised him. They were in their seventies, were very traditional, and spoke only Ojibwa.

Coming out beyond the immediate family was difficult as well. Sharon and Lee were not public about their sexuality when they returned to the reservation. Trinity Ordoña, the woman I met in San Francisco, had noted that coming out in the close-knit Filipino community on the West Coast was similar to coming out in a small town. She could never have lived openly as a lesbian in San Diego, where her family came from, she said. She noted that in a racist society, what a person of color did as an individual was seen as a reflection on their race. "You risk being called an embarrassment to your race by your own people," she said. "I don't think white gays experience that same kind of risk of rejection."

Ironically, it was AIDS that offered Indians and other gay people of color a chance for legitimacy within their own cultural and racial communities. Members of BWMT in Memphis served on the statewide AIDS task force. In Minneapolis, Lee and Sharon were hopeful that the Native American community would begin to view their fledgling group as a resource for AIDS education. Lee, in fact, was going to participate in a tribal panel on AIDS the following week. His dilemma was whether or not to bring up the word gay. "I just don't know how to deal with the issue," he said.

And, in all these minority groups, I found an effort to merge cultural and sexual identities. Trinity and Desiree's wedding was the ultimate example of that. The fuller, richer, more open life that white gays were attempting to achieve beckoned to people of color too. As Sharon put it, "I want to be as full a person as possible by acknowledging all of who I am."

Work was one area in which Sharon was attempting to do just that. She had told her two supervisors and other government officials involved in Indian affairs that she was a lesbian. But her department's advisory council, made up of seventeen people (mostly Indian men), apparently had problems with an open lesbian representing them. According to Sharon, some council members had complained to her supervisor that she was not communicating well with them. When her supervisor asked them pointedly if they were concerned about the fact that Sharon was a lesbian, they denied it. The flap had died down, but Sharon was worried that as their gay and lesbian group became increasingly visible in the Indian community, it might resurface. Despite the governor's executive order banning anti-gay discrimination, she still felt vulnerable.

Lee for his part was attempting to accomplish his personal integration through spirituality. "Getting back to my beliefs and race-spirit has centered me," he said. Some years before, he had been given a leadership role in tribal ceremonies. He spoke the tribal language perfectly and returned to the reservation every spring and fall to participate in the rituals. When he first took on his ceremonial role, he was concerned about the way his homosexuality would be viewed. Should he reveal it to other tribal members and perhaps upset people and undermine the ceremonies, or should he keep quiet? He opted for silence—one thing had nothing to do with the other, he reasoned.

Now, as he achieved sobriety and began to view his sexual identity more positively, he was changing. Recently, in the sweat lodge, he had talked openly about his sexuality with other Indians in his AA group. "There is such a liberating feeling in bringing these parts of me together in a setting [the sweat lodge] that was given to us as Indian people," he said. "People tell me to stifle it and not be public. But the more I am public, the happier I feel." He was not about to announce his sexuality on the reservation—yet. But, even there, he thought, "I may have to more and more come out." That was recovery, too.

SAN ANTONIO, TEXAS

We were dancing, Gloria and I. Moving, if not exactly gliding, across the floor of the outdoor pavilion at Rosedale Park on the west side of San Antonio. I had never danced to a polka before, but that was what the music most resembled, a polka with a Mexican flavor. "Just shuffle," Gloria advised. Around us swayed forty or fifty Mexican-American couples of varying ages, the men wearing Panama hats against the fierce south Texas sun, the women in cool pastel dresses. "Faster," Gloria urged. By now, the couples around us seemed to be soaring, becoming bolder, doing ever more elaborate turns.

The occasion was San Antonio's seventh annual Conjunto Music Festival. Conjunto, the popular music of the *gente pobre*, the Chicano working class of south Texas, is a curious blend of Mexican rhythms and German and Eastern European polkas and waltzes. It is usually played by a four-piece band composed of an accordion, a *bajo sexto* (a twelve-string, guitar-like instrument), a bass, and drums.

The festival was a major cultural event in San Antonio. The mayor had issued a proclamation announcing "Conjunto Music Week"; there was a panel discussion on conjunto music at a local theatre, featuring musicians and historians; there were inductions into the Conjunto Hall of Fame. Those events were just a prelude to the appearance of forty-eight different conjunto bands, performing throughout the afternoon and evening on that weekend in May. A fair-like atmosphere surrounded the stage and dance floor; there were booths selling fajitas, *gorditas*, tacos, and beer. Families picnicked on park benches, listened to the music, and watched the dancers from lawn chairs.

The conjunto festival was not a gay or lesbian event, of course. There was certainly nothing noteworthy about a man and woman (in this case me and Gloria) dancing together. But members of Ellas, San Antonio's fledgling Latina lesbian group, were present, helping sell beer at the concession booth and generally having a good time. That meant dancing—sometimes in a group of women, sometimes two women together. Women dancing with other women at a public event was an important statement in itself, Ellas members felt, one that hadn't been made before in Latino San Antonio. It represented a discreet coming out, at least to those in the crowd who chose to notice.

I had come to San Antonio, that most Mexican of U.S. cities, for more than the music. I wanted to look at the impact of Latin cultural traditions, with their rigid notions of sex roles, on Chicano gays and lesbians. In the *lesbianas Latinas* of San Antonio, I found a group of women struggling with the basic issues of identity and self-esteem, women at the earliest stages of creating community. And as I tried to understand their experiences, I also discovered that the issues of sexuality, gender, social class, and culture were so complex and intertwined that it was hard to puzzle out the part that homosexuality played. Nothing was very clear-cut.

Gloria Ramirez was my contact. Gloria, thirty-eight, was a small, thin woman, her dark hair parted in the middle. She used to be a doctor's wife. She was well-spoken and so serious-minded as to be a trifle intimidating. Gloria taught four year olds at a public school in one of the city's poorest districts. I had met her a couple of nights before the festival at the Esperanza Peace and Justice Center, a low, white-washed brick building that is built Mexican-style around a courtyard with a fountain. The center houses a variety of different organizations, all vaguely on the liberal-to-left end of the political spectrum—an anti-hunger group, a Quaker social-action group, an organization opposed to U.S. intervention in Central America. Ellas shares a small office there.

Gloria and two other women active in Ellas—Irene Rodriguez and Graciela DeLeon—took me out to a Latina lesbian bar called the Reminisce. On that Thursday night, the bar wasn't populated by *lesbianas Latinas* but by a group of apparently straight men playing pool. They were in the middle of a tournament, and they ignored us. A Mexican song, *"Volver, Volver,"* was playing on the jukebox. "When you hear that song, you have to order another round," explained Graciela, who liked to poke fun at the artifacts of Mexican culture.

The women were talking about their mothers. Irene had told her mother a year and a half before that she was a lesbian; her mother hadn't spoken to her since. Irene, who was twenty-seven and worked as a dental assistant, was an attractive woman with long black hair and sparkling dark eyes. She never went anywhere without her trademark Panama hat. That evening she was wearing a blue bowling shirt with "Westinghouse" printed on the back and was drinking a large schooner of beer. "My mother has to accept me as I am," she continued. "I don't want to play any more games." Her only sister, also a lesbian, hadn't been as forthright. The sister, who worked as a schoolteacher, had been living with a woman for eight years whom she referred to as her roommate. As a result of her discretion, apparently, she was still in her mother's good graces.

Irene observed that her mother lived a very secluded life. She couldn't read or write and didn't know how to drive. All three women remarked that their mothers had never learned to drive. "Write that down!" Graciela said to me. Gloria also found it significant. "We grew up taught that we had to depend on men," she said.

Graciela talked about the confusing and contradictory expectations placed on young Mexican-American women. Graciela was thirty-four and worked as an X-ray technician. She was a plump woman with braces on her teeth and a perpetual twinkle in her eyes. She wrote poetry and had a poem published in an anthology of Chicano poetry. On the one hand, she noted, Anglo society had no expectations of young Chicanas. In high school, she had been encouraged to be a secretary. (Irene said that she had been advised to work at K-mart.) Their mothers did have higher aspirations for their daughters. But, at the same time they encouraged their daughters to go to college, they also wanted them to be traditional—to marry and have babies. For that reason, daughters who left home and didn't get married had a "real struggle," Graciela said. They were viewed as having failed to meet the expectations of their culture.

Clearly, lesbians fell into that category. Graciela was already considered an "old maid." All her mother's friends' daughters were married. And the other day, her mother—who knew that Graciela had just ended a twelve-year relationship with another woman—was urging her to get married. "There will be no one to take care of you when you get old," she warned. Graciela, who was feeling vulnerable enough at the moment, had been upset.

In the midst of these cultural complexities, Ellas had been formed eight months earlier. Thus far, members had put most of their efforts into organizing two statewide retreats for Latina lesbians. The women had virtually no contact with the other gay organizations in San Antonio, all of them overwhelmingly Anglo. They seemed to see their allies in the left-wing Latino organizations they shared space with at the Peace and Justice Center, not in the mainstream gay and lesbian groups and churches.

The women stressed the importance of a separate Latina group. "The majority white groups don't know what we're about and don't seem interested," Graciela said. "We are different, we eat different food, dance to different songs. There are so many differences that stem from poverty, from hard work, from people being down and out and trying still to be happy and make the best of their lives. We need to keep reinforcing our cultural heritage."

But, why not at least get together with Latin gay men in San Antonio, I suggested. That had been tried once and failed, Gloria informed me. And she noted that in Houston, where they did have a sexually mixed Latino gay organization, its woman president had quit the week before, accusing the men of sexism. The younger women in Houston were leaving the organization. Latin women had been brought up, even brainwashed, to take care of their brothers, Gloria said. That was part of their culture. For women to walk away was a very radical step. Graciela agreed. "We need to build up our strength as women first and then get together with our brothers," she added.

But Ellas had a long way to go before it made an impact even on the Latina lesbian population in San Antonio. So far, only twelve women were involved in the organization, five of whom seemed to do all the work. Everyone agreed there had to be a grass-roots effort to reach the mass of *lesbianas Latinas*. The question was how. "There is a park where you can see two or three hundred Latina lesbians on a Sunday afternoon walking around and holding hands," Irene said. "But none of them will come to our group."

The pool players had given up for the night, Irene had finished her schooner of beer, and it was time to go. Gloria was off to a late-night copying place to pick up flyers for a concert by an all-woman salsa band from San Francisco. The event would be a joint benefit for Ellas and the local Guadalupe Cultural Arts Center. "Come to the festival on Saturday afternoon," Gloria said to me as she got into her car. "We'll all be there. We can talk more."

And so, two days later, we were shuffling awkwardly across the dance floor, me in jeans and clunky work boots, Gloria in a lavender T-shirt, white shorts, and sneakers. When the band took a break, Gloria and I found a picnic table away from the music. Over chicken *gorditas* and beer, she told me a bit about herself.

She had grown up in nearby Austin, the eldest daughter of a father who worked in an auto-body repair shop and a mother who was a cleaning woman in a state hospital. Neither parent had gone to school beyond the third grade. She was the first girl in her family to graduate from college; two of her sisters never finished high school. She had gone to the University of Texas in Austin, received a master's degree in education, and followed her college sweetheart to Harvard Medical School. In 1977, they married and returned to San Antonio, where he was chief resident at a hospital. Both were politically active—he worked to get Chicanos admitted to medical school, she worked for bilingual education. But the couple had problems communicating; something in her "wouldn't accept being married," she said.

Eventually, Gloria became attracted to a woman she worked with. The attraction was mutual. After two years, they finally acted on their feelings. For both, it marked their first sexual experience with another woman. Gloria and her husband were divorced. She was thirty-one. Gloria lived by herself for two and a half years, and then she and her lover bought a house together. This was the most acceptable way for her lover, a woman from a traditional Chicano background, to leave home, Gloria said. The two lived an isolated, closeted existence in the suburbs, and the woman finally left Gloria for someone else.

Gloria met her current lover two years ago at a private showing of John Sayles's *Lianna*, a film about a lesbian relationship. The woman, a full-time activist had been in Cuba for the past year and a half, studying at the International School of Film and Television. She was presently working on a documentary film about lesbians and gays in Cuba, and Gloria had visited in Cuba earlier in the year.

I was amazed that the Cuban authorities would permit Gloria's lover to make a film about gay people. In recent years, Cuba has been less than sympathetic towards homosexuals. Fidel Castro ordered gays put in internment camps shortly after he came to power (they were later released); in the spring of 1988, I read newspaper reports that his government was quarantining people who tested HIV-positive. But Gloria insisted that being gay was accepted in Cuba's film community. In fact, her lover had come out at an international film festival there. "People were more upset at her identifying herself as a working-class person, not at her being a lesbian," Gloria said. "They said no one in the United States could really call themselves working class because Americans were so much better off than people in the Third World."

With this woman as lover and mentor, Gloria seemed to have finally begun to integrate the different parts of her personality. She became politically active again, as she had been in the days when she was married. In fact, the statewide Latina lesbian retreat had originally been her lover's project before she had known she was going to Cuba. In her absence, Gloria had taken it up. She was trying her own wings as a lesbian organizer.

As Gloria and I were talking, another woman sat down next to us and asked if she could listen to our conversation. She was overweight, her hair was cut quite short, and she looked as if she couldn't be more than eighteen. Gloria had never met her before. She introduced herself as Pat Fischong Gomez, and said she was twenty-seven years old and studying political science at the University of Texas at San Antonio.

When there was a pause in the conversation, Pat jumped in. She had been born in Nuevo Laredo, Mexico, and had grown up just across the Rio Grande in Laredo, Texas. Her mother was Mexican and her father a U.S. Air Force officer. Her parents were divorced when Pat was four. As a child, she crossed the border every day to go to Catholic school in Mexico. Her English was not perfect; although her accent sounded as if she had grown up in the United States, she still used words incorrectly — "conversate" instead of "converse," for example.

Pat had spent most of her childhood hanging out with her male cousins.

"We border-crossed. We rode motorcycles. I had girlfriends like they did," she recalled. "I did my own living." During her "boyish" childhood, as she called it, she said that everyone was convinced she would turn out gay; she had always accepted herself as such. But all that came to an abrupt end when she was thirteen and her mother became a Jehovah's Witness. Her home life became extremely strict. Pat spent her teenage years failing to fit in with the young women at her high school, most of whom ignored her because she was overweight.

At age twenty-two, she came out in Laredo, the border city whose gay community, she said, was very much into traditional butch-femme cultural roles, especially the women. Pat entered a drag competition at a local bar, wearing a tux and singing "You Light Up My Life." She was a smash and was named Mr. Gay Laredo, 1982. "I always liked men's suits and clothes," she told us. "I liked dressing, behaving like a man." Her relationships were always with heterosexual women. "I have never been involved with a lesbian," she said.

Now the masculine identification of her early coming-out years was beginning to change. Pat had decided it "wasn't good" to be into roles. She had done some reading, and had spent five years madly in love with a lesbian lawyer in Monterrey, Mexico. She proudly showed me the woman's card. The relationship was unrequited; the lawyer was "into fashion and very sophisticated" and only liked "feminine" women. But if Pat was moving away from her butch persona, she still had a way to go. When I asked her what she wanted to do when she finished college, she said she was thinking about immigration or law enforcement. "Any job," she said half-jokingly, "where I don't have to wear a dress."

Talking with Pat recalled a conversation I had had the day before with Michael Stevens, publisher of a San Antonio weekly gay newspaper that had closed down earlier that year. He said that in Latino culture, with its well-defined sex roles, it was acceptable to act in homosexual ways as long as you stayed within gender-behavior guidelines. "That means that homosexual Latino men tend to assume a feminine identity and persona," he said. "Lesbians are the opposite." According to Michael, if a young Latino gay male took on a female role, he had a better chance of being accepted into the family structure, but as a girl, not as a gay man. That was why, he said, transvestism was so common among gay male Latinos. "It is often a twenty-four hour a day persona," he emphasized. "I could take you downtown and show you half-a-dozen transvestites going about their daily business." Perhaps Pat's family's acceptance of her as a "boy"—at least in the days before her mother became a Jehovah's Witness—and her later taking on a butch role was similar to the phenomenon Michael described among Latino gay men.

Pat's description of her childhood struck a chord in Gloria. "As a child, I always wanted to be a boy, too," she interjected. Everything changed for her when her family moved from an all-Chicano to an all-Anglo neighborhood when she was eleven. "From then on, I couldn't deal with anything except the racial issue," she said. In school, she was made an example of bad speech. The teacher would call her to the front of the class and command her, "Gloria, say 'chicken' now," so the other kids would learn how not to pronounce the word. She was chased home by Anglo kids on their bicycles who threw stones at her.

Her attitude quickly became "I'm going to show them!" And she did, becoming an expert at assimilation. She perfected her English. In fact, when she first went to the University of Texas, she felt alienated from other Chicanos. While they spoke flawless Spanish, she spoke flawless English.

Gloria's relationship to her own sexuality was subsumed in the complexities of being Latina in an Anglo society. She knew there were women called "dykes," but they were "big, white, and drove trucks," she thought. Like Sharon Day, the Native American woman from Minneapolis, Gloria was out of touch with her own sexuality and had no concept of her sexual identity. She only felt discontents she didn't understand.

When she finally acted on her sexual feelings and moved in with her first female lover, the two never saw themselves as lesbians. They had no contact with the lesbian or gay community. "I am angry at the homophobia on both our parts that destroyed that relationship," she said. Only when they had broken up and she became involved in her current relationship did she begin to change. When she and her new lover first got together, Gloria told the more politically conscious woman that she would never use the word lesbian. Within a few months, the word became second-nature to her.

The same kind of thinking—that homosexual acts and gay relationships were acceptable (or at least, less reprehensible) as long as you didn't give them a name—was reflected in the experience of Graciela DeLeon, the woman I had met at the lesbian bar earlier in the week. As Gloria and Pat returned to the dance floor, Graciela showed a different side of herself than the woman of the other night with the perpetual twinkle in her eye. She had just ended a twelve-year relationship with another woman and was very unhappy. The woman, Maria, was ten years her senior and had five children, four of whom she and Graciela had raised together. (The children ranged from age five to twelve at the time when Graciela, twenty-two, first became involved with their mother.) But the kids, particularly the girls, had never accepted Graciela, whom they viewed as a rival for their mother's attention. And Graciela admitted she was not a good parent figure for girls who were entering their teens. "Maria wanted to maintain the proper, maternal image, but I was wilder, not really maternal," she said. Her difficulty in getting along with the kids was largely responsible for the breakup of the relationship. She felt that one of the reasons the conflict with the children was never resolved was that Maria wouldn't tell them what was going on. Maria denied being a lesbian not only to the children, but to Graciela as well, even though they slept in the same bed. "She felt comfortable with me but not with *it*," noted Graciela.

In the seven months since she and Maria had broken up, Graciela had become involved with a married woman at work. It was the woman's first lesbian experience. Once again, Graciela had chosen someone who wouldn't consider herself a lesbian or as being part of a lesbian relationship. "It is a bad trend," Graciela admitted.

But perhaps her choice of women had more to do with Graciela's own lack of comfort with her lesbian identity than she would admit. She conceded that she had difficulty with the term lesbian when the word was used at the retreat for *lesbianas Latinas* that she attended. "I do enjoy women's company. That is my preference," she said. But if a man came along and there was the "right chemistry," she would be willing to get involved with him. "I want to be able to enjoy all of humanity," she said.

Graciela and I walked back towards the musicians, and she seemed to forget her momentary lapse into heterosexuality (or bisexuality). "The thing about this kind of event, for us, is that you can't express yourself," she was saying. "Everyone is having a good time, but you can't even dance with your girlfriend." We found our way to the edge of the crowd where Gloria, Pat, and a few other women were standing. They were looking at the dancers with surprise and delight. For there were Irene Rodriguez and another woman, both in big straw hats, moving cheek to cheek across the floor.

On my first evening in San Antonio, Graciela and Irene had had a disagreement. Graciela had been telling me that many of the older, working-class Latinas who came to the Reminisce were into traditional butch-femme roles. She described one night when a woman she called "Juana la Cubana" had been punched out by her lover. The two continued their battle outside, and "Juana" locked herself in the car. The women in the bar either ignored the incident or watched from a safe distance.

Irene was not amused. She felt strongly that the other women present should have intervened. The issue of lesbian battering was very complex, she said. Because Latina lesbian women had not met the "expectations of our culture"—to marry and raise families—there was "such a great weight on our shoulders." When someone got hit, she argued, the person might unconsciously believe she deserved it. Graciela, who had originally told the story to be entertaining, tried to hold her ground. The incident was between the two women, she said. "They probably do it all the time." But Irene was unmoved. "We are concerned about people dying in Central America," she said passionately, "but we won't intervene here."

I hadn't paid much attention to the exchange, except for thinking Irene was a bit self-righteous. I chalked up the dispute at the bar to abstract polemic, rather than personal experience. When I met Irene in Olmos Park the day after the conjunto festival, I realized there was nothing abstract about it.

Olmos Park, on the east side of the city, was the place where Irene had said you could find large numbers of Latina lesbians on a Sunday afternoon. She wanted to give out flyers for the upcoming salsa-band performance that Ellas was co-sponsoring, and she invited me along. We could talk for a while first, she suggested. Irene was driving a battered Chevy with directional signals that didn't work and a "Jesse Jackson '88" bumper sticker on the rear fender. I followed her in my car. Once inside the park, we drove until we came to an area where lines of cars were parked on both sides of the road. There, as promised, were perhaps a hundred gay men and women—mostly young, mostly Chicano—sitting on the hoods of the cars, talking, drinking, eating, playing loud music on their radios.

We sat a hundred feet away under a live oak tree whose branches bent almost to the ground. On the other side of us, Chicano families were picnicking and small children were playing on swings and seesaws. Irene removed her Panama hat but kept it comfortably nearby.

We talked for almost three hours. First, Irene told me about her childhood—about the sexual relationship with another girl that began when she was twelve and lasted for four years; being in gangs; hanging out with rough kids; finally, becoming lovers with a "pimp-style Mexican guy" with whom she hustled pool to make money to buy booze and drugs. She had graduated from high school with no job, no prospects. Her mother had kicked her out of the house, and she had moved in with another guy and his family. She was only eighteen, and her life already seemed at a dead end. But there was a way out. The army kept calling her once a month, urging her to enlist. Finally, she signed up for a four-year stint. The military promised to train her to become a dental assistant, training she couldn't afford on her own.

After basic training, where she discovered that "half the army was gay or lesbian," she wound up in Korea. There she was invited to brunches at the officer's club with high-ranking lesbians. She also found rampant alcoholism and drug abuse (beer was ten cents cheaper than Coke in the vending machines). It was a hard life but she learned to play "the military game," she said. After a year, she was assigned to Fort Hood in Temple, Texas, three and a half hours north of San Antonio.

From then on, she said, her life became "nothing but trouble." She became involved with a woman who had been in prison, had tattoos down both arms, and was three months pregnant after having been raped by four Mexican men. The woman, Dee, liked to do methadone—"crank," as Irene called it—and Irene discovered she liked it, too. Dee's pregnancy was difficult (she was suffering a lot of internal bleeding), and she and Irene were drinking heavily and doing more and more drugs. The baby was born with slow reaction times. Irene was present at the birth, "the neatest experience of my life." But the baby was given away for adoption, and Irene was crushed.

Her descent into drugs and alcohol continued. With her term in the army coming to an end, she didn't show up for any of her duties. She was doing drugs morning, noon, and night and had stopped eating. Her rank plummeted from sergeant to private; her weight fell from 115 to 95 pounds. The low point came shortly after her discharge when she spent two weeks hitchhiking up and down the interstate, "strung out" and sleeping with anyone who would give her a ride.

Eventually, she was back in San Antonio, going to gay AA, working as a dental assistant. Her parents only let her stay with them for a week. Her father, an aircraft mechanic at a military base, was an active alcoholic; two of her uncles had been alcoholic as well. Her parents gave her no support for getting sober, she said. Basically, they wanted her out of their sight.

That was when the abusive relationships began. She had no money and no place to live. First, there was the Anglo woman taxi driver who pressed Irene to move in with her. Irene agreed. "I had slept with fifty million people anyway," she said. "I was doing it to survive." Soon, she started dating another woman and moved out of the taxi driver's house and in with her new lover. The next day, the cabbie showed up at the dental office where Irene worked. Irene accompanied her outside; the woman pulled a knife and forced Irene into her taxi. They drove for what seemed like hours (Irene was trapped by the driver-controlled electronic door locks). The woman drove her to an abandoned warehouse district where Irene managed to get out of the car. The cabbie tried to run her over.

Meanwhile, Irene's new lover was also abusive. The abuse increased as the relationship, which lasted a year and a half, dragged on. If Irene said the wrong thing, her lover would force her out of the house in the middle of the night and lock the door. "I would sleep in my clothes, just in case," Irene said. The woman had a baby, whom they raised together.

Finally, Irene was able to move to her own apartment. She had been sober for two years by that point, and things were beginning to look up. Then, out of the blue, her old army lover Dee showed up. She moved in with Irene. A week later, Dee lost her job and vanished. She returned again, but this time Irene kicked her out for good.

Her decision to show Dee the door was a turning point. Shortly after, Irene started dating Susan, a "teacher involved in politics," as she described her. Susan was the woman—tall and blonde and wearing a T-shirt emblazoned with the initials of a Salvadoran rebel group—with whom Irene had been dancing at the conjunto festival. "When we first met, we really dated," Irene recalled. "It was a romantic thing. We would have lunch in the park. We would got out to dinner." Susan gave her books on abusive relationships. Irene became influenced by Susan's strongly feminist and left-wing political views. "She opened up a whole new world to me. She helped me with my self-esteem," Irene told me.

They lived together for a year. But Susan wanted to sleep with her ex-lover occasionally; Irene, once she was involved in a relationship, couldn't conceive of not being monogamous. They started drinking. Six months before I met Irene, they separated. Although they still "leaned on each other a lot," they were no longer lovers. Susan was moving to Chicago in the summer.

When I met her, Irene said she was happy living alone. She didn't feel she needed to get into a new relationship right then. "I have been a slut for so long," she said. "It feels neat to be able to say no to sex." She was working on her reading and vocabulary, she said. Although she was still drinking, she said she was drinking less and wasn't doing it every day. (I was suspicious, however, recalling that schooner of beer at the Reminisce.) Things were far from perfect, of course. She was unhappy that she hadn't had any contact with her family for a year and a half, since she came out to her mother. Her lesbian sister, the schoolteacher, wouldn't have anything to do with her either, viewing her as an embarrassment to the family. But Irene felt "lucky to be alive. I am looking forward to the future. It is a whole new world."

It was a classic survivor's tale, although the ending wasn't as tidy as one might wish. What would happen to Irene when Susan left for Chicago? How much did Irene really depend on her? How serious was her alcohol problem? Would she backslide or had she developed a strong enough sense of herself to continue on?

I asked Irene where being gay fit into all this. She wasn't sure. There were so many factors that had made her life what it was—coming from an alcoholic family, growing up poor, being Chicana, being lesbian. As a child, she noted, she had gone to a different school every year because of school integration. "I was always the new kid," she said. "I started drinking in the fifth and sixth grades." She was always moving around in the military, too—Fort Polk, Korea, Fort Hood. As a result, she never had a chance to develop much stability or a sense of self-worth. Then there was the guidance counsellor who suggested that she was best suited to work at K-mart. Irene simply couldn't sort it all out. Everything merged together; it was her life.

She pointed towards the young gay Chicanos and Chicanas, hanging out on the hoods of their cars and drinking. Their conversations were wild, she said. "You'll hear them say things like 'I beat up my girlfriend last night.' It just enrages me to hear that." I asked her if she wanted to go and pass out the flyers. "It's too late now," she replied. "It's not worth it. Everyone here is probably drunk or stoned by now."

If Irene had been able to achieve some sense of identity and self-esteem, she was convinced that most of the other gay people in the park were stuck at the stage she had been at a few years ago. "It is hard to get the people here to go anywhere, to do anything other than drink," she said. That included the salsa-band benefit that Ellas was planning. She predicted that attendance at that event would be ninety percent heterosexual. Most of the people in the park were lower-income Chicanos, she said, for whom any kind of organization was "too white." The more educated Latina lesbians, the ones who weren't in the park, would say, "Why should I come to Ellas? I don't need it." The poorer ones would ask simply, "What will you do to make my life better?" And Irene noted, "I don't know how to make their lives better."

Creating a positive sense of community — one not characterized by drink and drugs and abuse — was no easy task, even if it looked hopeful at that moment at the conjunto festival when Irene and Susan were dancing cheek to cheek and the other women looked raptly on. Earlier that day I had talked with a gay Chicano who had been involved in the formation of the now-defunct gay and lesbian group that had preceded Ellas. I had asked him why Latino gays were so apolitical. "When you don't see yourself as meaningful to organizational life and politics, you don't get involved," he said. "If it is hard to get a white middle-class person involved, it is two or three times more difficult to get a Chicano or Chicana involved. Sure, part of that is the racism they perceive on the part of Anglos. But they also have little involvement in institutions or appreciation for them. They feel powerlessness and isolation. Their only level of solidarity is in partying or the bars." He was referring to lack of Latin participation in the mainstream Anglo gay organizations in San Antonio, but he could just as well have been referring to Ellas. And what he said about Latinos and Latinas could easily be applied to blacks and Native Americans and other people of color in other places.

Dusk was falling. I looked at the kids sitting on the cars, playing their radios, probably drunk or stoned by now if Irene was right. The fuller, more expansive, more prideful gay and lesbian life was far away. The following day I was flying to a city where the gay community was politically and materially light years from Latino San Antonio. As I looked at those kids under the live oak trees in the San Antonio dusk, the distances between people—and the distances between gay communities—seemed very great indeed.

RELIGION

▼ ▼ ▼ ▼ ▼ ▼ ▼ ▼ ▼ ▼ ▼ ▼ ▼

DOVER, NEW HAMPSHIRE

On a late summer day in 1987, I attended an ecclesiastical trial in the vestry hall of a southern New Hampshire church. The accused was a forty year old ordained United Methodist minister named Rose Mary Denman. She was charged with being a "self-avowed, practicing homosexual," a characterization she did not deny. As such, the prosecution contended that her continuing service as a United Methodist minister was in violation of the *Book of Discipline*, the volume of rules that governs the church. The jury was composed of thirteen other United Methodist clergy.

The Reverend Denman was not charged with misconduct of any kind. No parishioner had complained; she hadn't preached a sermon in favor of gay rights. Her bishop had learned she was a lesbian when she wrote him a letter and told him so. Her offense appeared to have been forthrightness about her sexual orientation.

An ecclesiastical trial seems archaic, more in keeping with the late Middle Ages than the last decades of the twentieth century. It seemed particularly so in the second largest Protestant denomination in the United States, a church known for its liberal social positions: opposition to U.S.

intervention in Vietnam and military aid to the Nicaraguan contras, support for black civil rights.

In view of what have been interpreted as biblical injunctions against homosexuality, churches and synagogues by and large have been extremely uncomfortable with the emergence of an open and self-affirming gay identity and culture. Generally, the more literally a religion or denomination takes the Bible, the less accepting it is of homosexuality and gay relationships. Conversely, the more oriented a church or denomination is towards social action, the more conflicted it tends to be on the issue. Some of the more liberal Protestant churches fall into the latter category. They are eager to improve the social status of gays and lesbians, but at the same time are wedded to notions of homosexuality as sinful or deviant that make it impossible to accept openly gay clergy into their ranks. Perhaps more than any event in recent years, Denman's trial dramatized the resistance of many mainline Protestant denominations to the full participation of openly gay and lesbian people in religious life—and the determination of gay people to insist on that very participation.

Until 1984, the Methodists had not explicitly barred gays and lesbians from the ministry. Although the *Book of Discipline* condemned homosexual practices as "incompatible with Christian teaching," it also stated that gay men and women were "persons of sacred worth." But that year, under pressure from a resurgent conservative wing, the General Conference, the church's ruling body of clergy and lay members, added "fidelity in marriage and celibacy in singleness" to the list of requirements for ordination. That language effectively barred gay people, at least those involved in relationships that included sexual expression, from the pulpit.

At the time the General Conference made that decision, Rose Mary Denman considered herself a heterosexual—"as straight as they came," as she later described it. In fact, she herself had expressed strong opposition to the ordination of lesbians and gay men. When the church was in the midst of heated debate over the issue, she had told the same bishop who was later to put her on trial that if the United Methodist church voted to permit the ordination of homosexuals she would leave the denomination.

The next year her life changed completely. She fell in love with Winnie Weir, the former wife of a Methodist minister, and realized she was a lesbian.

And thus she found herself in a church in Dover, New Hampshire, being judged by a jury of her ministerial peers for the very "offense" she had condemned so vociferously just a few years before.

When I talked with the Reverend Denman three weeks before her trial, she told me that only members of the United Methodist church would be permitted to attend the proceedings. To be admitted you would have to prove you were a Methodist by showing a certificate of church membership or, failing that, by giving the names of your church and pastor. The rules were so strict, she explained, that witnesses at the trial who were not Methodists would have to leave the courtroom immediately after testifying. Her counsel was required to be a Methodist. Her assistant counsel did not have to be (and, in fact, was not); although she could sit in on the proceedings, as a non-Methodist she would not be allowed to speak or examine witnesses.

As someone from a Jewish background, I faced an ethical and logistical dilemma. I wanted to attend the trial. But was it proper for me to pose as a member of a church, a religion to which I did not belong? To be honest, I didn't spend too many hours agonizing. I soon became so caught up in the mechanics of trying to get into the trial that any moral scruples receded into the background.

It was suggested that I purchase a certificate of church membership (available at any religious bookstore), fill it out, and present it when I arrived at the trial. I bought one that read: "This Certifies that _____ has publicly confessed Jesus Christ as Lord and Savior and has been received into the full membership of the _____ Church on this _____ day of _____ in the year of our Lord 19____" signed by "_____, Pastor." Not only would I have to certify that I had accepted Christ, but I would also have to forge a minister's name attesting to it. That was going too far. So I retreated to a less blasphemous strategy. I called my mother, who still lives for part of the year in the town where I grew up, and asked her to call the local Methodist church and find out the minister's name. When asked about my Methodist credentials, I would simply state I was a member of that particular church and see how far that could take me.

It was a beautiful day in late August when I arrived at St. John's United Methodist Church in Dover, New Hampshire. An hour and a half drive from Boston, Dover is a gracious town, with fine colonial mansions along its main street. But St. John's itself is out of a different era. Completed in 1970, the church is an ugly brick and cream-colored building that looks more like a fundamentalist church than a New England meeting house. The church is set off a main road, with a sweeping green lawn and large parking lot in front. There is a brass bell tower off to one side as well as a vestry hall where the trial was to take place.

Guarding the door was the bailiff, a large man of about fifty dressed in a light blue seersucker suit. He could have been a redneck sheriff were it not for his air of studied affability. I walked up to him, trying my best to appear as if I spent most of my life attending church functions. "Are you a Methodist?" he asked, in a friendly but firm manner.

"Yes."

"What is the name of your church?"

"Trinity United Methodist in Kingston, New York."

"What is the minister's name?"

"Reverend Darmstadt," I answered.

The test of my religious affiliation wasn't over yet. "Can you tell me the first hymn in the Methodist hymnal?" the bailiff asked, a big grin slowly moving across his face.

My heart sank. I turned a mild shade of red, tried to make a joke. I was sure I had impostor written all over my face. The bailiff thought it was all quite hilarious, though. "Go ahead!" he said so genially that I was sure he was about to give me a parting slap on the back. The correct answer to his question, I found out later, was "Holy, Holy, Holy."

After I received my ticket of admittance and stepped into the sunlight again, I could hear the bailiff quizzing someone else. "What happened on May 24, 1738?" he asked roguishly. The would-be spectator didn't know the answer, looked mortified, and was finally permitted to enter. The date in question marked the conversion of John Wesley, founder of the Methodist church, to evangelical Christianity.

Bishop George Bashore, the bishop of the Methodist jurisdiction that includes Maine, New Hampshire, and southern New England, was holding a news conference under an apple tree across from the church. The bishop read from a well-thumbed copy of the *Book of Discipline*. The proper place for a debate on the subject of homosexuality, he emphasized, was at the church's

General Conference, held every four years, not here. "This is an in-house, family trial for the United Methodist church," he said. I found the Bishop's use of the word family in this context to be a little odd.

Just across the lawn, in front of the vestry hall, Winnie Weir, Rose Mary Denman's lover, was being interviewed by a reporter from a Boston TV station. Winnie, who was forty-three, had a serious demeanor and commanding presence: she was six feet tall, thin but solid, with short dark hair. That day, dressed in a lavender military-style blouse, purple pants, and boots, she looked as if she were off to the Sapphic wars. A women's spirituality pendant hung from around her neck, and she wore a badge with a pink triangle on it — the insignia that homosexuals were forced to wear in Hitler's death camps and which has since become a gay symbol. She had grown up in the church, she was telling the reporter. Her father had been a church sexton; she had been married for eighteen years to a Methodist minister.

Then the Reverend Denman made her appearance, and the press and photographers rushed towards her as if she were a film star arriving at a premiere. A short woman with big round glasses and silver hair combed to one side, it was evident that she had taken great care with her appearance. She looked quite elegant in a purple paisley dress, tan scalloped jacket with matching pocketbook, earrings, and high heels. At her own impromptu news conference, she complained that three of her witnesses, scholars on theological and ethical issues regarding homosexuality whom the defense had paid to come to Dover, were being barred from testifying. She wanted to turn the trial into a discussion of the church's position on homosexuality, she said. As the Bishop's comments had indicated, the prosecution was intent on restricting it to the narrowest of grounds — specifically, whether the accused was a "self-avowed, practicing homosexual." The accused had made it very clear on a number of occasions that she was precisely that.

The Reverend Denman was relaxed as she answered reporters' questions. She had had plenty of practice in the previous month. Although she was on trial, her future was not really in jeopardy. She was already in the process of transferring her ministerial credentials from the Methodist to the Unitarian-Universalist church. The Unitarians would not be bound or influenced by the verdict here.

When I had talked with Rose Mary Denman a few weeks before in her home in Portland, Maine, she looked far more casual than on the day of the trial. My lover, Stephen, and I had been vacationing on an island in Casco Bay off Portland. One overcast day I took the ferry into the city. Rose Mary (as she insisted I call her) met me at the dock, dressed in a Sunkist Orange T-shirt and a pair of green shorts. She has a face that is sweet and funny, almost clownlike, and a direct, blunt manner that comes as something of a surprise. She is the naïf who woke up one day to discover that the world—particularly the church—was not as caring or as benign as she had assumed.

In her aging 1983 Subaru, Rose Mary drove me to the apartment she and Winnie shared in a two-family, shingled house on a side of town far from the trendy waterfront commercial district. The apartment was filled with plants and oriental rugs, photo albums and scrapbooks. On one wall was an Indian shaman's headdress; on another were pictures of Rose Mary and Winnie's children (Rose Mary had a nineteen year old son who was in college in California; Winnie had a sixteen year old son who lived with his father). In the back of the apartment was a room dominated by a large wooden pyramid placed over a futon on the floor. Rose Mary made the pyramid herself from a kit and sometimes lay under it and meditated. Plants grew faster than normal if you placed them beneath it, she told me; a friend of hers had cut herself badly, lay under a pyramid, and was healed in two days.

Rose Mary was born in Rhode Island to Portuguese immigrant parents and was raised in the Roman Catholic church. She was the dutiful daughter who believed what anyone told her, especially anyone in a position of authority. She grew up wanting to be a nun, the "only alternative," she said, for a young Catholic girl growing up in the sixties who desired a spiritual life. Going into a convent seemed an irrevocable step, however; once she graduated from high school, Rose Mary joined the air force instead. She was stationed at Travis Air Force Base, north of San Francisco. Still attracted to the religious life, she went on a Roman Catholic retreat and met a monk named Brother William. Three months later, Brother William called her on the phone. "This is Bob Denman," he said. "I left the monastery today." The year was 1967. They began dating and were married seven weeks later.

Soon after, the couple moved back to Rhode Island. Rose Mary was pregnant; Bob found a job as a bookkeeper. But within a few years the marriage was over. According to Rose Mary, Bob was having an affair with another woman; in

1971, they were divorced. Rose Mary was on her own with a small child to support and only a high-school education. She and her husband had left Roman Catholicism when they returned to the East and had joined the Evangelical Covenant church, an offshoot of the Lutheran church. One day, while discussing her situation with her pastor, she made the decision to enter the ministry. For someone who had always assumed that a spiritual life for a woman meant being a nun, it was a bold step. It was bold in still another way: her adopted Evangelical Covenant church did not allow female clergy. Her father opposed the idea. His "red flag" gave her the determination to go on, she said. For the next ten years she persevered, earning undergraduate and graduate degrees while living with her parents and working at part-time jobs that ranged from waitress to factory worker to a rabbi's secretary. In 1981, she graduated from Bangor Theological Seminary in Bangor, Maine, and was ordained as a minister in the United Methodist church.

During this time, Rose Mary apparently never considered that she might be attracted to other women. The reason it was so hard for her to discover she was a lesbian, she said, was that it just wasn't an option. "I was raised in a Portuguese Catholic household where my father's favorite saying was, 'I am the captain of this ship,'" she noted. "Thinking about being a lesbian is like thinking about being a prostitute. They are equal in that setting." Being gay wasn't something to be thought about in the religious circles in which she moved either. "If spirituality is an important part of your life and you understand God only as the church has told you to understand God, then homosexuality better not be one of the things you discover about yourself," she added. "So who would want to explore it?"

The new pastor's first parish was in North Anson, Maine, west of Bangor. She became friendly with the minister of the church in the next parish and his wife, who ran a Christian bookstore. The minister's wife was Winnie Weir. After a year or so, Winnie told Rose Mary that she was a lesbian, something she had known since high school. Rose Mary seems to have shrugged it off. By the spring of 1984, Rose Mary had a new parish, two small churches in the New Hampshire ski country at Conway. Winnie had divorced her husband and needed a place to live until she went off to her first semester at Bangor Theological Seminary in the fall. She, too, was studying for the ministry. Rose Mary said she could move in with her for a while.

Winnie stayed through the summer. Rose Mary recalled feeling that the time was passing all too fast, that she would miss Winnie when the time came for her to leave. By August, Winnie became moody and withdrawn. Finally, she told Rose Mary that she had fallen in love with her. Rose Mary's response was "I'm straight." Winnie didn't push it. The evening Winnie left to go off to the seminary, Rose Mary found a large bouquet of flowers when she came home.

At Winnie's suggestion, Rose Mary was reading Mary Daly, the feminist theologian who contends that many Christian ideas and rituals were borrowed, if not stolen, from traditional matriarchal religion. Daly became a major influence on her. Rose Mary was becoming less trusting of authority, religious or otherwise. She began to question all the assumptions that governed her life. As part of that process, she began to consider the possibility she might be a lesbian. "The thing that made me choose to look at it," she recalled, "was reading something that Saint Augustine said, that 'All truth is God's truth.' I told myself that if it was true that I was a lesbian, it has got to be God's truth."

Winnie returned to visit in October. On Sunday evening of that week the two made love for the first time. In the middle of lovemaking, Rose Mary began to cry. When Winnie asked her what was wrong, she answered, "I feel like it's my birthday."

Some time earlier, when Rose Mary was so strongly opposed to gays in the clergy, she had told Winnie, "When you are ready for ordination, you had better hope we are not in the same conference because I will stand in your way." I asked her why she had been so adamant on the subject. Rose Mary admitted her views came "from a place of homophobia." She added, "Who secures their house the best? Is it the person who doesn't believe anyone will break into their house or is it the person who is afraid of everyone in the neighborhood? So who will protect their sexual identity the best? The person who knows who they are or the person who is too scared to find out?"

Once she and Winnie became lovers, Rose Mary seemed to have quickly become at ease with her lesbianism. "It is like when the eggbeater stops, the water calms down," she said. "I have always believed the truth can't hurt you. It is running away from it that hurts you."

Rose Mary certainly didn't run—at least not from her newly discovered sexuality. Winnie left the seminary after one term and moved in with Rose Mary in Conway. At that point, Rose Mary gave notice to her congregation. She didn't want her parishioners to be caught in the middle of any potential conflict between her and the denomination over her sexuality. She then asked the New Hampshire conference for a leave of absence, telling church officials she needed to think through her theology. "That was half the truth," she said. Reading Mary Daly and other feminist theologians had, in fact, shattered her world view. She was increasingly convinced that the church was a patriarchal institution, hostile to women and gays, and one that could never change.

She and Winnie moved to Portland in June 1985. Winnie got a job running the printing department at a mental hospital. Rose Mary worked as a waitress and later as a cook for an elderly couple. She also became a nutritional counselor at a weight-loss clinic. During her first months with Winnie, Rose Mary had lost seventy pounds. "That fits the pattern," she observed. "When we are afraid of our sexuality, we cover up and use weight as a way of keeping people away from us." Weight issues still concerned her. She had put twenty pounds back on, she told me, and showed me a photograph of her son, noting that he had lost sixty pounds since the picture was taken. She showed me other photographs, too, including one of her new, svelte self in snazzy black slacks, a fashionably cut checked blouse, and a hair-do out of a forties movie.

In Portland, the couple began to attend services at a Unitarian-Universalist church. Of all mainline Protestant denominations, the Unitarian-Universalists are probably the most accepting of gays and lesbians, welcoming gay clergy and performing holy unions for male and female couples. One Sunday when Rose Mary and Winnie were in attendance, the church was celebrating the birth of a baby to two of its members. The child was the daughter of two lesbians and had been conceived by artificial insemination. The pastor asked the parents and the baby to come forward. Uncles, cousins, and friends gathered around. "The whole congregation was beaming," Rose Mary related. "Everyone stood up and clapped at the end. I realized this is where I needed to be." She went and had a talk with the minister; "Welcome home," he told her. Encouraged by the denomination's openness on the gay issue and because there was "no theology you have to buy into," she soon began the process of transferring her ministerial credentials from the United Methodist to the Unitarian-Universalist church.

Her decision to change denominations had come just in the nick of time. Rose Mary had written an article for a Maine gay newspaper in which she had been open about being gay. A jealous former lover of Winnie's had shown a copy to a Methodist official. When Rose Mary learned of this, she immediately wrote a letter to Bishop Bashore, telling him she was a lesbian and involved in a relationship with another woman. It took six months for the bishop to respond, she said. When he finally wrote, she went down to Boston for a two-hour chat with him. "George [Bashore] is a very loving man," said Rose Mary. But after the meeting, she realized that as nice as the bishop was, he was essentially offering her two choices—to end her relationship with Winnie and remain celibate or to leave the church.

Shortly after that conversation, she wrote to the bishop telling him that she was in the process of transferring to the Unitarian church and requesting another leave of absence until the transfer was completed. She expected he would agree; she was going away quietly, after all. Instead, Bishop Bashore asked for her resignation. She refused. The bishop then began formal proceedings to remove her accreditation as a Methodist minister and void her ordination.

Because the *Book of Discipline* bars "self-avowed, practicing homosexuals" from the ministry, friends had suggested that she get around the prohibition by declining to answer whether or not she was "practicing." That was the strategy of the Reverend Julian Rush, a United Methodist minister in Denver. A few years before, two conservative pastors had filed charges accusing him of being a "practicing homosexual" after a photograph of Rush and his lover's hands (both wearing wedding rings) appeared in the *Denver Post*. He challenged his accusers to prove it. The local board of ministry ruled the photograph was insufficient evidence to verify that he was "practicing" and to bring him to trial; a minister could not be asked to incriminate himself, the board ruled. Rush, today the head of the Colorado AIDS Project and increasingly open about his sexuality, remained a Methodist minister in good standing, although one without a parish. "The more public I get, the more embarrassing it is for them to kick me out," he told me when I talked with him in Denver. "I am finding I have a lot more clout than if I had played Custer's last stand and said, 'Here I am. Kick me out.'"

But Rose Mary refused to play legal games. She wanted to put the church's policy to the test. In a speech to eighty ministers at an executive session of the New Hampshire conference held on May 20, 1987, she opted for that extraordinary step—a church trial. Her reception at the gathering was hostile. "All of a sudden I was 'the accused,'" she discovered. "I wasn't Rose Mary anymore." When she and two friends, also Methodist ministers, had walked into the meeting, the church was about a quarter full. Rose Mary and her allies sat on one side; when the other ministers entered, they all sat on the other side. "If it were an ark, it would have capsized," she said. She added, "What hurt me the most was to see the church turn into an ugly creature. I thought that was in the past. I thought the church had grown."

When I met Rose Mary that afternoon in Portland, preparations for the trial were quite advanced. John A. MacDougall, a Methodist minister from Enfield, New Hampshire, near Dartmouth College, had agreed to be her counsel; Elizabeth Cazden, a lawyer from Manchester, New Hampshire, would assist him. Jury selection had already taken place. The defense had challenged the prospective jurors whom they believed were the most anti-gay and had succeeded in removing them. Rose Mary and her counsels were convinced that the thirteen who remained would be fair. She told me that the jury had no choice but to find her guilty given the church rules (she had already made it clear she was both "self-avowed" and "practicing"). But she hoped they would stop short of dismissing her outright, giving her a lighter sentence analogous to an honorable discharge from the military instead. It would not be an "automatic hanging," she believed.

Whatever the verdict, her aim was to transform the proceedings into a full-scale debate on church policy towards gay clergy. Hence the "expert" witnesses—a professor of Christian ethics, a New Testament scholar, a lay theologian who had authored a book about theology and homosexuality. Rose Mary didn't expect the trial would change the church's position overnight, of course. "I am part of a process," she maintained. "It will take years of pushing and pushing."

And so on August 24, 1987, in Dover, New Hampshire, the pushing began in earnest. Except for the mahogany flying buttresses and peaked roof, the Modern Gothic church vestry hall in which the trial took place looked strikingly like an elementary-school classroom. It had yellow and green walls ("happy colors," as one reporter covering the trial put it), a linoleum floor, green curtains, a piano off to one side. On one wall was an embroidered hanging proclaiming "Love Never Fails"; on another was a large poster that read, "Sign Up for Church Suppers."

Nonetheless, the hall was set up as if it were a courtroom. The presiding judge, Bishop Neil Irons, in a dark suit and red tie, gavel in hand, looked directly out at the spectators. Facing him, stage right, Rose Mary and her two counsels sat on metal chairs in front of a folding table. To her left were Bishop Bashore and his counsels. Pitchers of water rested on the tables and fans whirred above, making the atmosphere feel a little like a Southern courtroom.

Winnie sat in the front row. There were about fifty spectators. Some were members of St. John's or other nearby Methodist churches who had come out of curiosity; others were ministers who wore pink triangles pinned to their clerical attire to demonstrate solidarity with Rose Mary. The press was much in evidence—reporters from the *Boston Globe*, *Newsweek*, even *People* magazine. The male reporter for the arch-conservative *Manchester Union Leader*, a newspaper that until a few years ago referred to homosexuals as "sodomites," sported an earring in his ear.

The trial was slated to begin at one in the afternoon, but a juror was late, so there was more than an hour's delay. In the meantime, the always affable bailiff did his best to prevent the crowd from getting restive. "In lieu of a trial, we'll have a hymn sing," he joked, rather inappropriately. "And afterwards we'll pass the offering." Finally, we rose as the jury marched in— four women and nine men. They were young, with an average age of forty, the same as Rose Mary. They truly did appear to represent a jury of her peers. The jurors sat down to the right of the spectators, under the church suppers poster. Bishop Irons opened the proceedings with a prayer for "the wisdom to do what is right and the capacity to love one another in spite of differences." Rose Mary Denman's trial had begun.

The prosecutor, Dr. Stephen C. Mott, stepped up to the lectern to deliver the charge to the jury. Mott was a tall bearded man with sandy hair and glasses. In his grey suit, he looked like a corporate lawyer; throughout the proceedings, he spoke with little energy or wit. Mott's job was to prove that Rose Mary was a "self-avowed" and "practicing homosexual," a task not particularly difficult since she had made those facts public herself. Nonetheless, he did so methodically. It was also his job to object when testimony threatened to move in the direction of theological or church-policy issues. Under the courtroom rules, he never had to state exactly why he objected, which proved somewhat disconcerting. He read from the *Book of Discipline*: "Homosexuality is incompatible with Christian doctrine." A jury of thirteen people cannot determine Methodist doctrine, he asserted. "Your task," he told the jury, "is to determine if the defendant engaged in the practice of homosexuality."

At that point, the judge asked Rose Mary to enter a plea. She declined. The court entered one on her behalf: not guilty. Then Bishop Irons issued a note of caution to the jury. "The issue is not the wisdom of church teaching, but whether the accused is guilty of the offense," he said, echoing the prosecutor. His comments left little doubt that the defense's attempt to turn the trial into a forum on Methodist views on homosexuality was doomed to failure.

As the prosecution carefully presented evidence to prove the charges against Rose Mary, the trial took on a somewhat stupefying quality. Mott called two New Hampshire ministers, the chairs of the state conference's ordained-ministry and investigations committees. Both church bodies had recommended Rose Mary's dismissal. One witness read Rose Mary's original letter to the bishop in which she described her "struggles for self-identity." Another letter was read aloud in which Rose Mary related her own previous stance opposing gay ministers, using the phrase "Thou dost protest too much" in reference to herself.

The cross-examination of the Reverend Ann Partner, chair of the ordained-ministry committee, provided the only "human" moment in the monotonous and methodical early testimony. A grey-haired woman in her fifties in a blue suit and pink ruffled blouse, the Reverend Ann Partner appeared unhappy and conflicted. Did she consider Rose Mary Denman a "whole, good, and healthy individual?" the defense attorney gently asked. "Yes, personally I do," she said, at that moment seeming more than ever as if she wished she were somewhere else.

The afternoon livened considerably when Rose Mary's counsel, the Reverend MacDougall, rose to address the jury. MacDougall was a droll fellow, always ready with a quip. Like most of the other men involved in the proceedings, he wore the regulation seersucker suit. But MacDougall added his own characteristic sartorial twist, wearing the official tie of the New York City Department of Sanitation, which incorporates a design of garbage trucks and street sweepers on a field of blue. "I wear it when I deal with a lot of garbage," he said afterwards.

Noting Rose Mary's "loving, covenant relationship with another woman," MacDougall said that the defense wouldn't dispute that the defendant was a "self-avowed, practicing homosexual." Its purpose, instead, was "to understand God's message." He read the passage in the *Book of Discipline* that states that homosexuals are "persons of sacred worth." (Everyone seemed to quote from the *Book of Discipline* for their own purposes.) Should clergy be different in this respect from laypeople? he demanded. Then he criticized the 1984 church rule that restricted ordination to those who practice "fidelity in marriage and celibacy in singleness." Gays can't meet the criterion because the church won't allow them to marry, he observed. And he added, "I have blessed cats, dogs, insulation, and mobile homes but I am not allowed to bless two Christians who love one another."

The first defense witness turned out to be Bishop Bashore himself. Bashore looked like the CEO of a Fortune 500 company. He had a deep tan and bushy eyebrows and was perfectly color-coordinated: a light blue suit to match his blue eyes, a silver rep tie to go with his silver hair. After he made a point, he would close his eyes and smack his lips as if inserting a punctuation mark; at the end of a sentence he would tap one foot on the floor. Bishop Bashore made an adroit witness. MacDougall tried to engage him in a discussion of church policy but to little avail. The issue of gay clergy in the Methodist church had been settled at this point in history, said the bishop, and that was that as far as he was concerned.

Then the defense called Rose Mary herself. Looking respectful but firm, hands folded in her lap, she related the story of her relationship with Winnie and the discovery of her sexuality. When MacDougall asked her when she became a lesbian, she replied, "God created me to be a lesbian. Conditioning created a heterosexual. God won out." Did she feel that God made her a lesbian just as he had made her a woman? he asked. "Yes," said Rose Mary. The prosecution objected and MacDougall rephrased his question. Was her lesbianism "intrinsic" to her creation by God? he persisted. "Yes," she replied. Rose Mary emphasized that she refused to resign her ministry because to have done so would be admitting culpability. "I don't feel guilty," she said. "I believe that in God's eyes I am not guilty."

After she had been on the stand about ten minutes, the judge interrupted her testimony to call recess. Perhaps he felt that Rose Mary was making too effective a presentation; at any rate, it was getting close to five o'clock and the dinner hour.

The scene shifted to the Friendship Inn in downtown Dover, where the defense introduced the witnesses who had been barred from testifying. One, Dr. Burton Throckmorton, a scholarly gentleman who was a professor of the New Testament at Bangor Theological Seminary, called the proceedings "a very sad day in the history of the church." The Bible was being cited to support a prejudice, he maintained. "This whole trial is about preserving the patriarchal structure of our society," he said. For his part, MacDougall was still angry that the judge ruled that his witnesses could not be called. "We have the bizarre spectacle of ruling God out of order," he said, in reference to the court's decision to steer the trial away from theological discussion.

The bailiff had blown his whistle signaling that the dinner break was over, and Rose Mary was completing her testimony. When she realized she was a lesbian, she told the jury, she felt that "God was smiling and saying, 'You are beginning to recognize yourself for who you were meant to be.'" It was the first time she ever questioned the authority of the church, she said. When her lawyer asked her if discovering her homosexuality led her "to look at Scripture in a whole new light" the prosecution objected. MacDougall withdrew the question, and Rose Mary stepped down a few moments later. She had been on the witness stand for not much more than twenty minutes.

It was time for final statements. For the defense, MacDougall stated that while he understood the jury could not go against church regulations and find Rose Mary innocent, they could play the role of "restorers." For the prosecution, Mott emphasized that the only question to be considered was whether the accused had a style of life that included homosexual practices.

The jury went out. Nine votes were necessary to convict. When they returned an hour later, they announced (as expected) that they had found Rose Mary in violation of discipline by an eleven-to-two vote. Only when pressed by the judge would the jury foreman use the word "guilty." The jurors' next task — to decide the sentence — would be more complex. They had three options for sentencing: suspension from the ministry (Rose Mary would not lose her ordination but could not perform pastoral duties; this was the lightest penalty, and the one that the defense wanted); ouster from the ministry (requiring the revocation of her ordination; this was the decision the prosecution requested); or expulsion from the church ("being kicked out of the Kingdom of God," as Rose Mary facetiously put it).

Finally, at ten forty P.M. (the trial had gone on for nine and a half hours at that point), the jury returned with its decision. Everyone in the courtroom was at full attention. The jury foreman, the Reverend Janet Smith-Rushton, a frail-looking woman who was the pastor of a church in a small town south of Boston, read from a statement: "We affirm the social principles of the 1984 *Book of Discipline* that homosexual persons, no less than heterosexual persons, are persons of sacred worth." She continued, "It is not clear to us that the Reverend Rose Mary Denman has received the adequate spiritual and emotional care of such a reconciling fellowship within the United Methodist church." So, "In the interests of reconciliation," the jury had determined that Rose Mary would merely be suspended until the next session of the New Hampshire General Conference in June 1988. The vote was twelve to one.

For Rose Mary, it was a personal triumph. She had received the lightest penalty. She didn't lose her ordination, was not defrocked. The jury's statement implicitly criticized the bishop for his handling of the case. It was true that being suspended meant that Rose Mary couldn't perform weddings or funerals, but as she noted, she hadn't done either for the previous two years anyway. "The jury pulled through," she said. She was off to the Unitarian church with what her lawyer called "a hearty handclasp," instead of "being shot in the back on the way out."

The prosecution could claim victory, too, even though it had not gotten the penalty it wanted. Mott and Bishop Bashore explained that suspension would have "the same effect but be more merciful" than the "involuntary termination" that they had asked for. They had succeeded in preventing the trial from being turned into a debate on church policy. And the Methodist church had held firm. As generous as the verdict was to Rose Mary personally, the message of the trial was that if you were openly gay, you could not remain a minister in good standing. For gay and lesbian Methodists, the dilemma remained: they were still second-class citizens in their own church.

Rose Mary Denman would soon be a Unitarian minister, instead of a United Methodist one, but her future was still uncertain. Would she find a parish that wanted her or would she be perceived as "too controversial"? Some individual Unitarian churches, I was told, had rejected applicants because they were gay, despite denomination policy. "I will have to prove there is life after trial," she had said.

The afternoon I visited her in Portland, Rose Mary had sung me a lampoon of "Onward Christian Soldiers" written by a friend of hers. It went:

> Like a herd of turtles
> Moves the church of God.
> Brothers we are treading
> Where we've always trod.
> We are not united.
> Quite divided we.
> Many points of doctrine,
> little charity.
>
> Onward herd of turtles,
> Though it's quite a bore.
> We will boldly tread
> Where we have trod before.

The author of the parody was wrong in one respect. The jury had shown Rose Mary some charity. Its decision exemplified the strand in liberal church thinking that wanted to treat gay people decently. On the other hand, there were the Methodist rules and regulations—and the church's noisy conservative wing. The United Methodist church was stuck. It just didn't know what to do with a self-affirming, articulate, and appealing gay person who didn't fit the outmoded categories of "sin" and "practice." So the church tried to cope with the situation "boldly treading where it had trod before." When all was said and done, it had to get rid of Rose Mary Denman.

MINNEAPOLIS, MINNESOTA

I n Minneapolis, just a few weeks after Rose Mary Denman's trial, I met another clergyman who had been forced out of his church for being gay. Father Bill Dorn, a Roman Catholic priest, had been dismissed from his post after writing an article in a diocesan newspaper critical of the church's stance on homosexuality. A few weeks after his dismissal, when Father Dorn announced publicly that he was gay, he was ordered to take an indefinite leave of absence from the priesthood. The bishop of his home diocese then defrocked him ("removed his priestly faculties and functions," in Roman Catholic parlance). All this had been done behind closed doors: unlike Rose Mary Denman, he was not allowed to face a jury of his peers. Shortly afterwards, Father Dorn left the Catholic church altogether and became an Episcopalian. Two years later, the Catholic church excommunicated him.

Father Dorn's troubles began at virtually the same moment that Roman Catholic attitudes towards homosexuality were becoming more rigid under Pope John Paul II. In late October 1986, three weeks after Father Dorn was fired, the Vatican issued a document stating that homosexual inclinations represented "an objective disorder." Previously, the church had viewed homosexual acts as sinful but had labeled gay sexual orientation morally neutral in itself. Now that distinction had vanished. At the same time, the Vatican was ordering churches across the United States to withdraw support of and use of church facilities by Dignity, the national organization of gay Catholics.

When I called Father Dorn to arrange a meeting, he agreed to talk only within certain boundaries. He would not discuss the details of his firing or his personal life. He wanted only to talk about the Catholic stance on sexuality and homosexuality. I agreed to his terms, hoping he might relent once we sat down to talk.

I had read a number of articles about Father Dorn's case, including a lengthy interview with him in the daily *St. Paul Pioneer Press Dispatch*. I knew that he was thirty-four, was the son of Minnesota poultry farmers, and that he had been ordained in 1979. I had also read about a bizarre incident in which Father Dorn, then Director of the Newman Center at Florida Southern University in Lakeland, Florida, had been abducted at gunpoint by two men from the parking lot of a Tampa gay bar back in 1982. Father Dorn had apparently lied to the police about the incident in an effort to cover up his presence at a gay bar. As a result, he was fired by his bishop, who barred him from serving as a priest in the Orlando diocese.

He returned to Minnesota and, in 1984, was appointed co-pastor of the Christ Church Newman Center at St. Cloud State University, a school of fifteen thousand students located about seventy miles north of the Twin Cities. There, he served as adviser to the campus gay and lesbian group. He was a political activist, as well, and was jailed for protesting against U.S. policy in Central America.

Father Dorn had been at St. Cloud for two years when the editor of the diocesan newspaper, *The St. Cloud Visitor*, asked him to write an opinion piece for the paper's "At Issue" column, which treats controversial subjects. The topic was "How should the church minister to homosexuals?" In the newspaper's issue of September 18, 1986, Father Dorn took a position that put him in direct conflict with church teaching. The Roman Catholic church, he wrote, has "a responsibility to develop a theology of sexuality that sees sexuality as a blessing and understands homosexuality as being part of a gift." There was a flood of letters, mostly opposing his view; the bishop himself wrote a rebuttal to Father Dorn's comments in the following issue. Three weeks later, Father Dorn was fired from his post at the Newman Center. His parish council vigorously defended him; 150 supporters protested on the steps of St. Mary's Cathedral in downtown St. Cloud. But it was all to no avail.

Now, almost a year after his dismissal, Father Dorn was sharing a modest frame house in a Minneapolis neighborhood with a man I presumed to be his lover. Father Dorn was working as a chaplain at a Methodist hospital and teaching a course in human relations at St. Cloud State. With rugged features, dark hair, and mustache, dressed in a flannel shirt and jeans, Father Dorn could stand in for the Marlboro man. At the same time, he was gentle, soft-spoken, intellectual, and seemed most at home when engaged in philosophical discussion. Sitting in his living room, with its sparse furniture, polished wood floors, and sunlight pouring through the window, he gave the impression of being just a little lost, even disoriented.

Father Dorn emphasized that he had been an unwilling martyr. He said his bishop had periodically threatened him with the loss of his job while he was counselling gay and lesbian students at St. Cloud, warning him to restrict himself to advocating celibacy. But he hadn't thought that writing that newspaper column would actually put his job in jeopardy.

Like Rose Mary Denman, he had only come out of the closet because of fear of exposure. Shortly after Father Dorn's troubles with his bishop became public, a man who had worked with him at Florida Southern University tried to interest the media in the story of Father Dorn's abduction and subsequent firing. The man contacted the *St. Paul Pioneer Press Dispatch,* but the newspaper refused to print the report. Then Father Dorn began receiving calls from other reporters asking him about what had happened in Florida. Afraid of losing control of events, he gave the story to the *Pioneer Press.* The following day, in another *Pioneer Press* article, Father Dorn revealed he was gay.

He insisted that, in his case, the issue for the church was not one of sexuality but of institutional control. He noted that his bishop had called him "a source of irreparable scandal" for expressing dissenting opinions. But Father Dorn said that a couple of years before, the bishop's chancellor of a nearby diocese had been arrested for purchasing child pornography. The man was sent to a counsellor and was reassigned. His actions were not viewed as "a source of scandal," Father Dorn observed bitterly. But Father Dorn's own writings were labeled as such because they challenged church control. "Sexuality is not the issue," he said. "If I had done something illegal or indiscreet, I could be repentant and ashamed and have a new job. What I did was to challenge the process."

Because he was dissenting, not just misbehaving, the terms the church offered him were particularly harsh. He said the bishop had told him that no matter how the church investigation turned out, he could only remain a priest if he publicly retracted his writings and promised never again to challenge church teaching on homosexuality. In addition, Father Dorn was told he would have to reaffirm his own vow of celibacy and agree to move to a part of the country where no one knew him and to be silent about his past. "I realized at that point no matter how the entire process turned out, the final ruling would be unacceptable," he said.

Father Dorn contended that at the heart of Roman Catholic thinking on homosexuality was the continuing belief that all sexuality was evil and could only be acceptable in a controlled situation, namely marriage. The church saw sexuality as justified only if children were the end result. "The church keeps saying that gay sexuality lacks 'an essential finality,'" he noted. "What they mean is that it can't produce children."

In addition, the church found gay male sexuality particularly threatening, he thought, because it implied an abdication of male control over women and a renunciation of patriarchal privilege. Lesbian sexuality also resulted in a loss of heterosexual male power. And the bottom line of church thinking was that gays were incapable of real human love.

As a result of the church's view, he said, gay Roman Catholics were faced with a dilemma: they could either affirm themselves as human beings or affirm their faith within the church. They couldn't do both. There was a place in the Catholic church only for gays who wanted to "lie or repress being gay people," for those who refrained from forming relationships or identifying with or taking an interest in gay culture. But those people ran a risk. The Vatican position that even gay sexual orientation was a disorder could cause gays who stayed in the church a great deal of psychological harm. In telling gay people that they could not love completely and form relationships, the church was helping gay people to internalize the feeling that "I'm unloveable," he said.

What about all those gay priests and nuns who remained in the church? I had read an article in *Newsweek* that estimated the proportion of gay Roman Catholic clergy at twenty to forty percent. Father Dorn thought that figure was exaggerated. But he believed the number of gay Catholic clergy was higher today than in the past because of the massive exodus of heterosexual clergy who left to marry in the sixties and seventies. For the most part, gay clergy were closeted; some priests, he thought, were acting out sexually. "Whatever we are secretive about, we are compulsive about," he noted. "Repression comes out in unhealthy ways. You get some secretive, compulsive sexual behaviors. Today you get a group of folks [gay priests] who are at real high risk for AIDS. And because the church won't talk about sexuality, there is no way to get a handle on the behaviors that put people at risk for AIDS."

I asked him if he thought there was any future for Dignity, the organization of gay Catholics. Father Dorn recalled the final Dignity mass held at the Newman Center at the University of Minnesota. As in other places, the organization had been expelled by the bishop, who until then had been quite supportive of the gay community. Father Dorn had feared the occasion might be depressing. Instead, he found it an almost exhilarating experience. "There was a very joyful sense that we are here and we will stay and our fate isn't dependent on the church and the church can't invalidate it," he noted. "There was a feeling that we are a church in our own way."

At the end of the service, the altar was stripped and the chalice and banners and Easter candles and other symbols of the Catholic liturgy were taken down. Carrying the ceremonial ornaments in their arms and singing, Dignity members marched out of the church and across the street to the Episcopal university center, where they had been granted approval to hold services. "It was a real sense of empowerment, and a realization that we don't need the church to validate who we are," Father Dorn said.

Dignity's future, in Father Dorn's view, lay strictly outside the Catholic church. That was where his own future lay as well. Dignity members would be worshipping on Episcopal church property; Father Dorn had gone even further, joining the Episcopal church, which he saw as similar in liturgy and tradition to Roman Catholicism but far more accepting of gays and gay relationships. As with Rose Mary Denman, he saw no recourse but to go into spiritual exile.

And just as Rose Mary was going to find out if there was "life after trial," Bill Dorn, a year after his dismissal, was still exploring whether there was a place in the world for him after the priesthood. He remained committed to the ministry, he said. But there was still that lost, haunted look in his eyes, the sense of not quite knowing where he fit. "I need some time to sort out this stuff," he told me. "I am still deciding what to do in the next life."

LOUISVILLE, KENTUCKY

Once I got outside the large East and West coast cities, most gay people I met, like everyone else, were involved in some version of church. Previously, I had been puzzled by gays and lesbians who remained in churches and synagogues that condemned homosexuality and refused to recognize the validity of gay relationships. I questioned whether such individuals were doing much to influence policy by staying and suspected that it was often personally destructive. Now, despite my glimpses into the experiences of Rose Mary Denman and Bill Dorn, I was changing my view. I became increasingly convinced that as long as churches remained antagonistic, chances for overall social and political gains by gay people were limited. If religious attitudes changed, the status of gays and lesbians in society would improve significantly.

I was searching for signs that gays were making progress within established religions, and I took a look at the Presbyterian church. At first glance, matters didn't look encouraging. In 1978, as it was affirming that homosexuals should be treated with "profound respect and pastoral tenderness" and even as it was endorsing gay-rights legislation, the church's 190th General Assembly barred "unrepentant" gays and lesbians from serving as ordained officers of the church. The restriction did not apply just to clergy; it extended to elders and deacons as well. Overall, this didn't seem very different from the position of the Methodists, except that the Presbyterians had been six years ahead of Rose Mary Denman's church in relegating its gay members to second-class status.

But by the early eighties, a number of Presbyterian churches around the country were openly defying church policy. They proclaimed themselves "More Light" churches, pledging to reach out and minister to the gay community and to welcome the ordination of gays and lesbians as elders and deacons in their churches. (Individual More Light churches do not have the power to ordain ministers; only a presbytery, the Presbyterian equivalent of a diocese, can do that.) In late 1987, there were thirty-five More Light Presbyterian congregations in the United States, although not all had gay ordained officials. The More Light concept represented an effort to offer gays and lesbians a way to stay in the church, a kind of boring from within the denomination.

Central Presbyterian Church in Louisville had passed a More Light resolution in 1983. In July 1987, it ordained an openly gay man, Nick Wilkerson, as an elder. Louisville is not the kind of place where you would expect a church to challenge its national denomination on the subject of gay rights. It is both southern and midwestern (Indiana is just across the Ohio River from downtown), located "twenty miles from Ku Klux Klan country," as someone characterized much of the rest of the state. Still, Louisville has a tradition of acceptance of minority groups. The city was mostly settled by immigrants from the North, had a large Catholic population, a Jewish mayor, and a history of relatively harmonious race relations. Interestingly, Louisville was about to become the site of the national headquarters of the Presbyterian church; that prospect made the ordination of an openly gay elder there all the more significant.

When I stopped for a few days in Louisville, I telephoned Nick Wilkerson. We met for dinner at a restaurant located midway between Nick's house and his church in the Old Louisville district of the city. I had expected a church elder to be dour or perhaps the opposite—effusive, unctuous, trying to persuade you to cough up more money for the collection plate. Nick, at thirty-one, was neither. With a round face and big glasses, dressed in a polo shirt and jeans, he reminded me of a graduate student. He was smart, with a critical view of things, but his easy Kentucky drawl gave the feeling of someone who was at home with himself and the world.

Nick grew up in a small town in western Kentucky and had returned to Louisville four years before after graduating from Harvard Business School. When he finished business school, he told me that he had been tempted to move to New York or San Francisco. But his sense of regional loyalty won out: he opted to return to Kentucky instead. He got a job working for Brown and Williamson, the country's third largest tobacco company. Today, he was an associate manager for one of the company's cigarette brands, part of a corporate team responsible for advertising and promotion. (When I observed, with typical Yankee self-righteousness, that working for a tobacco company seemed a curious job for a church elder, Nick was not offended.

"That is the Kentuckian in me," he explained. "I grew up with it." On the other hand, he insisted he wouldn't work for a defense contractor.)

Nick had been raised as a Baptist but left the church while in high school. He had "written off religion, or at least Christianity," he said, because of the hostility to gay people he had encountered in the Baptist church. But when he returned to Louisville from Harvard, he felt the need to find a church. A gay seminarian he knew suggested Central. Nick liked the congregation immediately. "It was like an extended family," he said. "It reminded me of the small-town church where I grew up." What he especially liked was the variety of people he met there. "We have two or three millionaires," he said, "some very poor people, gays, blacks, a lot of feminists and peace activists, elderly people, a number of conservatives. There is a former president of the University of Louisville. It is really a nice mixture to be floating around with."

To understand why Central is so accepting of gays and lesbians, Nick said, you had to know something about Old Louisville, where the church is located. After dinner, he took me on a tour of the neighborhood. As we walked past beautiful tree-lined courts with gaslights and fountains and names like Belgravia and St. James, Nick explained that Old Louisville had been the city's fashionable district beginning in the 1880s. In 1937, a flood had driven the city's upper classes to the high ground of suburbia, and Old Louisville began to decline. In recent years, gays and young professional couples had begun to restore some of the turn-of-the-century stone and brick dwellings. Nick himself had bought a plain two-story brick house with a stained-glass window and geranium pots on the front step. Old Louisville had not been transformed into a Yuppie haven or gay ghetto. Grand in some parts but still seedy in others, it remained a diverse neighborhood that mixed rich and poor, black and white, gay and straight.

Central Presbyterian had followed the neighborhood's fortunes into decline and was now sharing in its revival. To grow, even to survive, its largely elderly congregation had to accept and reflect the diversity of Old Louisville. And as gays played an important role in the revival of the neighborhood, the church had to accept them too. At first, Nick said, the gay issue was simply an intellectual argument for the church. In fact, the congregation made its More Light resolution even before it had any openly gay members. It did so for two reasons, he said—because it was right and because of the composition of the neighborhood.

As word spread that they were welcome, gays began to join, although not in overwhelming numbers. Nick said there were only six or eight openly gay men and three or four lesbians out of 120 active members. Still, Central's acceptance of gays was no longer based on abstractions. "It has been a question of good experiences with individuals," Nick said proudly. "It is easy to hate gays and lesbians when it is just a word."

He had been a member for only a couple of years when a heterosexual couple, an investment banker and his wife with whom he is friendly, nominated him to be an elder. At church, his being gay was "a non-issue," he insisted. "We have two straight couples who are probably more radical on the gay issue than some of the gays in church."

In fact, the gay-rights issue was one of the church's major social concerns. Several heterosexual church members, some carrying Central's banner, marched in Louisville's gay pride parade. The minister testified on behalf of the proposed gay-rights ordinance at a hearing before the county human rights commission. (In a churchly city like Louisville, religious support has provided a crucial umbrella for the fledgling gay-rights movement.) Central was part of an ongoing project in which a group of Louisville Presbyterian churches was examining the root causes of social suffering and injustice. One church was looking at hunger, another at teen pregnancy, and still another at housing problems. Central's issue was homophobia. In addition, the church had hired as a student minister the gay seminary student who had originally directed Nick to Central.

While Nick's ordination was not a particularly divisive issue at Central, he told me that More Light ordinations of gays and lesbians had aroused controversy in other cities. In the Presbyterian church, individual churches have the right to challenge the ordination of officials by other churches within their presbytery. A couple of years before, a church in upstate New York had ordained a gay man as an elder. Soon afterwards another church filed a complaint. The judicial body of the the denomination ruled against the More Light congregation, and the elder was forced to step down. While attending a conference of More Light churches, Nick met a gay elder from San Francisco whose ordination was being challenged as well. No church in his presbytery had pointed a finger at Nick, although many congregations in the Louisville area knew he was gay.

I asked Nick if he felt any conflict about being active in a church that, at least in its national policies, formally excluded gays and lesbians from positions of authority. He was very much an optimist, he said; the situation was temporary. The fact that the people in his own church were so supportive tended to negate anything the national church said or did. And he noted that most of the people on Central's task force studying homophobia were heterosexual. "Things like that tend to make me feel eventually church policy will change," he said.

Even if church policy didn't change, Nick thought that as an openly gay church official he was making an important contribution to gay people in Louisville. "When you are gay and twelve years old in a small town in western Kentucky like where I grew up," he observed, "you don't know anyone else who is gay. The only [gay] people you hear about or read about tend to be unsavory. The extent of gay life as you know it are scribblings on a bathroom wall. That tends to warp people in a lot of ways. It may not be as big an issue in Boston or New York or San Francisco, but in a place like Louisville, being a positive role model for gays is important."

Central's welcoming attitude towards gays and lesbians was, it appeared, the product of a particular neighborhood — and a few courageous souls who were willing to stand up and stand out. For a more representative view of Presbyterian Louisville, Nick suggested I speak to his friend Matthew, who had been the student minister at Central for the past year. Matthew, also thirty-one, was soon to graduate from the Louisville Presbyterian Seminary, one of eleven Presbyterian seminaries in the country. He seemed to exemplify a new generation of gay clergy — relatively open about being gay, militant at times, hopeful about his future as a gay person in the church. Yet, Matthew too was caught up in the contradictions of the church's stance on gay ministers.

I met Matthew for coffee in a fast-food joint at the Galeria Mall, the atrium-like shopping center that is a cornerstone of the city's downtown revival. In a white polo shirt and bright green pants, Matthew looked like he was off for an afternoon at the golf course. He was quite personable, with the sort of genial earnestness they must teach at seminary. In his case, I believed it was genuine.

Matthew grew up in Iowa, where he attended a small conservative church, which even now regularly offered prayers for him to be "converted" from his homosexual ways. He went to Bob Jones University in Greenville, South Carolina, a school well known as a bastion of fundamentalist thinking. There he would date "nice Christian girls" who had no expectations of anything beyond a listless good-night kiss. At graduate school at the University of North Carolina at Greensboro, Matthew encountered openly gay people for the first time. He became involved with three different gay groups in town and spoke on the radio about homosexuality. He also left the denomination he was brought up in and became active in the Presbyterian campus ministry.

During this period, Matthew thought his sexual orientation made it impossible for him to even consider being a minister. But, as he put it, "Eventually you get the call and it doesn't go away." He became a candidate for the ministry in the Presbyterian church. When he applied, he didn't tell the candidate committee in charge of admissions to the seminary that he was gay, fearing rejection, although he thought some of them knew. "I took the attitude and still do that, until I get stopped, I am going to keep going," he said. "That is the direction I think God wants me to go in."

He was sure that almost everyone at the seminary knew he was gay. In the prophetic ministry class, which explored social issues including homosexuality, Matthew was very open. "I can't see not talking about an issue that you are intimately involved in," he noted. People have said things behind his back, he said, but he always confronted them when he learned about it. The most supportive people on campus, he said, were the feminists.

In the seminary, Matthew had learned counterarguments for the accepted theological viewpoint that the Bible condemns homosexuality. He emphasized that recent scholarship has shown that the Bible addressed only certain aspects of homosexuality, making no reference to homosexual orientation or relationships. Instead, it restricted itself to a condemnation of "rape and gross acts that neither I nor any of my friends are guilty of doing," he said. "It [the Bible] is not addressing me." The widely used Revised Standard Version, he noted, had removed the term "sodomite" from five passages where it had appeared in the King James Version, translating the original Hebrew as "cult prostitute" instead. That change, he said, was an example of how mistranslation and misinterpretation had distorted biblical teachings on the subject—and how it could be corrected.

Like his time at the seminary, his year as a student minister at Central had generally been a good one. Matthew had come out to the minister there and was sure most of the congregation had figured out he was gay. He was also leading the church's task force studying homophobia. Nick Wilkerson's ordination had taken place during Matthew's tenure there, and Matthew conceded that some members of the congregation had had to do some soul-searching in order to accept a gay elder. "It is a struggle for me to listen to people sometimes," he said. "I want to say, 'Why can't you just accept us now.' On the other hand, I know it is a big struggle for people to change sixty or seventy or eighty years of social conditioning. When they do, I find it really amazing and very encouraging."

I had attended Rose Mary Denman's trial a few weeks before, and it was never far from my mind as I talked to Matthew. I pressed him as to what he thought would happen once he started looking for ministerial positions. In the Presbyterian church, he explained, you are not ordained until you get your first job. So he was not planning to tell the congregations he was applying to that he was gay, lest that stand in the way of his ordination. (He was also looking for agency jobs and had thought about working as a chaplain or doing drug rehabilitation.) He said he was in a double bind. On the one hand, the presbytery or group of churches that ordains pastors is not supposed to ordain you if they know you are gay; on the other hand, they are told not to inquire. "It reminds me of going to a tea party with an old aunt," he said. "You are not supposed to talk about dead Uncle Harry."

But by remaining silent, wouldn't he be validating church policies? He insisted the situation was more complicated. "Why should I put myself forward as a scapegoat?" he demanded. "I would rather challenge things in a group than stand out by myself. I don't want to become so embittered and get so angry that I would say, 'The heck with the whole thing.'" He added, "The way I look at it is the more gays who leave the church, the more the church will be anti-gay. My choice is to be with people of like faith. Why should I let some prejudiced ideas kick me out?"

Nonetheless, he said that sometimes he felt like a traitor to other gay people by being part of a church that discriminated against gays and lesbians. "I am never embarrassed about being gay," he said. "But I am sometimes embarrassed about being a Christian."

Matthew was in a curious position. He was at ease with being gay and active in the gay and lesbian community; his face had appeared on the TV news after the gay-pride march. His sexual orientation was known to his fellow seminarians, to his teachers, and probably to some church officials. Yet to be ordained, he would essentially have to tiptoe back into the closet. I wondered what would happen when he finally did get that first job. How quiet would he be willing to remain? And if he did speak out, would he eventually face the fates of Denman and Dorn, become the embittered person he was determined not to be? Or would he keep quiet, closeted and conflicted, like so many gay clergy in the past? Was there a middle ground, say in working at Presbyterian headquarters in Louisville? If so, how satisfied would Matthew be limiting himself to being a church bureaucrat? These were dilemmas that perhaps Matthew couldn't and wouldn't come to grips with until he left the security of the seminary for the outside world.

Matthew told the story of Louisville's first gay-rights march, the March for Justice that took place in June 1987, following a series of events in which gay students at the University of Louisville were harassed and threatened by other students. The 325 participants proceeded along the sidewalk from Central Park in Old Louisville past Central Presbyterian and the Unitarian church. Both churches had put up signs greeting the marchers. Spectators cheered them on. The procession ended at the courthouse downtown. Since the Presbyterian headquarters was about to move to Louisville, that building, by coincidence, was draped with a large banner welcoming the denomination. "Thank you Presbyterians," it read. "We once were lost but now we're found." There, under the banner, stood Matthew and Nick with their More Light sign. There, too, stood the Central contingent—gay and straight. To Matthew, it was a moment of irony. But it also offered a glimmer of hope.

WASHINGTON, D.C.

n view of the hostility of most mainstream religious institutions towards homosexuality, it is not surprising that large numbers of gays and lesbians have ventured into the spiritual wilderness to establish their own churches and synagogues, even their own denominations. Most often, these have been along traditional lines. The largest organization of gay-oriented churches is the Universal Fellowship of Metropolitan Community Churches (better known as MCC), founded in 1968. There are some 270 MCC congregations in ten countries; in the United States, many are located in smaller communities where the church is often the only gay institution for miles around. (MCC's application to join the National Council of Churches was rejected in the early eighties.) An association of gay Pentecostal churches, the Community Gospel Fellowship, was recently formed, with congregations in Oklahoma City, Houston, and Dayton, Ohio. In addition to Sha'ar Zahav in San Francisco, there are gay synagogues in New York, Los Angeles, Miami, and other cities. The Washington, D.C., metro area alone boasts a gay synagogue and four MCC churches. It also has one of the few black gay churches in the United States, a congregation called Faith Temple.

I was curious to see how a gay church might function, especially a black gay church, given the historically influential role of religion in the black community. So on a warm Sunday afternoon in November, when the temperature was approaching seventy degrees and most Washingtonians were out for a stroll or sprawled on lawn chairs reading the Sunday papers, I attended services at Faith Temple.

Faith Temple bills itself as an evangelical, charismatic church and, when I arrived a few minutes late for the one o'clock service, the hallelujahs, thank you Jesuses, and amens were already filling the air. Worshippers were raising their hands heavenward, or at least in the direction of the pulpit, in the Pentecostal manner. Accompanied by an organ and a tambourine, a group of five members of the congregation (called The Psalms) were performing a foot-stomping rendition of the gospel song, "Just the Two of Us—Me and My Lord."

The pastor was asking members of the congregation to call out a name of God. They responded eagerly. "The Resurrection and the Life," offered one parishioner. "The Lamb of God," intoned another. "The Greatest Name I Know," shouted a third. Still another called out—with a deliberate dramatic effect—"In a world where we search for security, He *is* Security."

Then the minister requested each worshipper turn to the person nearest and proclaim, "God's will is best." Sitting next to me was a woman in her thirties with her hair in cornrows, wearing an argyle sweater and holding a baby in her arms. We repeated the phrase to each other self-consciously but with enthusiasm. At Faith Temple, you don't have much choice but to participate, and it is easy to get swept along in the fervor of the proceedings. Part of the reason may be the length of the service—almost three hours. At a certain point it appears fruitless to resist the fervor that is all around, no matter how skeptical the visitor may be. I capitulated almost from the beginning.

If you stumbled into the chapel of the Presbyterian church where Faith Temple holds its Sunday services, you would have little reason to think there was anything unusual going on. The chapel is small and intimate with several rows of wooden pews, white walls, a red carpet, and stained-glass windows flanking the pulpit. The day I attended church there were about twenty people in attendance, half men and half women. They looked like ordinary folks, dressed in their modest but respectful Sunday best.

The congregation represented all ages, from the small baby next to me to a few who appeared to be in their fifties or sixties. There were three younger women, students at Howard University, who were visiting for the first time. The organist, named Camille, was a buxom older woman in an short-sleeved aqua dress and rhinestone necklace. She was also the music director and an elder-in-training. Isaiah Poole, a man in his early thirties, led much of the worship service. In a pink button-down shirt, tie, and dress slacks, he looked studious and serious-minded; like Camille, he was an elder-in-training. I was the only white person present.

Much of the dynamic quality of the service came from Dr. James S. Tinney, the minister who had founded Faith Temple five years before. Dressed in a black robe and sporting mutton-chop sideburns, Dr. Tinney looked like an old-time preacher, not the slick, image-conscious evangelist of today. His style was pure revivalism: I pictured him under a tent on some lonely country road entreating weary souls to heed the call of the Lord. Except for his affirmation of homosexuality, the substance of his sermon was virtually the same as that of many evangelical preachers. He stressed the literal truth of the Bible, a personal acceptance of Jesus Christ as savior, and water baptism. At one point in the service, Tinney asserted that no salvation existed outside Christianity.

The pastor was nothing if not fervent. Midway through the service, a woman in a bright yellow sweater went to the pulpit to give a report on missionary work. Before she began, she told the congregation that she had traveled to New York City the previous weekend to undergo surgery of an unspecified nature. At the last minute, the doctors had told her the operation wouldn't be necessary after all. At that revelation, Tinney burst out in a rhapsodic chorus of "hallelujah"s. When this woman finished her report on a missionary crusade in Zaire and Zambia (fifteen thousand people had made decisions for Christ and two "cripples" had been cured, she announced), he shouted out, "I predict this church will send a missionary to Africa!"

But Tinney's preaching was more than just hand clapping and hallelujahs. He was smart and savvy, able to move his audience and provide some food for thought, too. In fact, his sermon had a strong pedagogical component. (In addition to being a minister, he had also been a high-school and college teacher.) In the booklets passed out at the beginning of the service, each worshipper received a pull-out sheet entitled "Sermon Notes" to be filled out and placed on the communion table after church. The topic of the week's sermon was "Getting with God's Will." In their sermon notes, church members were asked to list (1) three characteristics of God's will, (2) three aspects of God's will or three meanings associated with God's will, and (3) seven ways to know or confirm God's will in your life. All papers would be graded; high marks would count as credit towards a certificate from the church's Bible school. Bible verses referred to in the sermon were listed on a blackboard, and most people paid close attention to the preacher's sermon. The woman with the baby next to me was underlining passages in her Bible in magic marker, as if she were in a college lecture hall.

If the style and content of the preaching at Faith Temple were not very different from that of many other church services taking place in Washington that Sunday, its pastor did tailor some sermon examples specifically to a gay congregation. "Getting with God's Will" apparently included the avoidance of casual sex, at least with other members of the congregation. "Resist it," Tinney said of casual sex. "You can't have everything in the store window." He related the story of a newcomer who came to the church's Bible-study class and was "propositioned before he got out the door." The pastor strongly chastised the church member who had done the propositioning. In such a situation, the pastor suggested, the recipient of the advance should respond, "I want you to get to know the Lord better first, then me." (Later, Tinney told me that Faith Temple did not insist on monogamy; he opposed casual sex among church members, he said, because it alienated people and caused jealousy and embarrassment.)

In describing the "false gods" that were impediments to getting with God's will, he offered as examples a BMW automobile and the gay-rights movement. He decried people who gave their life for a cause but didn't bother to "clean things up" at home. "A church that is gay, on fire for God, will do more for gay folks than anything else," he said. And he asked rhetorically, "Is the gay community unclean?" "Yes!" he answered, his voice rising. "Is the straight community unclean?" Again, his answer was a fervent "Yes!" Everything depended on salvation, not on secular political and social movements.

Towards the end of the sermon, Tinney unfurled a large drawing of a thermometer and placed it in front of the stained-glass window on the side of the altar. The time had come to talk about money. The church was being forced to leave its present quarters in a few months and was trying to raise $10,000 to buy its own building. No black gay organization in the country owned property, he noted. So far, although a number of parishioners had pledged money, the thermometer indicated that actual giving stood at a chilly $250. This Sunday, however, the pastor announced that the organist, Camille, had made good on her promised $500. Later, he called on church members who were tithing to stand in a row in front of the altar. Six people rose, including Camille.

Members of the congregation offered personal appeals. A pious-looking man in a grey sleeveless sweater revealed that his older brother had recently entered the army and had quarreled with the family before leaving home. He asked the congregation to pray for family reconciliation. A husky man in a brown sports coat told the congregation that his former boss had died; he asked them to call on God to look after the man's family.

Then came testimonials. The man in the grey sleeveless sweater stood up. Jesus had saved him ten years ago, he said, but he hadn't yielded completely then. Now, he had done so. An older man in a checked suit took his turn. "Condoms, diets, exercise won't save you," he said. "Only Jesus can." And so it went. Everyone gave of themselves, without reserve or hesitation. There were no barriers between individuals and, it seemed, none between the congregation and Jesus either.

Through all this, I felt somewhat estranged, of course, and not merely because of race. Faith Temple is a long way from Temple Emanuel in Kingston, New York, where I had my bar mitzvah and where Jews tried to act like the Episcopalians just down the street, eschewing yarmulkes, praying almost entirely in English, and turning ancient Jewish melodies into passionless versions of Handel. I remembered, as a kid, going to the Orthodox shul down by the Rondout Creek, to which my grandfather still belonged. There, old men in prayer shawls chanted a mournful sing-song, moving their bodies rhythmically back and forth as they worshipped, wandering in and out of the sanctuary as if it were their living room. Not a word of English was spoken during the service. Even though this was my faith, it had all the fascination of a visit to a distant land. I felt the same at Faith Temple. I was gay and that provided a bond, but this was still a foreign country. Intrigued, even carried away at points, I was always the outsider in the midst of this rousing but alien Christianity, just as I had been at my grandfather's shul.

I met Dr. Tinney a couple of days later at the chapel where Faith Temple holds services. The chapel is in a church basement; in the early evening, as I waited for him to arrive, the offices were deserted except for a lone doorkeeper. Finally, Tinney breezed in wearing a leather jacket with a label reading "Member's Only," looking less like a saver of souls than a typical forty-five year old gay man heading off for a drink at the neighborhood pub. We sat in the front pew of the chapel. The shouts of "hallelujah" and "Praise the Lord" had long faded, but the pastor was as lively and as opinionated as he had been on the pulpit.

Tinney had grown up in Kansas City, Missouri. At age fourteen, he began preaching in black and white Pentecostal churches; by the time he was in high school, he was on the revival circuit. No drinking, smoking, movies, or dancing was his message for salvation. At eighteen, he was ordained in a small independent Pentecostal group called the Evangelistic Messengers Association. (The Pentecostal tradition emphasizes speaking in tongues, which Faith Temple does not, Tinney said.) While in Bible school in Tennessee, he pastored his first church. While in Bible school, too, he married and he and his wife had two daughters. Even then, Tinney was exclusively attracted to men but viewed his sexuality as a weakness that he had to resist. He thought marriage would help the situation. It didn't.

When he was in his mid to late twenties, the family returned to Kansas City. Tinney was teaching high school and waiting to become pastor of a church that was starting up in a nearby suburb. He was sublimating his sexual desires and redirecting them towards church involvement with teenagers, he said. On Saturday nights, he would take whole carloads of his students to Youth for Christ rallies. Then, they would go out for a bite to eat and hold long discussions until well past midnight. Tinney also apparently became involved sexually with one of the young men.

His wife knew that Youth for Christ rallies did not last until one and two in the morning. After one of his late nights, she accused him of being with another woman. In a moment of anger, he told her that her suspicions were correct but that the other woman was actually another man. She became distraught, "tearing her hair and screaming and beating her head against the wall and asking God to kill her," Tinney recalled. He walked out of the house. When he returned a couple of hours later, he found his pastor and the pastor's wife there. The man asked Tinney if what his wife had said was true. Tinney admitted it was. The pastor told him that he was possessed by demons. His ministry would have to cease immediately, and an exorcism would be performed.

The exorcism took place a few weeks later. The pastor had informed Tinney that at some point during a Sunday service he would call him to the front of the church and proceed to cast out the demons. Tinney prepared with prayer and fasting. "I didn't believe I was demon-possessed, but I thought it was a possibility," he told me. "I did feel I was wrong. I hadn't worked through any of these questions. I had no mental construction that would be at all accepting of being gay. I really wanted to have a home and be a minister and be just like everyone else. I was willing to do and go through what anyone thought was the solution to keep my marriage together." The year was 1969, the same year the gay-liberation movement began.

At the Sunday evening service, with five hundred people in attendance, the minister called Tinney to the front of the church. Speaking through a microphone, the pastor ordered the "demons of lust, homosexuality, and perversion" to leave his body. Nothing happened. Then, the pastor asked several others to come forward, gather around, and lay hands on him. Again, nothing happened. Finally, the minister ordered Tinney to kneel and pray. The minister told him later he thought the demons had departed but he should be careful not to have any other sexual experiences lest they return.

"I was disappointed," Tinney said. "I know the minister was disappointed. It just didn't work right." Tinney walked out of the church "dumbfounded," he said. "I had been at exorcisms where people screamed and hollered in what sounded like another voice, a voice of a demon saying 'I'm not coming out.' I was willing for that to happen, for whatever forces might be in control of me to let them display themselves. Nothing happened." On his way home, Tinney saw a man standing at a bus stop and was immediately attracted to him. It was a kind of epiphany. He realized that, whatever his problem, it was not one of demonic possession. Nothing had taken place in church to change the way he was.

Years later, Tinney could view those events at some remove. "It didn't have all the excitement that *The Exorcist* movie had," he said. "But at the time it was very traumatic." The incident did alter his life in dramatic ways. His marriage broke up, and his wife told his two daughters—aged four and five at the time—that their father was demon-possessed. To this day he had no ongoing relationship with them. Barred forever from pastoring in his church, Tinney moved to Washington, D.C., and went to graduate school. In 1976, he began teaching at Howard University, where he was a tenured associate professor of journalism. But he did not lose his interest in spiritual matters. He founded the first scholarly journal on black Pentecostalism and, in 1980, as he was being more open about his homosexuality, he started Pentecostals for Human Rights, a support group for gay Pentecostals.

Then, in the summer of 1982, his life took another direction. At four A.M. one sleepless night, God spoke to him, "not audibly but in a strong impression," in Tinney's words. He called on him to hold a citywide gay revival. Tinney and two black churchwomen—one the minister of an MCC church in Baltimore and the other a Baptist home missionary from Atlanta—led a four-night revival at a Unitarian church in Washington that September. Some fifty to a hundred people, black and white, were in attendance each evening; many came forward to make decisions for Christ, he said. On the eve of the revival, however, the bishop of the Washington diocese of Tinney's denomination, the Church of God in Christ, publicly excommunicated him. The following Sunday, seventeen of Tinney's supporters picketed the church where the bishop was attending Sunday services.

By the end of the week, Tinney's co-organizer, MCC minister Delores Berry, was encouraging him to start his own congregation. "James, you need to do what God wants you to do," she told him. "He wants you to start a church." When Tinney heard those words, he said, "I felt it had been given to her to say." The first service of his new church took place the following Sunday.

The early days of Faith Temple were stormy ones. As chronicled in a seventy-page account of the church's history that Tinney himself wrote, those first years were characterized by a series of challenges to the pastor's leadership. In addition, the establishment of Faith Temple 2 in Brooklyn, New York, proved to be a disaster. Apparently, the sister congregation was offering prayers to traditional African spirits and teaching reincarnation. Faith Temple quickly disassociated itself from the Brooklyn church. At the same time, the Washington church was struggling to find its own theological and liturgical identity. It was experimenting with approaches more characteristic of liberal Protestant denominations, including the use of inclusive, nonsexist language.

Tinney survived the turmoil and returned to his evangelical roots. In the process, he created a spiritual home for a close-knit group of people, with five worship leaders, an elder-in-training program, Bible-study class, and pastoral counseling and guidance. The pastor had found his flock and was determined to be the shepherd. And if the church viewed itself as a rallying point for the black gay community at the beginning, it soon moved away from an activist approach and began to stress personal salvation instead. "At first, a lot of people were coming out of curiosity or for political purposes, without a real focus on spiritual life. They weren't interested in church, just symbolism," said Tinney. Eventually, the more politically minded left and a core of committed worshippers remained. "You feel pressure to get very involved here, to get in or get out," the pastor noted. "People who don't get involved don't feel comfortable with just coming and hanging on. They realize it is a serious proposition."

In more recent years, the church faced another challenge. Ten persons who were either church members or occasionally attended services at Faith Temple had died of AIDS, an extraordinarily high number for a small congregation. Two of those who died were church leaders. But the deaths only seem to have turned the church inward.

I asked Tinney why he felt it was important for black gays and lesbians to have their own church. There were two reasons, he said. On the one hand, black gays couldn't be open in black churches; on the other, they didn't feel comfortable in the Washington area's largely white gay MCC churches. The problem with other gay churches was not so much one of racism but of cultural specificity, he maintained. Most black gays and lesbians had spent their childhoods in Baptist and Pentecostal churches. The MCC churches in Washington, he said, were more in line with the relatively reserved Methodist or Episcopal worship traditions. "When people come to our church, they feel at home," he said. "It is a lot like churches they grew up in."

The pastor also contended that a black gay church could play an important role in changing attitudes in the black community, particularly in the influential black evangelical churches. He noted that homosexuality was a very volatile issue among blacks because many saw homosexuality as a threat to the black family. "The whole thing in the black community is the feeling that homosexuality is 'caught' like a disease from white gays," he said. "If it weren't for that contamination, they think, there wouldn't be any homosexuality in the black community." As a result, he said, white gay churches have "absolutely no ability to bear witness to black churches about homosexuality." In the eyes of many conservative blacks, white gays were the problem.

As a result, Tinney attempted to use Faith Temple as a vehicle to reach black clergy, and this was the one area where his church had taken on a more activist role. In the spring of 1985, seventeen pastors, most of them black and associated with Baptist and Pentecostal churches, engaged in a three-hour dialogue with Tinney and other Faith Temple members. Since the church was founded, Tinney said that fifteen clergy from nongay churches had preached at Faith Temple. One speaker was a prominent minister who was both a pastor at the local AME Zion Church and the administrative assistant to Walter Fauntroy, the delegate from the District of Columbia in the U.S. House of Representatives. This clergyman had been known for his anti-gay views until conversations with Faith Temple apparently caused him to become more moderate. "The reason we exist," said Tinney, "is to challenge people like this and get them to confront the gay issue."

Two well-known preachers invited to Faith Temple were Jim and Tammy Bakker. Following their ouster from the leadership of the PTL (and after Jim Bakker, accused of having homosexual relations, made a relatively nonjudg-mental statement about gays), Tinney extended the Bakkers an invitation to preach during Faith Temple's fifth anniversary celebrations. According to Tinney's account of church history, Tammy Bakker responded with a hand-written letter. "We just received your precious letter of encouragement and it meant more to us than we can ever tell you," she wrote. "Thank you for your invitation for us to speak at your church, but at this time our plans are so uncertain that we do not even know where we will be at that time. We hope that your fifth anniversary celebration will be a tremendous success. In warmest Christian love, Tammy Faye."

Like other evangelical churches, Faith Temple believed that the Bible was "inerrant," that it represented the literal truth. Unlike most other evangelical churches, however, it contended that, on the subject of homosexuality, the Bible had been misinterpreted. A "careful reading" would show this, Tinney maintained. And because of this belief that every single word in the Bible was true, Tinney insisted that his church was in a unique position to challenge more conservative churches on the gay issue. "We are willing to engage in biblical exegesis," he stated. "We can relate to churches who want to really look at what the Scripture says. In that way, we get the ear of those churches. We say the same thing they are saying, except on the subject of homosexuality."

When I told Tinney I wanted to speak to one of the members of his congregation about the church, he suggested I talk with Isaiah Poole. Isaiah was the gentle and studious-looking young man who had led the worship service on the day I went to church. And, Tinney added, Isaiah had been involved for almost ten years with the Reverend Sun Myung Moon's Unification church before joining Faith Temple. Although he was no longer a member of the Unification church, today he worked as a reporter for the Moon-owned *Washington Times*, the ultra-conservative daily that Ronald Reagan once called his favorite newspaper.

I met Isaiah at a restaurant in Washington's Capitol Hill neighborhood. He arrived on a motorcycle, wearing a leather jacket. Instead of the sweet, serious, conservatively dressed worship leader I had seen in church, I found a tough, wiry street fighter. At thirty-three, with closely cropped hair and a handlebar mustache, he seemed the aggressive reporter who would push his way to the center of any event and never take "no comment" for an answer.

He had spent the day in the library digging into the legal decisions of Judge Douglas Ginsburg, the Reagan appointee to the Supreme Court who eventually withdrew because of revelations he had smoked marijuana. (That fact had not yet been made public.) Isaiah was annoyed. His editor had pulled him off an investigative piece he had been working on for two months to stick him in a library poring over Ginsburg's decisions on subjects like antitrust and cable television.

Isaiah wasn't aware that Tinney had told me he had been a member of the Unification church. He had come to talk about Jesus, not about the Reverend Moon. While the subject of his experience in the Unification church didn't seem particularly painful, his feelings were still complicated. As he talked about those days, he would frequently put his hand over his face, as if somehow to protect himself from being too exposed. When we changed the subject, he became more relaxed. He was once again Isaiah Poole, journalist and tough guy. I liked him better when he talked about the Moonies, though; his vulnerability was appealing.

He had grown up in Washington with a mother who was a fiery, Bible-believing fundamentalist. Early on, she had laid down the law: if Isaiah turned out to be a homosexual, she would disown him. She died when he was sixteen. Three months later Isaiah first met up with the Moonies. He gradually became intrigued with the Unification church; by the time he was eighteen and studying at Howard University, interest had become intense involvement.

His attraction to the Moonies, he maintained, was primarily intellectual. They satisfied his religious curiosity, and their view of themselves as establishing God's kingdom on earth corresponded to his notions of how religious ideas were supposed to work in the world. "I had grown up surrounded by religion," he noted. "In the Unification church, I saw myself as part of a movement that would change the world, that was God's active plan to change things." In the Moonies, he was an inner-city black among a bunch of white kids from the suburbs. If the socioeconomic difference was alienating, he was "convinced that this [the Unification church] was where God was." That belief kept him going.

During his years with the Moonies, Isaiah didn't see himself as gay. He believed his sexual desires were Satan's attempt to keep him from God. The Moonies' main concern, however, was not with homosexuality (of which they certainly did not approve) but with sexual abstinence before marriage. "For them, premarital sex is bad, the worst thing," Isaiah noted. "They equate the Fall with sex. So your sexual feelings become a great burden, whether gay or straight." He recalled the only reference he heard the Reverend Moon make to homosexuality. Moon made the comment during one of the five-hour speeches he would give beginning at six or seven A.M. on a Sunday morning at his Tarrytown, New York, estate. Homosexuals, Isaiah recalls Moon saying, "should be hit on the head with a baseball bat."

For Isaiah, his early years in the Moonies were a constant struggle with his sexual feelings. He "broke down" a few times and had sex with men in public restrooms. When he confessed to a church leader, he was told God would forgive him.

He did manage to avoid being married in one of the mass wedding ceremonies for which the Moonies were famous. He knew that, at least, was something he didn't want to do. Once, he was invited to participate in such an event. During the interview that preceded it, he was questioned as to whether he had had sex with a woman during the previous three years. He said he hadn't. Then, he was asked if he had had a homosexual affair in the previous three months. "Yes," he replied and was immediately disqualified. To this day, he has never been able to figure out why the Moonie marriage brokers differentiated between heterosexual and homosexual relations in that manner.

In 1977, he returned to Washington. Although still involved in the Unification church, he started picking up men in bars and bookstores with increasing frequency. He began to see himself as two distinct people. One was Isaiah Poole, loyal Unification church member and journalist. The other was the guy out cruising the bars and bookstores. In 1980, in one of those cruising situations, he met a man with whom he became romantically involved. As they continued to meet, Isaiah wouldn't tell him his real name or where he lived and only gave him a vague idea what his job was. But this relationship was clearly different from his previous anonymous encounters. "It felt good," said Isaiah. "It never felt guilty." Finally, he sat down in prayer and left the matter in God's hands. "If you want it to end, do something to end it," he challenged the Lord. The Lord chose not to intervene. In September of that year, Isaiah left the Unification church and moved in with this man, who remained his lover today.

During our conversation, Isaiah was reluctant to speak critically of the Moonies. He was never brainwashed, he insisted; he had simply latched onto something that worked for him. What he eventually found was that "the [Unification] church was no better than any other institution. I found no evidence that God was doing special work there." Still, he gained knowledge there he thought he wouldn't have gained otherwise. "I learned a lot about people in the Unification church," he said almost wistfully. "It was an environment where more often than not you were delving into people's lives, even if you were just trying to get someone to buy overpriced flowers. I met a broad range of people. I had grown up in an all-black neighborhood and I was able to move beyond that. I learned something about Koreans, Japanese, about whites."

It took him a year to wean himself away from the Moonies, but, once he did, he wanted to make sure he would never backslide. He wrote an article for a gay Christian magazine on being a black gay man and sent copies to everyone he knew. "I never lost a friend over that article," he claimed.

In 1982, he got a job at the *Washington Times*. His lifetime dream had been to work on a daily newspaper in Washington and this was his chance.

The person who hired him was aware he was gay, and Isaiah said he received assurances from the newspaper that his personal life wouldn't be a factor in determining his employment. Today, he said, everyone at the *Times* knew he was gay.

The day I met Isaiah, the *Times* had run a virulently anti-gay column on its Op-Ed page, blaming "promiscuous" gay men for AIDS and suggesting "Biblical laws of quarantine" be put into effect. I asked him how he could work for a newspaper that expounded such views. He admitted that the *Times*'s coverage of gay issues left much to be desired but thought it wasn't quite as bad as it might seem. "If gay activists rated the *Times*," he said, "they would give it high marks for coverage of local gay issues, high marks on AIDS news coverage, and low marks on national issues."

At the newspaper, he maintained, "you learn to pick your fights." One fight in which he did get involved took place during the 1984 presidential campaign. The *Times* had run a cartoon mocking Democratic candidate Walter Mondale for his support of gay rights; in the cartoon, Mondale was drawn wearing rubber gloves, a reference to AIDS. A petition of protest was circulated by the staff and Isaiah signed it. The next year, there was the editorial that said, in effect, that Rock Hudson deserved to die. (The actor died of AIDS in 1985.) Isaiah fired off a memo to the editorial page editor, and the editor later apologized personally.

By this point in our conversation, Isaiah's combative side was very much in evidence. "There are problems at every paper," he insisted. "I have never been confronted with a story being altered because of an advertiser's complaint. I have never been relegated to a low level of employment because of my color. I have never been thrown out of my job like Chris Madsen [the reporter for the *Christian Science Monitor* who was fired because she was a lesbian; she later sued the newspaper]." When I asked Isaiah what he thought about that day's anti-gay column, he dismissed it with a wave of the hand. "I laughed at it," he said.

A year or so after he had left the Moonies, Isaiah ran into Dr. Tinney at an MCC church service. At the gay church, Isaiah was feeling the same alienation he experienced at the Unification church—that "there are not enough of my people here." He had known Tinney from Howard University. When Tinney held his city-wide gay revival, he and his lover attended. And when Tinney founded Faith Temple, Isaiah and his lover were among the new church's first members.

Isaiah described the early days of the church before it found its current identity much as Tinney had. At first, it had "a protest edge to it," he said. "Half of it was to worship and the other half was to show off your sexuality and to show we could be Christians and gay too." But for Isaiah and for other members of the congregation, serious study of the Bible put matters in a new perspective. At Faith Temple, "We were ready to do business with the Lord," he said. "Sexuality and race takes care of itself after that."

Today, for Isaiah, everything revolved around his relationship with Jesus. "It took a long time for me to understand a relationship with Jesus was important, to accept that his sacrifice was a sacrifice for *me*, to bond directly with Christ," he said. Finally, he realized that God wanted him to enter into unity with Christ, to separate himself from the past and be reborn. That went far beyond God merely accepting him as a gay person. And so, on September 15, 1985, Isaiah underwent water baptism in the pool at the Calvary Baptist Church.

His new relationship with Jesus, he said, had given him greater strength to confront anyone who wanted to deny him his rights. "They can't mess with me," he said. "I am a child of the King. If God accepts me, you have to accept me, too." In some strange manner, being born again had become merged with gay pride. His relationship with Jesus meant that he simply refused to let social and political institutions tell him how to lead his life. "I am secure," he added. "Not only did Christ die for me, but once I accepted him, there is nothing that can be done to snatch it away."

It seemed an odd turning for gay liberation, this sense of individual salvation, of a personal relationship with Jesus as a shield against the homophobes. Collective effort became of minor importance. The world was no longer divided into gay and straight, but into those who had achieved salvation and those who hadn't. One might have expected that an acceptance of oneself as gay, an affirmation of sexual variety and diversity, would lead to a less rigid view of human beings and their place in the universe. But clearly, for Isaiah, a theology that left no ambiguities was essential. The Moonies had once provided him with that sense of certainty; now his relationship with Jesus did. And a black gay evangelical church provided the one setting that encouraged, even demanded, such thinking in absolutes, while also affirming his pride both in his homosexuality and in his blackness. That was what Faith Temple was about, what made it distinct, necessary. Through his struggles, the curious paths he had taken to arrive at the goal, Isaiah Poole had come home.

Postscript: Several months after my visit to Faith Temple, I picked up a copy of the *Washington Blade*, the city's gay and lesbian newspaper, to read that Dr. James Tinney had died from complications of AIDS. He had given no hint that he was sick when I talked with him. In the *Blade* article, Michael Vanzant, a member of Faith Temple, said of Dr. Tinney, "He brought into our community a unique understanding of the word of God. He was able to see past the prejudice of the world and understand the word of God as it was supposed to be, not as it is interpreted by mainline fundamentalist churches."

LAW, POLITICS, AND ACTIVISM

▼　▼　▼　▼　▼　▼　▼　▼　▼　▼　▼　▼　▼

SAN FRANCISCO

ob Almstead was working vice, and we were driving around the Tenderloin in a grey, unmarked Ford LTD. That evening, Bob wasn't looking for "serious runs." It was early, and he was keeping his eyes open for a prostitute who had an outstanding warrant. "She is fat; she can't outrun me," he said. At the corner of Jones and Ellis, he pointed out two prostitutes, chatting as they walked down the street. They turned away from us. "They'd know this car in a heartbeat," said Bob. "All the hookers and hustlers do. It's the antennas and the pigeon shit. The police parking lots are infested with pigeons and everyone knows it." Meanwhile, the police radio was reporting that, somewhere in the city, two men were beating up a third with a lead pipe.

We passed a couple of uniformed foot patrolmen "running" two suspects, a heavy-set American Indian in a San Francisco 49er jacket and a clean-cut, younger white man in a V-neck sweater. Bob pulled over to the side to provide back-up. "These officers don't know me from Adam," he said; stopping was a courtesy that cops did for one another. Even though they didn't appear to have problems, "It can happen so fast that it turns to shit," he said.

When the cops finally let the suspects go, one of the officers approached us and Bob rolled down the window. "Just standing by," said Bob, and the street patrolman nodded.

Now we were approaching Polk Street, where the male prostitutes hang out. They got older as you went down the street, Bob explained. Busting hustlers was one of Bob's major activities these days, and he had only contempt for them. Most were so "fucked up" on drugs, he said, that they wouldn't remember him from one occasion to the next. He often wound up arresting the same person more than once.

According to the police radio, "three black girls" were beating up a fourth in the Mission area. Driving with Bob, I was beginning to view San Francisco not as a city of cable cars and gentle hills and pastel colors but as a place where, at almost any moment, some violent crime was being committed—the perspective of cops and paranoids.

Bob was dressed in plainclothes—a grey and orange flannel shirt and green fatigues. He had strapped his gun under his blue denim jacket. Bob was thirty-six, with a military bearing and a beard, speckled with grey, that he was permitted to grow because he was on the vice squad. The San Francisco Police Department had begun hiring openly gay officers in the late seventies; Bob had been on the force for three years. He had started working vice in January, five months before. When I went with him to the police station that evening, I found a vice squad that incorporated some of the major constituencies of San Francisco. Bob's sergeant, a husky man with a beer belly, wearing a green military T-shirt and camouflage fatigues, was also gay. An attractive blonde woman in skin-tight jeans was preparing for an evening standing on street corners in order to arrest "johns." (In nonsexist San Francisco, both hookers and their customers are arrested.) There were two Asian men whose assignment was to infiltrate Chinese gambling in the city. And there was Bob. He was supposed to do a little of everything, including male and female prostitution—mostly male.

I was looking at gays and lesbians in positions of authority and wanted to meet an openly gay cop. The police and the gay community had a long history of antagonism dating from the time—not very long ago, in many cities— when the police used to raid gay bars; many gays saw the cops as the enemy. That was particularly true in San Francisco. In 1979, after Supervisor

Harvey Milk's assassin, Dan White, was convicted of manslaughter instead of first-degree murder, cops and gays battled one another in the streets in what became known as the "White Night Riots." Sixty-one police officers and one hundred gays were hospitalized. After that, the city made an effort to bring gays and lesbians onto the police force; by 1980, one out of every seven recruits was gay, as Randy Shilts reported in *The Mayor of Castro Street*, his biography of Milk.

I had visited Bob at his home earlier that day. He had told me to come about nine o'clock; he always got up early to do his pottery, he said. Bob's lover was leaving for work when I arrived. He was a lawyer and came from an old San Francisco family; he was dressed in a three-piece suit with a "Jesse Jackson '88" button on the lapel. They lived in an old Victorian house with high ceilings, chandeliers, and elaborate moldings; it was crowded with period furniture.

Bob led me to a room off the kitchen where he displayed his pottery. He made clay sculptures, some of which resembled Eastern European churches, while others seemed a cross between Meso-American pyramids and medieval fortresses. Bob took his work very seriously. At different points in his life, he had supported himself by selling his sculpture at crafts fairs.

He always wanted to be a cop, he told me. As a kid, he had a high voice and a bit of a lisp. He was sensitive about being called a "sissy." He wanted to make up for it. He had grown up in the Panama Canal Zone, where American police officers were highly respected. Bob's father was an officer in the U.S. Army; his mother was Panamanian, the daughter of a former chief justice of that country's highest court. Law enforcement was the family profession.

Bob won a presidential appointment to West Point. But he never graduated; he knew he was gay and was having a hard time accepting it. He enlisted in the military, where he worked in counterintelligence, penetrating companies with defense contracts in order to test their security systems. Later, he worked for the U.S. Drug Enforcement Agency, doing computer analyses of evidence collected in drug arrests.

Eventually, living in Washington, D.C., Bob got a job on a magazine published by the Organization of American States. When the magazine developed financial problems, Bob began looking for another job. He read an advertisement in the newspaper that the D.C. Police Department was hiring. In small print, the advertisement said that the department did not discriminate on the basis of sexual orientation.

It was 1981 when Bob applied to join the Washington police force. The officer who interviewed him told him he was perfect for the job: he had served in the military, was multilingual, and was in good health and good shape. Bob said there was something else they should know—"I'm gay." The interviewer assured him it was no problem and promptly started asking Bob all sorts of questions about his sex life. "They didn't expect someone like me," Bob said. "They thought that a bunch of hairdressers would apply who would shriek when they were told they had to carry a gun." In the end, Bob proved the perfect candidate to become the first openly gay police officer in the nation's capital.

He went through the police academy and won two awards, including one for best marksman. Some of his classmates knew he was gay and were protective of him; in general, the department tried to keep it all quiet. But word leaked out. Once he came on the force, a reporter from the *Washington Blade* wrote a story about him. Until the reporter started asking questions, Bob's sergeant hadn't been aware he was gay. When he found out, he assigned Bob to a kind of purgatory—working with a male-to-female transsexual named Bonnie, who was a senior officer and had continued on the force after her sex change. "I knew no one was assigned to work with Bonnie for more than three days," Bob said. "But three days passed, and I was still there. They thought we would drive each other crazy." In fact, he and Bonnie got along splendidly; they declared themselves partners. The two became known for domestic-violence work, their speciality. "We developed a kind of telepathy together," Bob told me. "Without speaking, we could tell each other things, like check the kitchen or the bathroom." The crucial element in domestic-violence work, he stressed, was "to get complete control of the situation."

Bob's fluent Spanish stood him in good stead, as well. At times, he was the only Spanish-speaking officer in the entire city, which was then experiencing an influx of immigrants from Central America. "Officers in Spanish-speaking districts were constantly having to call me," he said. "And I would be really nice to them, really professional. I would give them credit for splashy homicides and major assaults." It was, he admitted, "a calculated attempt to buy acceptance."

During his first months on the force, Bob was constantly being tested by the other officers: "Would I be the 'little fairy'?" He recalled one incident when he was sitting and talking to another cop in the line-up room. Thirty cops were present, all of whom were carrying guns. An older officer looked in Bob's direction. "Are you the queer cop?" he demanded. Bob stood up. "Yes, I am," he said. "But I prefer to be called homosexual." "Maybe it is time for me to retire," said the other. "Maybe it is!" Bob shot back. Another time, he discovered the word "faggot" written on the blackboard. He knew who had done it and confronted the officer. "It would be easy," he told him, "to stand up and say, 'There is no truth to reports you are having an affair with so-and-so.'" The officer never bothered him again. In still another incident, Bob was sent out alone on a dangerous assignment. He complained at roll-call, accusing his sergeant of discrimination.

Other officers were constantly taken aback, he said, when he handled these incidents calmly. The important thing was always to come out on top in confrontations, "to have a tough skin and throw it right back." He noted that police officers like to see their supervisors put down. "It makes you one of the boys," he said.

Bob said he had to work "extra hard" to prove himself. He would identify the cops who were uncomfortable with the fact that he was gay. When they radioed for help, he would make it his business to be the first one on the scene. It was another example of buying acceptance. He added, "In intense, life-threatening situations, officers forget about your personal life. They just want you to be competent. They forget you are gay. I think that is different from how they react if you are a black or a woman." He did want to be treated as "one of the boys," he said. But, at the same time, he wanted other cops to perceive him that way, fully aware that he was gay. "I would remind them," he told me.

As the first openly gay cop in Washington, D.C., he received intense attention, as well as money and even marriage proposals in the mail. In the gay community, his celebrity proved a sexual boon. "I could go to the D.C. Eagle and go home with anybody I wanted," he said. "I didn't even have to try. I would find excuses to wear my uniform to the bar."

After he had been a police officer for three years, Bob met Jim, his current lover, through mutual friends. Jim was living in San Francisco, and Bob went out to the West Coast to spend ten days with him. He decided that "I like myself a lot," enough to trade his job—and the respect he had worked so hard to attain—for a relationship. He quit his job, packed his clay pieces, and set out for San Francisco. After working for a year as a potter, he joined the San Francisco police force.

In San Francisco, Bob found a police department that was markedly different from the one he had left. The city had had openly gay police officers for a number of years. Bob was one of many; he was no longer the first, no longer a celebrity. He was assigned to the Mission-Castro station, which covered the predominately Latino and gay areas of the city. Most of the gay cops were assigned to Mission-Castro, he said, because gays and lesbians in the neighborhood demanded openly gay cops. As a result, he said, there were few openly gay cops in the rest of the city. But in terms of police work, the gay community didn't offer much of a challenge. "We got very few complaints from the Castro. Mostly they were noise and domestic quarrels," Bob said. "Generally, people in the Castro are well educated and know their rights. They can give you a hard time."

After a year at Mission-Castro, Bob was transferred to a beat that offered as much action as a police officer could ever want. It was the Potrero, an area of warehouses, up-and-coming residential areas, and run-down housing projects that had San Francisco's highest homicide rate. Bob was awarded the department's medal of valor for saving the life of his partner in a fight. "I was making a lot of arrests," he said. "I began to like it."

Then, six months before I met him, Bob was diagnosed with AIDS. He had informed the department in January, but he made it clear he wanted to stay on as long as he was able. He was reassigned to vice, "a plum job," he said. It wasn't clear if the department was being generous or whether it was simply afraid of a discrimination lawsuit if he was let go. In Bob's situation, it didn't hurt to have a lover who was an attorney.

At vice, Bob was determined to work as hard as anyone else. "They thought I was going to come in for two hours and make coffee," Bob said. They were wrong. He began to specialize in prostitution, particularly male prostitution, something that vice had generally ignored in the recent past. He went to gay sex clubs to see if there were drugs or prostitution. (There weren't.) He would work the video arcades where prostitutes and hustlers would get men sexually aroused and then demand money. Sometimes, he "wore a wire."

It made me somewhat uncomfortable that a gay cop would be assigned to arrest male prostitutes. A lot of these hustlers were straight kids out to make a buck and (sometimes) to rip off gays, and some of the gay hustlers were pretty unsavory characters. But others were runaways, kids who had been kicked out by their parents simply because they were gay and who wound up on the streets. To me, it seemed that the police department was exploiting Bob's insider status and knowledge to arrest teenagers for a crime that probably shouldn't be against the law anyway. On the other hand, prostitution was against the law, and how far did one's allegiance to other gays extend when one was dealing with people on the edges of the criminal world? Clearly, Bob didn't share my reservations. He was a cop first and a gay cop second. "You have to understand the sleaze factor," he said. "So many of these hustlers have warrants on them and they use the money they earn to finance other criminal activity."

For Bob, the important thing was doing something, anything, that made him feel he was valuable. "My own sense of self-worth," he said, "is critical to my health."

Bob talked for four hours. He told me stories of saving a kidnapped seven year old girl; of how he resuscitated a man after a gang battle and then, a couple of weeks later, the same guy's brother saved Bob's life in the middle of another gang fight involving two hundred people. "That kind of thing just never happens," Bob said with pride.

When he had gone through his stories, he started asking himself questions: "Does a gay cop have more compassion than a straight cop?" Bob's answer was yes. "I didn't think so when I first got into police work," he said. "But gays have been discriminated against. They know what it's like. They might say, 'Let's look a little deeper.' They tend to listen a little more, to take a stand if a straight cop says, 'Let's book the guy.'"

I asked Bob if I could go out on the beat with him that evening. That was fine, as far as he was concerned; he didn't think his boss, the gay sergeant, would object. I should come by his house at six o'clock and we would go down to the station together.

Bob's sergeant gave the okay, but with one stipulation. He wouldn't allow me to be present when arrests were made. But I could accompany Bob on his preliminary drive-around before the real work began. On our way to the parking lot to pick up the LTD, a burly officer in a cruiser stopped to talk to Bob. They chatted about impending layoffs. When Bob mentioned he was working vice, the other cop expressed surprise. "I got sent over there because I have AIDS," Bob said, matter-of-factly. I was amazed at his openness. They didn't have any openly gay cops in Boston, as far as I was aware, let alone cops who would announce they had AIDS to a fellow officer.

So we were driving around, checking out prostitutes. But it wasn't really the Tenderloin or Polk Street with their "sleaze factors" that interested Bob. He wanted to show off the Potrero, his old beat. Once on the expressway, we were there in no time. Bob took me past Geneva Towers ("so awful most cops won't go there—a pickle jar thrown from the eighteenth story can cause tremendous damage") to the low-rise Sunnydale and Hahn projects. These were all largely black areas. People scattered as the LTD drove by; they instantly recognized it as a police car. "There are drug deals going on over there," Bob pointed. "Look at that Mercedes! And what is that guy doing walking along the side of the road in the dark with a baseball bat?"

When Bob was first assigned to this part of town, he memorized maps of all the projects. "I have chased people all through here," he told me. "I know this area like the back of my hand."

He couldn't merely be the tour guide. He wanted to establish some kind of police presence. He squealed his tires. He stopped beside a couple of cars that were double-parked and told the drivers there were parking spots further up ahead. They obeyed politely, never questioning his right to order them around. "My boss would kill me if he knew I was out here alone," Bob said. A woman was calling out to her boyfriend from a parked car, "Don't forget to call your P.O. [parole officer]." Bob drove up next to her and told her to move on. "I'm sure I could bring her in on some charge—driving without a license or registration," he said.

It was dark now and I felt uneasy driving through these projects, even though I knew Bob wouldn't make any arrests. "You can get hooked on adrenalin," Bob said. "I used to get ten to fifteen rushes of adrenalin a night.

I would get cranky and anxious when I started withdrawing." He added, "I wonder if adrenalin rushes might be a cure for AIDS."

We drove through the Hunter's Point project, past the spot where Bob's life had been saved by the brother of the guy to whom he had given CPR. "The guy spewed blood and bile in my face," said Bob. "Maybe that's how I got AIDS. He was a well-known drug user. There are a lot of times when I've had people's blood all over me."

There was something depressing about the whole experience. Of all the people I talked to during my travels, Bob had accomplished one of the most difficult feats; he had managed to find his place and find respect in an organization that was a bastion of homophobia. His experience on the D.C. police force was, in many respects, the gay equivalent to the experience of the black kids who broke down the color bar in the fifties and sixties. And here he was, prevented by his illness from doing the work that meant so much to him, reduced to busting hustlers and to squealing tires in a housing project—angry and impotent. In a way he was a romantic figure, the soldier-artist who has fought his last battle and returns to the scene for one final glimpse.

He drove me back to the place where my car was parked. "You never know," Bob said. "Things were going great. I had money in the bank. Jim did too. Then I got AIDS." We were far from those housing projects now, back in the San Francisco of tourists and boutiques and spectacular views. As I got out of the police car, Bob told me, "You can leave two things in this world— children and art. I don't have kids. I just have my art, my little vision, my imagination." And then he went back to Polk Street to make some arrests.

WASHINGTON, D.C.; ST. PAUL, MINNESOTA;

AND KEY WEST, FLORIDA

was sitting in the office of Congressman Barney Frank, when the announcement came that it was time to vote. Barney stubbed out his cigar. "Come over to the House chamber with me," he said. "It should only take a few minutes." Barney was casually dressed in a red-checked shirt and grey trousers. Despite his well-publicized transformation from rumpled, overweight legislator to svelte, Nautilized man-about-town (the local glossy, *Boston Magazine,* had given him its 1986 Best Dressed award), Barney looked as if he might be putting on a few pounds again.

As we walked over to the Capitol, we passed a number of congressmen on their way back from voting. And everyone felt they had to banter with Barney. Most of their comments centered around the fact that he wasn't wearing a tie. "The new Frank style," kidded one. Another offered to let him borrow his paisley tie for the vote. "Do you have one in stripes?" Barney deadpanned. In the elevator up to the House chamber, he was trading Yiddish jokes with Congressman Gary Ackerman of Queens.

I mentioned all that joshing to Barney when we returned to his office. He had publicly come out of the closet five months before, and I couldn't help but notice how relaxed everyone seemed with him. "I discovered when I left the Massachusetts legislature, I wasn't as well-liked as I thought," he confided. "People thought I was too acerbic. I've tried to be more liked here." That surprised me. I thought everyone loved Barney.

I had known Barney Frank for years. During my tenure as editor of *GCN,* Barney (as everyone called him) was the state representative from the Back Bay section of Boston. He was still in the closet at the time but he was a great supporter of gay and lesbian rights and the gay community. Occasionally I would hear a rumor that he was actually gay, but no one paid too much attention. He was just Barney—blunt, wise-cracking, fast-talking, the darling of the media. He tended to appear so dishevelled that even his own campaign organization made fun of him. During one legislative reelection bid, his campaign poster featured a particularly rumpled-looking Barney with the slogan, "Neatness isn't everything." Nothing about his image suggested he might have a sex life—or sexual feelings.

It was when he came to Washington in 1981, representing a Massachusetts congressional district that extended from suburban Brookline and Newton to blue-collar Fall River, that a different Barney Frank began to emerge. In Boston, Barney had always been the sympathetic observer at gay events, remaining just a little at a distance. Now he was determined to have a lot of gay friends, not just as a supportive politician, but as a gay person. He cautiously began coming out to people, both gay and straight. He began to go to gay bars. As we chatted, he recalled the first time he had gone to a popular gay bar called the Lost and Found. He was attending a dinner party hosted by Judge Douglas Ginsburg, President Reagan's ill-fated nominee to the U.S. Supreme Court. At half-past eleven, he excused himself and headed for the bar. "I had forgotten all about that!" he said.

In 1982, shortly after being reelected, a constituent asked him, "How does it feel to have a safe seat?" Barney realized the man was right. It represented a green light of sorts. Soon after he returned to Washington, he started losing weight in earnest and "living my private life as a gay man without too much concern."

At the Human Rights Campaign Fund Dinner in Boston in 1985, I got my first glimpse of the new Barney. It wasn't just that he was thin and that his suit was pressed. He was dancing with another man.

After that, like so many people who had watched Barney's career over the years, I was waiting for the inevitable—his public coming out. Thomas P. "Tip" O'Neill, then Speaker of the House, was waiting too. Barney tells the story that at the time, rumors were circulating that he was about to acknowledge he was gay. O'Neill was heard to say, "Well, I guess I am going to have something else to deal with. Barney Frank is going to come out of the room." Gerry Studds, the congressman from Cape Cod, had acknowledged his homosexuality in 1983 after he was censored by the House of Representatives for having an affair with a teenage page; Barney had no such questionable incident in his past. He was just waiting for the right moment.

And then in late May 1987, I picked up my Saturday morning copy of the *Boston Globe* to read the front-page headline, "Frank Discusses Being Gay."

And after all that buildup, there seemed to be little consequence. Barney held a series of town meetings throughout his district to assure his constituents he was still concerned with their issues. There were a couple of follow-up stories in the newspaper, of course: "Many Unperturbed by Frank's Disclosure" and "Frank Still Has Clout in House 6 Months After Saying He Is Gay." But mostly, when I saw Barney's name in the paper in the months that followed, it concerned something other than homosexuality—public housing, Israel, Soviet refuseniks. A year and a half later, he was reelected to his fifth term with seventy percent of the vote.

When Barney gave that interview to the *Boston Globe*, he hardly stood alone as an openly gay elected official. There was Gerry Studds (D-Massachusetts), the other publicly gay U.S. congressman. There were gay city councillors in Boston, San Francisco, Rochester, New York, and Chapel Hill, North Carolina. Gay mayors had served or were still serving in Santa Cruz and West Hollywood, California, and Key West, Florida (and Bunceton, Missouri). The town clerk/tax collector/treasurer of tiny Lunenburg, Massachusetts, was openly gay—one of the few Republicans among the group.

There were plenty of places around the country that would never elect a gay man or woman to public office, of course. Gay-baiting was still a factor in political campaigns. In Barbara Mikulski's 1986 race for the Maryland U.S. Senate seat, her opponent referred to her as a "San Francisco Democrat," a characterization whose inference was lost on no one. And the Republican party was, by and large, hostile to gays and gay issues. Bruce Decker, a former advance man for Jerry Ford who had helped found a group of gay Republicans a few years before, told me gay people were "about as welcome in the Republican party as a turd in a punchbowl." (At the 1988 Republican National Convention in New Orleans, GOP delegates physically attacked gay protesters, with some shouting, "AIDS is the cure!"; during the presidential campaign, Senator Orrin Hatch (R-Utah) called the Democrats "the party of homosexuals.")

Still, the number of gay public officials was climbing. And although Massachusetts won high marks for gay and lesbian officeholders (Elaine Noble, an open lesbian, had been elected to the Massachusetts House of

Representatives in 1974, the first to break the barrier), the place where it seemed easiest for openly gay candidates to gain election to public office was not Boston or even San Francisco but Minneapolis. That city boasted an openly gay city councillor, Brian Coyle, and the only two openly gay state legislators in the entire nation — State Senator Allan Spear and State Representative Karen Clark. (In November 1988, Calvin Anderson, a gay man, was elected to the legislature in the state of Washington.)

Spear, the granddaddy of openly gay public officials, was first elected to the Minnesota Senate in 1972, while still in the closet. He came out two years later and had been reelected four times since. He currently serves as chairman of the Senate Judiciary Committee, one of the most powerful positions in the Minnesota legislature.

When I was ushered into Spear's office at the capitol in St. Paul, he was sitting in a swivel chair behind an immense mahogany desk. A balding man with big glasses and a reddish, fleshy face, on first impression he looked like a politician of the old school. I could just as well have entered the domain of Richard Daley or Boss Crump. On the wall behind his desk was an ornately framed picture with little oval portraits of all the chairmen of the Senate Judiciary Committee — from the greybeards of the nineteenth century to Allan Spear. On another wall were large, framed photos of Floyd Olson and Elmer Benson, the populist Farmer Labor party governors of Minnesota in the thirties. When Benson died a few years ago, it was Spear who was chosen to give his eulogy in the Minnesota Senate. It was a proud moment.

As his admiration for those populist governors of the Great Depression indicated, Spear is far from being a traditional pol. He is candid, friendly, and very precise and detailed, as befits the chairman of the Judiciary Committee. He told me he was probably the most liberal member of the state senate. The first question I asked him was a simple one — "Why Minnesota?" Why did that state have two openly gay state legislators when no other state at the time even had one and hadn't since Elaine Noble left the Massachusetts legislature in 1978? One reason he offered was the active and organized gay and lesbian community of the Twin Cities. Equally important was that in Minnesota, the legislature was relatively large, and legislative jurisdictions were smaller than in some of the more populous states. Spear's district had sixty thousand people; Karen Clark's had thirty thousand. "If you were to run for the state senate in California, you would have to run in a district with hundreds of thousands of voters," Spear pointed out. "Here it is much more concentrated. When people see you face to face, they are less afraid of you than when you are some abstraction out there—the gay candidate."

When Spear first ran for office in 1972, he was a thirty-five year old professor of U.S. history, strongly identified with peace and civil rights issues and with the liberal-left wing of the Democratic party. He was also in the midst of coming out on a personal level. Although people in his campaign knew he was gay, the electorate didn't. Spear's district was a liberal one—the area surrounding the University of Minnesota campus, as well as some senior-citizen high-rises and ethnic pockets. (It should be noted that it did not include the bulk of the city's gay population.) He narrowly won that first race—"one of the few candidates in the country who ran on George McGovern's coattails," he observed wryly.

Spear came out in a front-page interview in the *Minneapolis Star-Tribune* midway through his first term. The senate majority leader had encouraged him and made it his business to shield him from adverse consequences. (The majority leader's girlfriend, later his wife, was an editor at the *Star-Tribune* and did the coming-out interview.) Spear's colleagues took the position that what he said about his private life wasn't their business. But they were sure he'd never be reelected.

He surprised them, winning sixty-eight percent of the vote over a Republican opponent whose refrain was, "Allan Spear's homosexuality is not an issue in this campaign." In 1980, he won with seventy-five percent, and despite the redistricting that "cannibalized" his district, was reelected by substantial margins throughout the eighties. (His new district was made up of a more affluent area on the west side of the city, plus areas where the gay population was concentrated.) Except for that 1976 campaign, Spear said his homosexuality had never been made an election issue. "They realized the issue was a loser in a liberal district," he said.

That was not the experience of State Representative Karen Clark, Spear's legislative colleague. A former ob-gyn nurse-practitioner and health-care activist who had never held political office, Clark was elected from a low-income, south Minneapolis district in 1980. With redistricting, her district was now the poorest in the state—with a high concentration of American

Indians, Southeast Asians, poor blacks and whites, and twenty-two senior-citizen high-rises. Starting with that first race, Clark's opponents—usually right-wing Republicans—have tried to make her lesbianism an issue. (Unlike Spear and Barney Frank, Clark made her homosexuality known before she was elected to public office.) She has always won by large majorities, though—seventy-four percent in the 1988 election, for example. "I have always counteracted it [lesbian-baiting] by sticking to the issues," Clark said when we talked in a conference room across from her capitol office. Although Clark didn't dwell on the use of the gay issue by her opponents, Spear felt it was extremely difficult for her. "Karen always knew she would win," he said. "But to have to deal with that kind of thing constantly! You go home and think, How can I go through another day of this?"

I asked Spear if he thought that being gay had hampered him in the legislature. Right after he came out, he said, people were hesitant about giving him bills to carry. But once he was reelected, that changed. He ranked high in terms of seniority, he noted, and was the first nonlawyer to head the Judiciary Committee. For her part, Karen Clark said there were two members of the Minnesota House who, despite her eight-year tenure, still couldn't see past the lesbian label. Beyond that, she had experienced as many roadblocks in the House being a woman as being a lesbian. (There were only twenty women representatives out of 134 in the Minnesota House.) "Any woman in public life has to work twice as hard, be twice as competent, be twice as innovative," she noted. Her sexuality added still "another layer to it," just as race did for people of color. It was a constant proving ground. But she was now entering her eighth session in the legislature. "I still have to produce 150 percent," she said, "but at least I don't have to begin behind the starting line anymore."

Clark noted that expectations about her before she entered the legislature didn't fit with her personality. The "news" that circulated soon after she arrived was that "Karen Clark is a nice person." "They expected someone who would be a stereotypically tough woman, a scary kind of person," she said. Delicate but determined, her oval face out of a pre-Raphaelite painting, Clark comes across as firm, committed, but hardly frightening. Spear, thanks to his superficial resemblance to an old-line pol, goes against stereotype too. So does Barney Frank with his perpetual cigar, his blunt manner, and street smarts. "It helps not being stereotypical because you are dealing with a prejudice," Barney noted. "People have this inaccurate view of what it is to be gay. If you superficially conform to that, it is harder to get them to see beyond it. So if you are very different, it really helps."

One of the keys to his success, Spear maintained, was that he (and Clark and city councillor Brian Coyle, as well) did not spend the majority of their time focusing on gay and lesbian concerns. As chairman of the Judiciary Committee, his agenda was dominated by issues related to the legal system — criminal law, sentencing law, DWI (driving while intoxicated) issues, due process for people committed to mental hospitals, child abuse laws. He was also on the division of the Finance Committee that concerned itself with welfare appropriation; he had been trying to hold the line on cutbacks in income-maintenance programs, he said. For her part, Clark has stressed housing and health issues, which are important to her low-income district. One of her proudest accomplishments, she said, was the enactment of a "worker right to know" law in Minnesota, one of the earliest in the nation. Under that legislation, workers who handle toxic chemicals and other hazardous substances must be informed of the fact by their employer, given protective gear, and given the right to refuse to work in dangerous situations.

Both Spear and Clark have stressed childcare issues. On Spear's wall, next to that ornate picture of the past chairmen of the Judiciary Committee, was a modest plaque given to him by the Minneapolis Daycare Association. The year he received the award, the other person honored was Karen Clark. He noted the irony: The two legislators who, in the public mind, were least likely to have children had received recognition for their work on family concerns.

For all these public officials, incumbency (and their relatively liberal districts) seemed to cancel out many of the political negatives of being gay. But there clearly were drawbacks. Spear observed that no one would consider him as a possible candidate for higher office because he was a gay man. He had been in the legislature for fifteen years and held an extremely influential position. Yet in any discussions about who might run for mayor or for Congress, his name was never mentioned. Barney Frank seemed to take it for granted that his coming out made it impossible for him to consider higher office. "If I had any interest in running for the Senate, this would hurt me," he said. The state of anti-gay prejudice was such that people who knew you, specifically your constituents, weren't going to turn away from you because you were gay. But there was still enough bigotry, he thought, that "when it comes to people who don't know you, being gay can block them off from you." And Barney seemed concerned that his gayness might prevent him from rising very high within the House of Representatives. "I don't know if I ever had a chance to get into any kind of leadership position here," he said. "I might have. I probably don't now."

For her part, Karen Clark emphasized the personal costs. She had recently attended a meeting of gay and lesbian elected officials from across the country. One thing that struck her, she said, was that "a majority of us had lost a significant long-term relationship in the first year after we were elected. I was one of those people." It was well known, she said, that, given the demands of elected office, the personal lives of many politicians suffered. Gays and lesbians were no exception. The difference, she said, was "we don't have the support that other families do." That fact made sustaining gay and lesbian relationships difficult in general; when you added the pressures of political life, it could well be fatal.

In all this, a question remained. What was the value of openly gay political figures for the gay and lesbian community? In Minnesota, for example, despite the very visible presences of Allan Spear and Karen Clark, the gay-rights bill had gone down in defeat year after year. That was in contrast to neighboring Wisconsin, which a few years before had become the first state in the nation to enact civil rights protections for homosexuals. And Wisconsin, I pointed out to Spear, didn't have any openly gay legislators.

"Why *not* Minnesota?" I asked. Spear had given the matter a lot of thought. The state's religious right, he said, was extremely well organized around the issue of abortion. As a result, the legislature was one of the most strongly pro-life bodies in the country. And the same people who were so vocal on abortion lobbied strongly against gay rights. "Whenever the gay-rights bill comes close, all hell breaks loose," he said. Phone lines were jammed; legislators were inundated with mail opposing the legislation. That was difficult to counteract, he said, because gay people in the state tended to migrate to the Twin Cities. Those who remained in the small towns and rural areas were often closeted. So legislators convinced themselves there were few gays and lesbians in their districts. For a gay-rights bill to have a serious chance, "We need more openly gay people in places like Clara City or Sleepy Eye, Minnesota," Spear said.

And while Spear thought that the openly gay and lesbian elected officials were a rallying point for the gay community in the Twin Cities, the fact they had risen as high as they had might breed complacency. "People think that because we are here, we can do it all," he said. He noted there was no ongoing gay and lesbian political organization in Minneapolis–St. Paul as in other cities. "Karen, Brian [Coyle], and I can't do it all," he insisted. "We can't do organizing."

Gay political figures would contend, of course, that they were in politics to represent all their constituents, not just to further the gay community. Barney Frank told me he was rationing his visibility on gay issues, especially because he had come out so recently. In Karen Clark's campaign literature, support for gay and lesbian rights was listed number six in her human-rights category—between reproductive freedom and protecting American Indian burial grounds. Allan Spear even had a gay opponent in his 1982 race who claimed that Spear had made too many compromises in trying to gain passage of the gay-rights bill. (His gay opponent, who called himself a Socialist, got about two percent of the vote and made Spear appear more moderate, Spear told me.)

But clearly, part of their agenda was to improve the social status of gays and lesbians. Spear said that when he, Karen Clark, and Brian Coyle spoke on gay issues, they were identified as gay elected officials and that gave them legitimacy. They were also able to do a lot behind the scenes. Despite the failure to pass a gay-rights bill, Spear took partial credit for persuading Governor Rudy Perpich to issue his executive order banning discrimination against state employees on the basis of sexual orientation or AIDS status. "That was basically Karen, Brian, and I working with the governor, although there were others, too," he said.

On the national scene, Barney Frank thought his presence in the House of Representatives made it more difficult for his colleagues to take positions opposed to gay rights because of their personal relations with him. While the U.S. Senate was approving anti-gay amendments to AIDS-appropriation and housing bills in the spring and summer of 1988, the House was defeating similar amendments. Congressman Frank, for example, had introduced an omnibus immigration bill that, among other provisions, removed existing restrictions barring gay foreigners from visiting or immigrating to the United States. An attempt by Congressman William Dannemeyer (R-California) to retain the anti-gay prohibition was defeated in the House Judiciary Committee. Some conservatives tried to remove the gay category from legislation sponsored by Congressman John Conyers, Jr. (D-Michigan) that required the Justice Department to keep statistics on crimes motivated by prejudice. The full House defeated that amendment, too.

Barney Frank didn't take credit for all these victories, of course. During the Reagan years, the U.S. House of Representatives, with its large Democratic majorities, was generally more liberal than the Senate. But as Barney noted, "The personal approach can make a tremendous difference. Legislators don't like to deal with face-to-face hostility." And that, in part, was what the joshing on the Capitol steps was all about the day I walked with Barney towards the House chamber.

In Key West, they didn't seem to care very much about gay rights—or at least about having gay-rights protections made into law. I could understand that in Bunceton, Missouri, with its six gay residents; in Key West, the city that a lot of people viewed as gay paradise, I found it odd and just a little smug.

I was having coffee with the former mayor, a gay man named Richard Heyman. We sat outside at a restaurant on Duval Street and watched the parade of tourists and locals. Heyman told me he and a friend had once counted the number of shops and restaurants in Key West that were gay owned. "We got to 120 or 130 and stopped," he said. "And we didn't even start counting the guesthouses." One of those businesses, an art gallery located a few doors down, was owned by the former mayor himself. He was asking seven thousand dollars for a painting by Tennessee Williams.

After the U.S. Navy left in the early seventies, Key West fell into an economic depression. Duval Street was all boarded up and the "old conchs," the long-time residents, were forsaking the architectural gems of downtown for the concrete monstrosities of the suburbs. It was the gays who were credited with reviving the city. There had been a gay community in Key West for many years, but it was not until the seventies that gay men began to migrate there in large numbers. Gay investors played a major role in the revitalization of downtown; the new arrivals bought up the charming conch houses that were going for a song. By the end of the decade, gay tourists started arriving in droves, helping to fuel the town's expansion.

Heyman, who had been running the family farm in rural Ohio, was one of those arrivals. In 1979, after being in town for only six years, he ran for one of the five slots on the city commission. He was the first gay candidate to try to translate gay economic prominence into political clout. He won, carrying nine out of the fourteen precincts. In 1983, Heyman was elected mayor with almost sixty percent of the vote. In 1985, illness prevented him from seeking a second term. A reticent and slightly bohemian man with a neatly clipped beard, he was out of office when I met him, running his gallery and planning an international performing-arts festival. Meanwhile, people kept urging him to run for mayor again, and he was considering it. (He was elected to his second term in November 1987.)

During his two campaigns for public office, it was well known that he was gay and lived with his lover (an artist, whose work Heyman exhibited in his gallery). But the reason for his political success, Heyman said, was not that gays dominated the voting rolls. In fact, they only made up about twelve percent of registered voters. The key to the acceptance of a gay candidate was the live and let live attitude that prevailed in Key West. The original settlers, he noted, were "a bunch of pirates who would use the lighthouse to guide ships into the rocks so they would run aground. Then they would salvage the cargo." In Key West, the prevailing view had always been "Whatever anyone does is OK as long as it doesn't hurt your neighbors." Today, that attitude translated into "It isn't who you are but what you contribute."

Heyman began to tick off the accomplishments of his term in office: a height limit and architectural review board, a new sewer plant.

Had he tried to get a gay-rights bill enacted? I asked. No, he said. Moreover, he saw "no need for gay issues in Key West." In the past, when the idea had been proposed, Heyman had asked for evidence of discrimination first. Apparently none was forthcoming. "Why bring up something and make it a law when there isn't even a need for it?" he demanded. "If there was ever a need, fine. I'm sure everyone would pass it here. In the meantime, it is superfluous." Ironically, that was the very same argument opponents of gay rights had always used in the Massachusetts legislature.

I stopped by to see Jim Stokes, a youthful fifty-six year old architect who was the co-owner of one of the city's largest gay guesthouses. Shortly after he was elected, Mayor Heyman had appointed Stokes to the city's architectural review commission.

As we sat by his pool, Stokes told me he had no doubt that Heyman's tenure in office had a tremendous impact on gay people in the town. In part because Heyman's election had demonstrated gay political power, any candidate running for office in Key West would be committing political suicide if he took an anti-gay position. When the present mayor had launched his campaign, Stokes noted that he had made the rounds of the gay guesthouses and cocktail parties.

I asked him about a gay-rights bill. His position was the same as that of the former mayor: Key West didn't need one. But what was to prevent someone from losing their job or being kicked out of their apartment because of anti-gay discrimination? I asked. Couldn't such things happen, even in Key West? Stokes replied, "There is enough residential space in Key West that is owned or controlled by gay people to house all the gay people who want to come down here and are willing to work." Consequently, there was no need to worry about housing discrimination. As for employment bias, "If all the gays in this town who were working for straight establishments stopped work at four P.M. today, they would have to shut down, I guarantee you." In short, gay economic power meant there was no need for gay civil rights protections.

That was the same reason there was no gay-pride parade in Key West, in Stokes's view. In Key West, he maintained, "We have gay pride all the time. We don't need to demonstrate our numbers because there isn't any one in town who doesn't know our numbers and appreciate the value of our numbers—or the value of our money!"

As we were talking, Stokes was called to the phone. When he returned, he told me it had been the current mayor on the line. Key West had been experiencing power blackouts during the previous few days. The mayor had just called to assure Stokes that everything possible was being done to correct the situation.

But I was determined to get beyond boosterism, beyond the party line, so I called on Peter K. Ilchuk, the man who had managed Heyman's campaign. Instead of taking me beyond the party line, Ilchuk turned out to be its author. What I found was a new breed of gay politician—tough, savvy, adept at using the political process.

Ilchuk, a stocky, curly-haired man of forty, had worked for former New York congressman Mario Biaggi for many years, eventually becoming his chief of staff. In 1978, he moved to Key West and bought a guesthouse. Within a year, he was urging the Key West Business Guild, the local organization of gay businessmen, to run a candidate for city commissioner. Heyman came forward, and Ilchuk became his campaign manager. In 1981, Ilchuk was elected chairman of the Democratic party of Monroe County, the county that stretches from Key West up the Keys to the Everglades. Two years later, he managed Heyman's successful mayoral campaign.

I visited Ilchuk in the restored clapboard conch house he owned, located across from the old cemetery with its whitewashed above-ground burial vaults. When Heyman had first run for city commissioner, he told me, gays were not as secure as today. There had been some street harassment. "We wanted to make a statement," he said. Still, Heyman had run on the basic issues—"fix the streets, get the sewer system working, get the government functioning better, lower taxes." By the 1983 mayoral campaign, the gay statement had been made. In that vote, the issue was not one of gay versus straight, but one of newcomer versus native Key Wester. "That is what the whole election hinged on," he maintained.

Because of what he called the "amalgamation" of gay people into all segments of society—from boards of banks and the Chamber of Commerce to the local theatre guild—Ilchuk agreed that the city didn't need a gay-rights ordinance. In Key West, people hadn't stereotyped gays, he insisted; because of gay participation in a wide range of civic groups, people had come to understand that gays were like themselves. So there was no discrimination. In fact, Ilchuk didn't even see a need for a separate gay organization such as the Key West Business Guild. He thought that gay businessmen should just work through the Chamber of Commerce. The Chamber recognized different market segments to which it appealed for tourism: sports fishermen and skin divers, for example. In his view, gay tourists were just another part of the market.

I asked Ilchuk what the response was to his election as chairman of the Monroe County Democratic party. "I controlled all the votes so there wasn't any problem with response," he replied. Fifteen out of the nineteen votes on the Democratic committee were beholden to him. He had worked to get them elected. "I went out and got them to run and told them we wanted to change the party and to get them involved," he said.

The message, he said, was that if you wanted to become an insider, to make changes, you simply had to be active. Of course, "There is no question that being gay, being a woman, being black, you have to work a little harder."

Ilchuk was willing to admit that things could sometimes be somewhat more complex than he made them out. He had been appointed to be the commissioner of elections in Monroe County by Governor (now Senator) Bob Graham. At about the same time Graham appointed him, a vacancy came up on the school board. "I am not going to suggest I would have as equal a shot at getting on the school board as of being appointed commissioner of elections," he admitted. "There would probably be another standard applied in my case. I am sure the outcome would have been different. There are some doors closed. But gradually, by being involved, we are going to change that."

Was this the great gay and lesbian future—gay integration into the general community, little need for the gay community to have its own institutions, and no reason for civil rights protections when money talks? Or were gay politicians like Heyman and Ilchuk just trying to avoid rocking the boat by bringing up a controversial gay-rights ordinance that might call attention to the town and threaten the gay community's comfortable economic and social status? I didn't know the answer. And I certainly questioned what might happen if the economic situation changed or if an anti-gay bigot ascended to power. Alliance with mainstream economic and political forces clearly was important for gay progress; some degree of "amalgamation" made sense. But it seemed naive to leave yourself defenseless, without institutions or laws to protect you. Even in paradise.

JOHNSON CITY, TENNESSEE

The student strip in Johnson City, Tennessee, home to East Tennessee State University and the ETSU Buccaneers, is lined with fast-food, health-club, and tanning franchises. There isn't a bookstore or even a stationery store in sight. On weekend nights, the atmosphere turns rowdy. Students congregate in the parking lot of Zak's Famous Frozen Yogurt and spill out of Quarterback's Barbecue and Carry-Out; others drive past and shout out of car windows.

If you drive a few blocks down West Walnut Street, where the New South begins to yield ever so imperceptibly to the Old, past the General Mills flour plant with its looming silos, you come upon a blue frame building that is of the strip but at the same time apart from it. It is the Connection, the gay bar that serves the Tri-Cities of East Tennessee (Johnson City, Kingsport, and Bristol). The Connection is the only gay gathering place in an area that stretches from Knoxville on the west to Asheville, North Carolina, on the south and Bluefield, West Virginia, on the north.

The bar is an unappealing place—a large, dark, smoky room with a discolored carpet and cheaply paneled walls decorated with fading posters of Venice and Florence. There are tables scattered about, a dance floor, flashing lights, and a noise level that makes conversation virtually impossible. The customers—a mix of clean-cut students and Appalachian faces—all seem remote from the trendiness of big-city life. On the stage, flanked by pseudoclassical statues and a curtain of crepe-paper, drag queens with names like Vanessa Diane and Sable Chanel lip-synch to disco tunes they stopped listening to in Atlanta and New Orleans two years before.

On the night of Friday, September 5, 1986, a man named Larry and two of his friends drove about two hours to the Connection from the small towns in the mountain valleys of southwestern Virginia where they lived. There, Larry ran into a student at East Tennessee State named Tim whom he had met before. Around midnight, the two left the bar in Tim's car and drove past McDonald's and Domino's Pizza and Quarterback's Barbecue and Carry-Out to a deserted parking lot on the campus of East Tennessee State University. A half an hour later, a police officer drove up, shined his lights, and brought the two in to the campus security office.

The officer later testified that he saw Tim performing oral sex on Larry. According to Larry's account, they were assured at the security office that if they cooperated with the campus police, they wouldn't get into trouble. The pair signed a statement admitting to the act and promising they would never come back to the campus again. Tim drove Larry to the bar where his friends were, and Larry returned home to Virginia.

Two or three days later, Tim called Larry on the phone, in tears. He had been served notice that he had been arrested, he said, and Larry had better go down to Johnson City to receive his papers, too. The two had been charged with a felony under the Tennessee "crimes against nature" statute. If convicted, they could receive five to fifteen years in prison.

Almost ten months after the arrests, I went to see Larry's lawyer, Eric Johnson, in his office in downtown Johnson City. Eric reached back and removed a heavy volume from the shelves of law books behind his desk. In his deep east Tennessee drawl he began reading: "Tennessee Code Annotated: 39-2-612. Crimes against Nature, either with mankind or any beast, are punishable by imprisonment in the penitentiary not less than five years, not more than 15." Included in the offense, he said, were fellatio, cunnilingus, and anal intercourse—any sexual acts that did not result in conception. This was Tennessee's sodomy law, enacted in 1858 and unchanged since.

"Basically, it is what we call a status offense," Eric explained. "You punish people because they are homosexual, not because what they do has any impact on society." If Larry and Tim had been a man and a woman, Eric was highly doubtful that the district attorney would have considered prosecution.

Twenty-five states still have similar laws on the books. In *Bowers v. Hardwick*, decided on June 30, 1986, the United States Supreme Court voted five to four to uphold the constitutionality of such laws. The Court ruled that private sexual activity between consenting adults was not protected by the U.S. Constitution, not even when "private" meant one's own bedroom, as in the case of Atlanta bartender Michael Hardwick. Although the laws were rarely used in most states, their existence—and the potential for their application at the whim of a district attorney—underscored the vulnerability of homosexuals to possible felony conviction for their ordinary sexual practices. These laws could also be trotted out in other cases to prove that homosexuals were "felons" undeserving of basic civil rights.

I had gone to Johnson City with Sue Hyde, a former *GCN* news editor who was the head of the Privacy Project of the National Gay and Lesbian Task Force. In the wake of the Hardwick decision, the Task Force was attempting to organize gay and lesbian communities around the country to work to overturn the sodomy laws, on a state-by-state basis. Sue was going to give a talk in Johnson City, where she would use Larry and Tim's case to direct attention to the legal situation in Tennessee. Here was a state where the sodomy law was not just still on the books but where at least one district attorney was more than willing to use it.

After Sue left town, I stayed in Johnson City for a few days to look into the case. Johnson City, a town of forty thousand, was not exactly a congenial place for homosexuals. The year before, for example, automobiles in the streets near The Connection had been vandalized. When individuals filed complaints with the police, they found their names and addresses in the newspaper the next day as part of a story about the incident. Since the bar was also named in the story and was known to be a place where gay people congregated, the implication was that the people whose cars were vandalized were also gay.

When Eric Johnson agreed to take Larry's case, the young lawyer was convinced he would have no difficulty getting the charge reduced to a misdemeanor. "I knew of cases in Memphis where guys soliciting cops in Overton Park had gotten off with a fifty-dollar fine," he told me. "I didn't think this would be any different." His client had another advantage: Tim's lawyer was the former district attorney of Washington County (which includes Johnson City). Eric assumed the other lawyer's prominence and links to the power structure would assure a deal could be made.

But he was soon to discover otherwise. At the preliminary hearing, the assistant district attorney flatly rejected the defense's proposal that their clients plead guilty to a misdemeanor. Eric was stunned. Although the DA stated his office wouldn't oppose probation, he would not back down on the felony charges. "It was no sale," Eric said.

The lawyer knew that it would be extremely risky for his client to plead innocent. He had a weak case. The only witnesses to the "crime" were a police officer and the two defendants. It would be the word of two gay men against a police officer in a Tennessee town where gays were viewed as deviants and sinners. The officer's testimony could not be rebutted without calling Larry and Tim to the stand. Under cross-examination they would have to admit they had committed the act. If they denied the charge, there was always the confession the two men had signed that night at the East Tennessee State University security office.

Only the generosity of the DA could save Larry and Tim from felony convictions. So Eric, accompanied by an American Civil Liberties Union attorney from Memphis, went to see David Crockett, the district attorney of Washington County. Crockett was a DA with a reputation for toughness; Eric told me his office had put more men on death row than any other in Tennessee. He was popular with most of his constituents, but others who had come up against him more directly thought he was dictatorial, sometimes irrational.

The two lawyers gave Crockett "every reason in the world" to reduce the charges, in Eric's view. The deterrent effect had already been met, they argued—none of Washington County's gay citizens were about to have sex in automobiles anytime soon, you could be sure. In addition, Larry was willing to sign an affidavit stating he would never come back to Johnson City for any reason. "We told the DA if this had been Memphis or Nashville, these guys would have had a fifty-dollar fine and it would have probably been expunged from their records," Eric said. Then he recalled Crockett looking at them with "the most disgusted look on his face" and saying evenly, "I don't think we would want to be like Memphis or Nashville."

When Crockett asked about his client's occupation, Eric felt a glimmer of hope. Perhaps he could prove to the DA that Larry was a hardworking fellow. But when he told Crockett that Larry worked for his town government, Crockett replied, "I'm not sure if I would want a gay working in that kind of job! There is a possibility of AIDS being transmitted." At that comment, said Eric, "Both of our mouths hung open. It was like arguing with a brick. We left totally disgusted."

Eric, a red-haired, athletic man in his thirties who climbed mountains on his vacations (and who made a point of telling me about his girlfriend and the wild time he had had the night before), soon became deeply involved in the case. He saw the prosecutions as "a blight on Tennessee." "I am proud of this area," he said. "I grew up here, and I have lived here all my life. I don't think Johnson City is any more homophobic than most places. But this is getting back to hillbilly time."

The reasons for the DA's determination to pursue the harsh charges were a subject of debate in Johnson City in the months that followed. Eric himself was sure the DA was homophobic and cited comments he made in their conversation such as "I don't care what anyone does in the privacy of their own home but I'll be damned if I let two queers do that in the parking lot of the school I went to."

In the months that followed, Crockett made a series of public statements on the case that underscored his views on homosexuality. "It's high time the gay community realizes it [homosexuality] is not simply an alternative lifestyle— it is a crime," he told the daily *Johnson City Press*. "If they don't like that . . . they can go to Nashville and seek to change the law." And he added, "I am concerned about it [homosexuality] in this community. In the light of the apparent ease of which I have observed many of these people to engage in homosexual encounters . . . they are endangering everyone by spreading AIDS."

But political and turf battles—and a much larger and far-reaching sex scandal—may have played a more significant role in Crockett's insistence on prosecution than his views about homosexuals and homosexuality. During the spring of 1986, just a few months before Larry and Tim were arrested, East Tennessee State University security officers had mounted a vice opera-tion that netted close to fifty men who had had sex in a library restroom in the basement of the medical school. No one was actually arrested or charged, although the men involved were all forced to sign confessions. Rumor had it that a number of prominent individuals, some associated with the university, were among those caught. As a result, the university did its best to hush up the entire affair. The *Johnson City Press* went to the state's highest court to gain the release of the names of the men involved; although the paper won its case, the names were never printed. "When Crockett found all this [the ETSU scandal] was going on behind his back, he was furious," said Eric. "He was never consulted. We heard from the grapevine that Crockett said if something like this happens again, we are going to prosecute, no matter who it is." According to those who viewed Larry and Tim's arrest in the context of this larger scandal, Crockett was determined to reassert his position as the scourge of "crimes against nature" in Washington County, Tennessee. And he soon got his chance.

On May 29, 1987, nine months after their arrest, Larry and Tim pleaded no contest to the felony charge in Washington County Criminal Court. Judge Arden Hill sentenced the pair to five years in prison, the minimum sentence under the law. (Pleading no contest instead of not guilty was the only concession the defendants' attorneys could obtain from the DA.)

As he sat in the courtroom and listened to the judge pronounce the sentence, Eric Johnson felt he was witnessing "the most disgusting thing I've ever seen. I was thinking these guys were getting a greater sentence than a third-degree burglary, a statutory rape. A guy has sex with a fourteen year old girl and gets a lesser sentence."

Probation for the men was still an option, and a hearing was scheduled for the end of summer. When I talked to Eric in his office, a few weeks after the convictions, he told me he was "ninety-nine percent sure" the judge would grant probation. The main basis of his optimism was that Crockett had stated he would not oppose probation. But Eric had also been confident he could get the sentences reduced to a misdemeanor early on. So far, nothing in the state's handling of the case inspired confidence.

That same day, I drove to meet Larry in his hometown, two hours drive to the north. Just across the Virginia line, I stopped for lunch in a proud old Georgian town that features a playhouse, a large nineteenth-century hotel, and crafts shops. But as I continued on through spectacular mountain scenery, past farms with bales of hay laying out in the fields, ramshackle shacks, and one-story brick houses that looked all out of proportion, it became increasingly evident I was entering the depressed coal country of Virginia's Appalachia. A recent study by researchers at Virginia Polytechnic Institute found the seven counties of southwestern Virginia to have rates of poverty, unemployment, and disability two to three times those of the rest of the state.

I called Larry when I arrived in his town, and he met me across from the barber shop. Larry is an utterly modest-looking person with stooped shoulders and bright blue eyes. He had a beaten-down look about him, but a kind of doggedness, too; I wondered if both those qualities were present before his arrest. Larry was the sweet and naive small-town boy who had never left home to see what life was really all about, who had never really had to face the cruelty of the world. When he graduated from high school, he was hired for his present job, which he had held for fourteen years. His mother, who relied on him for everything, lived in the town, as did his sister and his two brothers. He was the deacon of a gay church in nearby Bluefield, West Virginia.

Larry and his lover, Andy, lived in a small frame bungalow on a steep street, with views of wooded hills across the valley. Their living room was dominated by a large aquarium. Our conversation was punctuated every few minutes by the sound of train whistles.

Except for contact with Larry's family, Larry and Andy lived an isolated life. They weren't used to having guests. Larry admitted he didn't know what to offer me to eat or drink. "I had Andy run out and buy some Coke before you came," he said apologetically. "I didn't know what else you might like."

When Larry was first charged with violating the Tennessee crimes against nature statute, his whole life seemed to fall apart. "I thought about just going out and driving and not looking back," he told me. "And when I ran out of gas, to just keep walking. I didn't care where I ended up, what happened to me. I just didn't care. I couldn't believe they were willing to do this to me. Not in America, not in the United States." Andy added, "If he had had a gun in the house he would have used it on himself. He was on the edge of a breakdown."

Larry's fragile mental state led Andy to move from his home in Charleston, West Virginia, to live with Larry. The two had only met a few months before the arrest and had been seeing each other occasionally at the time. A stocky, street-wise former coal miner who worked in hotels and restaurants in Charleston after being laid off from the mines, Andy seemed far more worldly than his small-town boyfriend. He was now working at a nearby fast-food joint; there just weren't any other jobs around. They don't do much except watch TV (they had a VCR but had gone through all the movies available in town, they said), visited Larry's mother (who had adopted Andy as one of the family), drove up to Bluefield, just across the West Virginia line, to visit the minister of Larry's church or maybe over to Charleston on weekends.

Since Johnson City was some distance away and the *Johnson City Press* (which printed Larry's name and address three times in stories about the case) didn't circulate in Larry's hometown, very few people there knew anything of his run-in with the law. In that sense, he had been very lucky. Still, two weeks after he was charged, Larry went to tell his supervisor about "some problems" that "might not enable me to keep my job," as he phrased it. When his supervisor asked him, "What kind of problems?" Larry replied, "I don't know if I should tell you. All I can tell you is that I am in trouble and could go to jail." "Are you trying to tell me you're gay?" asked his boss. "I've always kind of thought you might be." His supervisor stood behind him throughout the affair, even offering to testify on his behalf at his probation hearing. But Larry was still worried what might happen if higher-ups in town government heard about the case. And although he had been able to keep his job, the case had been a financial disaster for him. Thus far, legal fees and court costs had amounted to four thousand dollars.

Larry's mother didn't know about his arrest, only that he had been in some kind of trouble. Larry led her to believe it was all over now. His brothers didn't know either. Telling his sister involved a conversation similar to the one he had with his supervisor at work. When he mentioned he was in trouble, she asked him point-blank if it had to do with being gay. "It doesn't make any difference and mom knows, too," she told him. For Larry, the coming out he was forced into provided a major surprise. People made it clear to him that they liked and respected him, even though he was gay.

Nonetheless, the whole affair had been a kind of emotional roller-coaster. Shortly after his arrest, he experienced intense feelings of loss of control. It seemed that the district attorney had "all the power" over him and his destiny. "I was nervous, I was scared all to hell," he said. "It even affected my work. I got physically sick from worrying too much. I passed out once at work. I was so worried that I didn't think I would have anything left. It is hard to put into words." He had been wary about Andy moving down from Charleston and giving up his job and his life there when his own future was so unsure. "I didn't know if I could be here the next day, if they wouldn't come and drag me out of my own house," he recalled.

As time passed, he began to cope better, due in large part to his many sources of support—Andy, his family, his supervisor at work, and his friend

Jordan Weiss-Bartok, the minister of the Open House Fellowship, the tiny gay church in Bluefield. At Christmas, six months after Larry's arrest and a couple of months after Andy moved in, Larry and Andy were joined in holy union in Jordan's living room, where the church holds services. Jordan officiated. An ordained minister, Jordan was in the process of converting to Judaism—she was studying with a rabbi in Bluefield—and was integrating Jewish prayers and rituals into her services. So, as an Israeli flag fluttered from the mantel above, she married Larry and Andy in a traditional Jewish ceremony. Although they had no intention of becoming Jewish themselves, they showed me their *ketubah* (the traditional Jewish wedding contract) and said they had even broken the glass, as is the custom at Jewish weddings. "We still have the pieces of glass," they told me.

Still, with his probation hearing due to come up in two months, Larry was uneasy. "I worry about going to jail," he said. "I still worry about the kind of future I am going to have. I worry that if I go to jail I will turn out to be bitter and not want anything to do with society, not want to have anything to do with Andy. If I go to jail I don't think I'd be worth having, just don't think I'd be worth anything."

Although he felt the whole affair "has more or less strengthened me as a person," Larry declined to play the role of political martyr. The National Gay and Lesbian Task Force (NGLTF) had hoped that Larry and Tim would plead innocent and, in so doing, provide a test case to challenge Tennessee's crimes against nature statute. NGLTF's Sue Hyde had been in touch with Larry and his lawyer. But Larry would have nothing to do with it; not only was he unwilling to be a test case, he deliberately stayed away from the talk that Sue gave in Johnson City.

When Sue told him he was a hero, Larry's reply was "No, no way. I don't want to be a hero. I just want this to be over with and to be able to go on from where I left off, just to be able to look forward to another day and not worry."

Larry's friend and minister, Jordan Weiss-Bartok, was angry with both NGLTF and the American Civil Liberties Union for trying to use the case to help bring about changes in the Tennessee law. "The concept of a cause can overtake the human approach," she told me, when I visited her in Bluefield. "The person gets lost. Maybe Larry doesn't feel like saving the world, but that doesn't mean he is letting gay people down. If you have a man who is strong enough, let the Civil Liberties Union hit it with everything they got. Larry is not that person. But he shouldn't be made to feel he is a coward because he is not."

Jordan noted bitterly that if Larry and Tim had had their tryst in her state of West Virginia, nothing would have happened to them. The state had abolished its sodomy law years before.

Some time later, I called Eric Johnson and found out that Larry and Tim had finally been given five years' unsupervised probation; they didn't have to go to jail after all. The only condition of probation, Eric said, was that neither one could enter the grounds of any educational institution — elementary or secondary school or college — in the state of Tennessee during that five years. An exception was made in the case of Tim, who had transferred to the University of Tennessee in Knoxville after being expelled from East Tennessee State. Tim could continue to attend classes, but if he set foot on any other college campus in the state he would be violating his probation. As for Larry, he got his wish. He picked up his life where he left off. Meanwhile, as of this writing, the Tennessee crimes against nature statute remains on the books, as it has since 1858, with little prospect of repeal in the near future.

KNOXVILLE, TENNESSEE,

AND WASHINGTON, D.C.

A few days before my visit to Larry, I had accompanied Sue Hyde to a meeting of Knoxville's Ten Percent (KTP), the Tennessee city's gay organization, to hear her rally the troops against the sodomy laws. It was late June and her speech was part of Knoxville's Gay-Pride Week events. The meeting took place in a renovated church that had been turned into a theatre. A large banner touting the upcoming National March on Washington for Lesbian and Gay Rights had been unfurled over the speaker's platform. T-shirts with the group's gay-pride slogan, "Nothin' Can Stop Us," were on sale. In the back of the room, in boxes, was a sampling from the organization's gay and lesbian mobile library. You could borrow a copy of Rita Mae Brown's *Rubyfruit Jungle* or Gore Vidal's *The City and the Pillar* at one meeting and return it at the next. It was pouring rain outside, which kept the crowd down to about fifty.

Dynamic, personable, darting around the podium, Sue exhorted the crowd. "We're not gonna let them get away with it. That's the story," she said, in reference to Johnson City convictions and the Tennessee sodomy laws. She blasted Massachusetts Governor Michael Dukakis's foster-care policy (she had been one of the founders of the Dukewatch, the group of gays and lesbians that had dogged the governor in his appearances around the state). "When the Duke comes to Knoxville to campaign, ask him about it!" She cheerfully admonished the audience, noting that the men and the women weren't sitting together. "It seems to me that Knoxville's five percent is on one side, and Knoxville's five percent on the other."

When she asked the crowd to "tell me some Knoxville stories," a blond, mustached man in shorts and suspenders stood up. At Gay Pride Week four years before, he had asked a DJ at a popular local bar to play Jerry Herman's gay anthem from the Broadway musical *La Cage aux Folles*, "I Am What I Am." The DJ refused to play such a "militant" song; it was too controversial. Now, he noted, there was a full week of pride events, including Sue's talk.

Nonetheless, a woman in the crowd made the observation that a lot of lesbians were reluctant to come to KTP meetings out of fear of losing custody of their kids. Tim Kuchta, the organization's president, rose and asked how many in the crowd were Knoxville natives. Only six or seven hands went up. That caused a stir. As in a number of prosperous Sunbelt cities, a large number of out-of-staters had moved to Knoxville. But where were all the gay people who were born there? Were they too frightened to join KTP, to come and hear the representative of a national gay and lesbian organization?

As for the sodomy laws, not much was said, despite Sue's energy and enthusiasm. The group did not seem eager to take on the issue. I could understand better why Larry, facing five years in prison, didn't have much faith that the gay movement could save him in the end.

I went to another KTP pride event—a picnic at Big Ridge State Park, near Norris Dam. The organization had rented a pavilion on one side of the park where they displayed the March on Washington banner. The picnickers played volleyball, swam and canoed, ate pasta salad and cheesecake. Unless you wandered over to the pavilion and noticed the banner, you would never have known it was a gay-pride celebration. It was just a bunch of folks in their twenties and thirties getting together for a Sunday picnic—and "Wendy," who showed up in drag. Wendy, I was told, was a married heterosexual lawyer in Knoxville, but she was far more flamboyant than any of the gay people present.

They didn't have a pride march down Gay Street in Knoxville that week in June. Had they done so, KTP president Tim Kuchta was sure no one would have come. People were simply too afraid of the consequences. "In a larger place, you can do things anonymously," he said. "Here, even if we had a huge turnout for a march, it would only be a few hundred and that could be very intimidating." Instead, there was the picnic, a tea-dance, a pool party, and Sue's talk. There was also a gay and lesbian art exhibit at a local gallery, featuring, among other works, a series of brightly colored breastplates that a local lesbian artist had made by taking plaster casts of her friends. The show was called "Hidden Talents."

In Knoxville, the local gay and lesbian population was attempting to work in the community in a "positive, nonthreatening way," Tim told me after the picnic. For example, the city's Beautification Board had inaugurated an "Adopt a Spot Program" in which different local organizations took over pieces of property that the city owned but didn't maintain. KTP adopted an area at a well-trafficked intersection and planted it with flowers and shrubbery. There was a sign explaining that the spot was maintained by Knoxville's Ten Percent. No further identification was given. (That winter, a vehicle drove through the spot several times, destroying the plantings.) KTP was involved in other civic activities, too—selling balloons at the Arts Council's "Saturday Night on the Town," one of Knoxville's major annual cultural events; providing volunteers for the annual Dogwood Arts Festival; contributing to a local food bank at Christmas.

Tim, a stocky, Slavic-featured man of twenty-eight, had come to Knoxville from Milwaukee to work as an Elvis impersonator at the 1982 World's Fair; he now sold industrial robots. Tim admitted that their civic activities didn't put KTP in contact with large numbers of people. But he was convinced the organization's approach was productive. "When people see you doing some-thing for the community in a positive sort of way, any arguments they might have as to why you shouldn't exist or problems they might have vanish before they start," he maintained. And that approach particularly made sense in Knoxville, where religious fundamentalism was strong ("Jesus is Lord over this City," was the billboard I noticed as I came into town). Tim was convinced that being more vocal or confrontational "would polarize the situation and make things more difficult."

So KTP was trying to build a solid gay community now and leave political change for the future, when the organization would, it was hoped, be stronger and more cohesive. "It is a process," Tim said. "We are trying to build our group, trying to interact with the community we live in in a positive sort of way so we are not isolated, eventually developing a political consciousness in the gay community. That is down the road a ways." Perhaps Knoxville, in contrast to other cities, could enjoy the luxury of time. The police didn't harass the gay bars; the mayor's administrative assistant spoke at a KTP meeting and told the group to contact him if there were any problems. Tim had been the youth-group coordinator at a Roman Catholic church where people knew he was gay (he quit when he became president of KTP). AIDS seemed far off, even though there was a fledgling AIDS social-service organization in Knoxville. No one associated with KTP had become sick, and Tim didn't know anyone with AIDS personally.

At the time I visited, KTP was barely three years old. The group had about 110 members. Only twelve out of that number were "out, out" as gay people, in Tim's words. Yet, some more visible activity might not be too distant. As Tim noted, "Sue Hyde's speech was the most political speech this group has ever heard. I think she stirred some thought. Maybe the March on Wash-ington will, too. Who knows? Maybe people will come back from Washington and change the community."

Something was stirring in Knoxville, quietly, cautiously, but stirring none-theless. The same thing was happening in Louisville, two hundred miles to the north. The month I visited Knoxville, Louisville was holding its first gay-pride parade (with Presbyterian elder Nick Wilkerson and Matthew, the seminary student, marching with their More Light banner)—even as a biplane, paid for by a fundamentalist group, was trailing the words "Homosexuals Spread AIDS" over the heads of the marchers. Across the Ohio River, Cincinnati was holding a pride march, too.

As the mid-size cities in the heart of the country were beginning to organize, the national gay and lesbian movement was undergoing a transformation of its own. In the exhilarating period before and after the 1987 march, I went to Washington and talked with the heads of the major national gay organizations.

In the past, the gay and lesbian movement had tended to stress two major issues—the repeal of the sodomy laws and the passage of antidiscrimination legislation. Organizing around these relatively abstract issues proved difficult. Legislative change just didn't seem to galvanize people. The major organizations were weak; over the years, no visible national gay leaders emerged (the charismatic Harvey Milk, assassinated in 1978, had come the closest). Factionalism was rife. Women and people of color often felt excluded, as did many working-class gays. Outside of the large metropolitan areas, gay activism was in its infancy, if it existed at all. Only when there was an external threat—Anita Bryant's "Save Our Children" campaign or the Briggs Initiative in California (which would have barred gays from teaching school)—did the community mobilize.

As time passed, the movement could point to at least a mixed record. As of this writing, only one state, Wisconsin, had enacted gay civil rights protections into law. The national gay-rights bill, despite seventy-three cosponsors in the U.S. House of Representatives and ten in the Senate, had never come up for a vote; its supporters knew it didn't have any chance of passing. Nevertheless, many cities (New York, San Francisco, Baltimore, Raleigh, North Carolina, and others) had passed gay-rights ordinances or included gay-rights protections in comprehensive human-rights ordinances. And a number of states had repealed their sodomy laws, some (like California) by an up-and-down legislative vote, most others as part of a general overhaul of their criminal codes.

By the late eighties, however, the landscape of gay politics was being altered dramatically by the AIDS crisis and the serious civil rights concerns that the epidemic raised. Gay issues and AIDS issues increasingly began to overlap; at the same time, gay activism and AIDS activism were fueling each other. It was increasingly hard to see where one ended and the other began. According to Kevin Cathcart, the executive director of Gay and Lesbian Advocates and Defenders (GLAD), the New England public interest law firm on whose board of directors I served, "There is nothing left in gay and lesbian civil rights issues anymore that is not connected to AIDS. All you have to do is raise something about homosexuality, and people think about AIDS. That even happens in lesbian-mother cases. And you can't come up with a more low-risk situation than that."

The two most influential national gay and lesbian political organizations, the Human Rights Campaign Fund (HRCF) and the National Gay and Lesbian Task Force (NGLTF), are headquartered in Washington, D.C. Between the two, they divide up most of the political issues facing the gay movement. (There is occasional overlap.) The Human Rights Campaign Fund, which has come into its own in the past few years, is a political action committee set up much like other PACs. It raises money through high-ticket dinners and other fund-raisers and contributes to the campaigns of congressional and senatorial candidates who support gay issues. On most issues, it functions as the gay community's lobbying arm with Congress. It has also taken on the task of pressing for the passage of national antidiscrimination protections.

For its part, the National Gay and Lesbian Task Force, which has been in existence since the mid-seventies, is a membership organization with an estimated 7,500 members nationwide. It has a grass-roots orientation (although it has never had a field organization of any consequence) and, perhaps in response to a reputation for elitism in its early years, it has particularly tried to be responsive to the disparate groups that make up the gay and lesbian population. The issues NGLTF stresses include sodomy-law repeal, anti-gay violence, and, increasingly, gay and lesbian family issues. The organization has also played a major role in discussions on AIDS-related issues with the U.S. Public Health Service and the Centers for Disease Control.

I quickly discovered that, despite the overall anti-gay climate engendered by AIDS, the epidemic had given both organizations greater visibility and credibility than ever before. Suddenly, the power structure was paying attention. "One way or another, a human face has been put on us," said Jeff Levi, who became the executive director of the Task Force in 1986, shortly after the organization moved to Washington from New York City. "Who would have thought that the administration or the U.S. Public Health Service would give two seconds' thought to what the gay community thinks? I am sure all those bureaucrats never thought in their wildest dreams they would be dealing with us the way they have."

Over at the Human Rights Campaign Fund, the organization's young and enthusiastic political director, Eric Rosenthal, was having much the same experience. The political system had "opened up" to gay organizations, he said. Gay lobbyists met with sympathetic senators and congressmen to plot the defeat of the punitive anti-gay AIDS amendments that Senator Jesse Helms (R-North Carolina) and Congressman William Dannemeyer (R-California) were trying to tack onto a variety of bills. In the process, they were forging close ties with important figures on Capitol Hill. One of those people was Congressman Tony Coelho (D-California), the House minority whip. Until AIDS, Rosenthal noted, the gay community had never had any contact with Coelho, whom he described as "a major political leader in the House with a bright future ahead." They now had a good working relationship with him, and it was the AIDS issue that "had provided the opportunity to build that relationship."

The AIDS issue was doing more than helping gay lobbyists make friends in high places. NGLTF's Jeff Levi contended that AIDS discrimination and anti-gay discrimination were so tied together that the national organizations now had a unique opportunity to educate legislators about gay issues in a nonthreatening way. Often when you were talking about AIDS discrimination, you were really talking about anti-gay discrimination, he pointed out. As a result, "Whenever you talk about civil rights concerns associated with AIDS as a public-health issue, you have the opportunity to give a 'Homosexuality 101' course to the legislators," he said. "AIDS has provided us with a tremendous vehicle to educate people about gay rights without talking about gay rights."

The issue of anti-gay violence—a phenomenon dramatically on the rise since the advent of AIDS—provided a similar opportunity, Levi said. At a hearing of the House Judiciary Criminal Justice Subcommittee the year before, he found a number of legislators who were not in favor of a gay-rights bill to be very receptive on the issue of violence. "It is a building process," he said. "We need to bring people along from one issue to another, so that when we come to them with the gay-rights bill, that no longer seems so outrageous. We can say to them, 'You supported us on AIDS discrimination, you supported us on anti-gay violence. Here is the next step.'"

In all this, the gay organizations could point to some very real achievements, actions that went beyond fending off anti-gay and hostile amendments. As the HRCF's Rosenthal put it, "Five years ago or three years ago, who would have thought the organized gay community and our allies would have gotten $1.2 billion from Congress to fight AIDS?" he asked. On the other hand, Congress did view AIDS as more than just a gay issue. And Rosenthal conceded that while his organization had been successful in its push for more AIDS funding, it had been less so in affecting programs and policy. For example, Congress had failed to enact comprehensive legislation barring discrimination against people with AIDS; there had been no overall attempt to address red tape in research and drug testing.

In the midst of the constant press of AIDS-related concerns, the traditional boilerplate issues—national gay civil rights protections and sodomy-law repeal—were increasingly being put off to the future. Although HRCF was continuing to round up sponsors for the national gay-rights bill, Rosenthal admitted "we view the bill as a long-term project." A national gay-rights bill had always been regarded as a distant goal, of course. But, with the advent of AIDS, its chances of passage were more remote than ever, despite all the new allies on Capitol Hill. For his part, NGLTF's Levi insisted that his organization had made a commitment that the demands of AIDS issues wouldn't eclipse the other things that the Task Force had worked on for years. He cited Sue Hyde's Privacy Project to repeal the state sodomy laws, although that, too, was now a "long-term organizing tool." The Supreme Court's *Bowers v. Hardwick* decision, which found sodomy laws constitutional, dashed any hopes of a "quick fix," Levi said, forcing the Task Force "to do the hard work of organizing on a state-by-state basis." The problem, however, was that few legislators in socially conservative states like Tennessee were likely to vote for sodomy-law repeal lest they be accused of contributing to the spread of AIDS.

One of the most significant ways in which AIDS had changed gay politics had been the advent of gay fund-raising. In the past, gay and lesbian organizations had tremendous difficulty raising money; they just weren't seen as legitimate causes, even by other gay people. That was all changing. In response to the tremendous toll of the epidemic, many gay people around the country had opened their pockets to the local AIDS social-service organizations. Now, that generosity was extending to national gay organizations as well. The National Gay and Lesbian Task Force had retired an $85,000 debt. And by the spring of 1988, the Human Rights Campaign Fund ranked ninth nationwide in fund-raising among independent political action committees. In 1983, the organization raised $325,000; for the 1988 calendar year, its budget was $2.1 million. During the 1988 congressional and senatorial campaigns, the organization hoped to contribute as much as $400,000 to candidates who supported gay and AIDS issues.

HRCF's donations of $5,000 and $10,000 gave the gay community "access" to congressmen and senators, according to Vic Basile, the organization's executive director. "In the minds of a candidate, it makes us seem like just another player in the arena, an inside player," he said. And in Basile's view, playing inside made all the difference. "I really believe," he told me, "that once you begin to have a dialogue it is very hard for senators and congressmen to say no. It is like any other human dynamic. It is harder to say no to people who are sitting opposite you."

Back in 1984, when HRCF gave money to congressional candidates, ten of its sixty-four contributions were returned. Candidates were fearful of the political consequences of taking money from a gay-rights PAC. In the 1986 campaign, no one sent back any checks. Basile conceded that there might be times when gay contributions could be used against a political candidate. He cited the 1984 North Carolina Senate race in which Jesse Helms, the Republican incumbent, was opposed by Governor Jim Hunt. In view of the nastiness and gay-baiting of the race, Basile thought an HRCF contribution would have been counterproductive. Maryland Senator Barbara Mikulski also signalled HRCF that she would rather not have any contributions to her 1986 Senate bid, because of fear of gay-baiting by her opponent. In the 1988 campaign, nearly 125 senators and congressmen accepted HRCF contributions. (Twenty-five percent of those receiving donations were Republicans, leading HRCF political director Rosenthal to assure me, "This isn't a question of affirmative action for Republicans. These candidates are genuinely supportive of our issues.")

Vic Basile claimed that most voters really didn't care about gay rights one way or another. The social issue that had the greatest overall impact, he was convinced, was abortion. "There are gradations around gay rights that don't exist around choice," he said. "So people might oppose job discrimination against gays but at the same time might not want homosexuals teaching kids. Most politicians who are also pro-gay are pro-choice and they were pro-choice first. The votes they would lose on the gay issue they had probably lost on the choice issue anyway." At the very worst, the gay issue was "a neutral," he insisted. In the vast majority of elections where the issue had come up or been a factor in the campaign, the candidate identified as being pro-gay won, he said. In the 1986 election, no members of Congress who were cosponsors of the gay-rights bill and who sought reelection were defeated; in the 1988 vote, only one cosponsor—Senator Lowell Weicker (R., Conn.)—lost his seat.

Those fancy dinners where HRCF raised its money (twelve hundred dollars a plate in Dallas and Columbus, Ohio; one hundred fifty dollars in Boston) brought the gay middle and upper classes into the movement, Basile said. That was vital. He was amazed at how many people could easily write a twelve hundred dollar check. "If all someone is willing to do is to write that check and fund the movement," he said, "we should give them the opportunity."

But, by the end of the Reagan years, as the AIDS epidemic began to affect the lives of so many gay people and there was so much frustration with the federal government's response to the epidemic, many clearly felt a need to do more than write large checks and attend lavish dinners. In New York City, an organization called the AIDS Coalition to Unleash Power (ACT UP) was formed to protest government AIDS policies. ACT UP tactics primarily involved street demonstrations, sit-ins and "die-ins," and civil-disobedience actions. In March 1988, the group celebrated its first birthday by snarling rush-hour traffic in New York's financial district, shouting slogans critical of President Reagan's lack of attention to AIDS. One hundred protesters were arrested. As New York's ACT UP made headlines, similar organizations were established in cities all over the country. In October, groups from fifteen cities joined together in an attempt to shut down the suburban Washington headquarters of the Food and Drug Administration, to protest the delays in testing and approving experimental AIDS drugs.

Soon enough, civil-disobedience tactics spread from AIDS issues back to gay and lesbian issues that weren't directly related to AIDS. Early in 1988 in Boston, four hundred people disrupted state house proceedings for several hours to protest the State Senate's refusal to pass a gay-rights bill. Fourteen demonstrators were arrested, including eight who handcuffed themselves to chairs in the visitors gallery. In New York City in the summer of 1988, ninety people were arrested in a demonstration to protest the stabbing and beating of two gay men and the murder of another.

One of the effects of the rise of the activist AIDS organizations was to bring about a rare political unity between gay men and lesbians. The novelist Sarah Schulman (*After Delores* and *The Sophie Horowitz Story*), who was involved in New York's ACT UP, said that working in that organization made her feel for the first time that there was a "totally unified gay and lesbian community." Most of the men in ACT UP had never been politically active before, she observed, while many of the women had a history of involvement in feminist and traditional Left organizations. It was the women who knew how to facilitate meetings and organize demonstrations, who had a broad political analysis. "There has been incredible respect and mutual sharing," she said. "Now it is much more equal inside the organization. For these men to become politicized has opened them up in such an incredible way. It has really changed things." Sarah pronounced ACT UP—which operated on consensus and drew hundreds of people to its weekly meetings—to be "the most exciting political movement I've ever seen in my life."

Boston gay legal advocate Kevin Cathcart saw civil disobedience as "a turning point in tactics" that mobilized people and shined a badly needed spotlight on gay and AIDS issues. He noted that many of the people involved in civil-disobedience organizations like ACT UP were in their early twenties. "It is as if gay political organizing had skipped a generation," he suggested.

Cathcart felt that the rise of civil disobedience was tapping into the underlying anger about AIDS. In fact, he was surprised gay people weren't showing more rage. "On the one hand, everyone is being mobilized and we are doing a lot," he said. "On the other hand, we aren't doing anything. When you think about the fact that AIDS is decimating the gay community, how many of us are spending the amount of time you would think people would spend under the circumstances?"

Part of the explanation, he believed, was that gay people, like most Americans, lived in a world "where politics is frowned upon." There were other brakes on activism, too—fear of losing jobs and children, fear shared by large numbers of gay men about whether they were HIV-positive, whether they or friends or lovers might get sick. Despite all that, Cathcart said, "What we are seeing is a very difficult move towards politicization."

It was Columbus Day weekend, 1987, when that "difficult move towards politicization" was made most dramatic. The occasion was the gay and lesbian March on Washington, the largest political event of its kind in the nation's capital since the Vietnam Moratorium of 1969. It began with a mass wedding—two thousand same-sex couples, some wearing tuxedos and others in jeans and T-shirts, exchanging vows under an arc of black and white balloons in front of the Internal Revenue Service building. It ended with mass civil disobedience—some 650 gays and lesbians carried from the steps of the United States Supreme Court and arrested in a protest against the court's decision upholding the constitutionality of the sodomy laws. Off-stage, there were receptions and religious services, dances and meetings, a forum on sex and politics, a concert of gay marching bands and choruses. Washington was transformed overnight into a city that seemed to be populated almost entirely by homosexuals.

I had attended the first gay March on Washington in 1979, with its respectable turnout of 75,000 or so, but nothing then prepared me for the 1987 march. This time, the numbers were overwhelming—200,000, according to the estimates of the U.S. Park Police, 600,000 according to march officials. (CBS News reported there were 800,000 people in attendance.) It took the Massachusetts contingent three hours before we finally left the Ellipse and completed the twenty-block journey down Pennsylvania Avenue to the Mall.

At times the march resembled a vast traffic jam. At other times it seemed like the departure of a noisy citizen-army of crusaders to take Jerusalem, the flag of Texas as its standard (with bravado characteristic of the state, Texas flags were everywhere), and the black and white T-shirts (with a pink triangle and the "Silence = Death" slogan) of the New York City contingent as its uniform. I looked for a Tennessee banner and caught a glimpse of the blond man who had stood up that night at Sue Hyde's talk and related his attempts to get a local DJ to play "I Am What I Am." It was easier to march down Pennsylvania Avenue in Washington, D.C., where nobody knew you, than down Gay Street in Knoxville, of course. But maybe it was good practice.

The unveiling of the memorial AIDS quilt for the first time provided a somber adjunct, as did the AIDS victims in wheelchairs who led the march. There were small and poignant reminders of loss, too, like the lone South Dakotan whose T-shirt stated simply, "I'm Marching for Michael Hackett — He Didn't Make It." The quilt itself, the size of two football fields, was composed of almost two thousand rectangular panels. Each was inscribed with the name of someone who had died of AIDS, and many panels were decorated with flowers, palm trees, and intimate touches such as poems, pictures, and embroidered guitars and tennis rackets. On display just a few hundred feet from where the speakers (including presidential candidate Jesse Jackson, United Farmworkers president Cesar Chavez, and actress Whoopi Goldberg) were exhorting the crowds, the quilt left everyone in tears. The quilt was both monumental and personal, and with the Washington Monument on one side and the dome of the Capitol on the other, its brightly colored panels stood out boldly in the afternoon sunshine.

The collective joy and grief, the exhilaration and the sadness, the cere-monies of marriage and memorial expressed many of the complexities of being gay in America. Another degree of complexity became evident when neither of the nation's two leading newsweeklies mentioned a word about the march. And the march's exhilaration turned to anger three days later when both houses of Congress voted overwhelmingly to ban the use of federal funds for educational projects or programs that "promote or encourage, directly or indirectly, homosexual sexual activity." The votes represented the most significant defeat the gay community had ever suffered in Congress.

But these disillusionments were far from the minds of those who came to Washington that Columbus Day weekend. The enthusiastic applause that greeted the waves of marchers as they paraded past the White House and down the hill to the Mall provided a euphoria that contrasted both with the terrible character of the AIDS epidemic and with the lonely and fearful coming out experiences of so many lesbians and gay men across the country. There was a feeling of being part of a proud people who had survived struggle and adversity and were finally coming into their own.

For me, the most striking moment of the day did not come during the march or even at the rally that followed it. It happened when the scheduled events were over and I was leaving a subway car packed with marchers returning to buses, hotels, and hometowns. As we streamed out of the train at Dupont Circle and headed for the escalators, there was a momentary pause. Inexplicably, in one of those rare moments of spontaneity that tell more about an event than any description of the event itself, everyone on the packed platform raised their fists in unison and let out a thunderous cheer. From the midst of the crowd, a woman shouted, "Aren't we beautiful!" And then another cheer went up.

AFTERWORD:
IN SEARCH OF
GAY AMERICA

▼　▼　▼　▼　▼　▼　▼　▼　▼　▼　▼　▼　▼　▼

owards the end of my travels, I returned to Brown University, in Providence, Rhode Island, the college I had graduated from more than twenty years before. When I was at Brown, there was no gay student organization. But this time, as I walked across the College Green and looked up at the brick student union building, there, plainly visible in a third-floor window, was a large pink triangle. It was a signal that the office of the Lesbian and Gay Student Alliance was open. Change can seem so simple once it finally occurs—a sign in a window. I wondered how different my life would have been if there had been that pink triangle in the window when I was at Brown.

As I looked back on all I had experienced and the people I had met over the previous year and a half, I saw gay life as a continuum. At one end was a greater sense of openness, the acceptance and self-acceptance, that fuller, richer life that comfortably combined sexuality with the rest of one's identity. The continuum was personal, political, cultural. Individuals and groups of people were at different points along its progression. Some were just beginning to grasp at a gay identity, to develop a sense of community, like the Latina lesbians in San Antonio and the Native Americans in Minneapolis. Others were so far along that they seemed to be creating an autonomous culture all their own, as in San Francisco. Still others were stalled along the way or hadn't even begun the journey—the gay men in Selma, Alabama, so deeply in the closet that they were "back behind several racks of clothes"; the guys in Morgantown, West Virginia, who lived to get drunk on the weekend; the gay married men having furtive, guilt-ridden sex at X-rated bookstores in North Dakota.

But overall, I perceived a momentum—the ability of at least some gays and lesbians to lead relatively open lives in small towns, the organizations springing up in mid-size cities, the gay churches and synagogues and sports leagues, the lesbian "baby boom," the militant AIDS activism. As the Knoxville gay-pride motto went, "Nothin' can stop us now." Even AIDS, despite its toll, was accelerating the movement towards community-building, towards politicization, towards those hundreds of thousands marching past the White House on Columbus Day weekend.

A major factor in that momentum was the growing interaction between lesbians and gay men, replacing the divisions of the past. Once again, that varied from place to place. During Gay Pride Week in Knoxville, visiting activist Sue Hyde rose to speak and found the male and female members of Knoxville's Ten Percent sitting on opposite sides of the room. At least they were in the same organization. In New York City, on the other hand, the novelist Sarah Schulman could boast that, based on her experience in AIDS activism, the relationship between lesbians and gay men had been transformed. "We've gone co-ed!" she said. There were other indications of a newly found unity: the beginnings of a confluence of sexual attitudes between men and women; the college women I met who listened to British gay male punk groups instead of women's music and informed me they had "a gay male identity." In smaller places—Bunceton, Bismarck, Fargo—separation between men and women had never been an option. There, the numbers were so few that they had to band together. In general, the separatism of the past was fading; the men and the women were finally realizing they were part of the same community.

There was almost always the personal struggle, the agony and joy of self-discovery, the sense of coming through. I was struck again and again by the tremendous changes in the lives of so many of the people I met as they came to grips with issues of identity and sexuality. A Denver psychotherapist named Britt Alkire, who had gone from being a schoolteacher, to marriage, to divorce, to the military, to coming out, to becoming a psychotherapist and lesbian activist, saw this as central to the gay experience. "There is a requirement for gay people to be more inventive or flounder forever. We are thrown on our own resources," she said. "I think gay people have this assignment in life to invent ourselves and our own relationships. We are in the definition business—to energetically and creatively invent new institutions, relationships, ways of being with each other in the world. That is how I give meaning to gay life."

I noted, too, a general attempt at healing the wounds of the past—of gays and lesbians trying to overcome the effects of years of believing all the negative things society had told them about themselves. The rise of gay spirituality—from churches and synagogues to alternative approaches like women's spirituality—was a sign of this. Another indication was the proliferation of gay twelve-step groups, modeled on Alcoholic's Anonymous. In the listings section of the monthly San Francisco newspaper *Coming Up!*, I counted a total of thirty-five gay and lesbian self-help groups, ranging from gay AA and Children of Alcoholics groups to those for survivors of incest and abuse. Even in isolated Rapid City, South Dakota, where there was virtually no organized gay and lesbian life, a woman I met was planning to start a group for addicted gay people. This development was in part a response to AIDS; many men were concerned that the use of alcohol and drugs undermined the immune system and could encourage unsafe sex. But it also reflected a growing sense of pride and self-acceptance that translated to an effort to build a healthier community, both physically and mentally.

Everywhere, I found people reevaluating what was important in their lives. Sometimes, this was part of the resolution of issues of self-acceptance. Thus, after much struggle, Jan, the West Virginia coal miner, had decided to leave the mines because her increasingly strong self-image as a lesbian made it impossible to continue to work in an environment where she felt she had no recourse but to hide her sexual orientation. For men, AIDS was often a major factor in this reexamination, in ways that went beyond simply changing sexual practices. So Frank, the computer entrepreneur in Boston who had lost his two best friends to AIDS, was putting a new value on a committed relationship, reconsidering whether professional success was providing sufficient meaning for him, and generally asking the question, "How should a man live?" In Los Angeles, I encountered a forty year old vice president at a major studio who was quitting his job to search for other sources of satisfaction, a decision precipitated in part because so many of his friends had been diagnosed with AIDS. This premature mid-life crisis was a phenomenon I saw repeated among gay men across the country.

There were changes I had hoped to discover but never did. I didn't find many indications of a new kind of gay male culture emerging out of the AIDS crisis. I had speculated that with the decline of recreational sex as a main focus of life for many gay men, we would begin to create a culture similar to that of lesbians—one centered around music, theatre, and the arts in general. Perhaps this would evolve gradually; the rise of gay sports leagues (even a gay and lesbian version of the Olympics, called the Gay Games) was one sign of a search for alternatives to the social patterns of the past. But this kind of cultural change was clearly a slow process. And despite the pronouncements of the movement, I didn't see the gay community coming to grips with issues of racism and social class. The divisions between black, white, Latino, and Asian and between middle- and working-class remained deep, reflecting those of America in general.

I found no single vision of the gay future. Instead, I saw various gay and lesbian communities taking different paths, adopting their own strategies as they attempted to create an atmosphere of openness and a sense of security. How they went about it depended on numerical strength, on the quality of leadership, on particular local factors. There was the approach of conservative, mid-size Knoxville, where the gay and lesbian group eschewed the visibility of a march down Gay Street and instead was trying to prove itself through neighborly participation in arts festivals and city beautification programs. There was the model of Key West, where a gay community strong in numbers and in economic power argued that no civil rights protections and (in the view of some) no gay institutions were needed, that assimilation and "amalgamation" were the best ways to win a place in the sun.

In Los Angeles, the gay students at UCLA had formed a gay fraternity and a lesbian sorority—with rushing, pledging, and all the trappings of the Greek letter societies. Although frats and sororities had traditionally been symbols of elitism and homophobia, the students were determined to do things differently—stressing community service, "not beer parties and MRS degrees," as one sorority sister put it. It was still another strategy, one that was particularly inventive and risky—taking an institution that had been oppressive to gays and lesbians in the past and molding it to one's own needs and vision.

Finally, there was the model of some of the larger cities, notably San Francisco, with a sense of gays and lesbians as a people in their own right, with distinct family structures, religious, social, and cultural institutions. In New York City, Richard Burns, executive director of the city's Lesbian and Gay Community Center, saw a similar development. "We are beginning to develop a sense of responsibility for our gay youth and our gay elders," he said. "In the future, you will increasingly see us develop our own social-service agencies, our programs to take care of those portions of our community who are in crisis. We are realizing that we can develop an identity as a people and we can take care of our own."

To my mind, that big-city approach was probably the most promising, but it required a critical mass of gay people; in many respects, it didn't apply to smaller communities, to parts of the country less congenial to gays and lesbians. In the end, most likely, each gay community would continue to find its own solutions, some not even thought of yet.

But there were other, more ominous prospects that could not be discounted. It was still quite possible that the progress and the increasing options gays and lesbians were beginning to enjoy would eventually be overwhelmed by the magnitude of the AIDS epidemic. A man in New York City related that almost all his closest friends had succumbed to AIDS. "I feel like the bomb has already hit," he said. "I went to Seattle for a few days and was amazed that life was still going on." That was another line that extended into the future, a continuum that dramatized how deeply individuals and gay communities had been affected by the AIDS crisis. Everyone fell somewhere along it. The epidemic and its relentless progression was part of the gay present and the gay future, as well, side by side with the gains, the increasing openness. How would the gay community, a fragile community still, cope with the estimated quarter of a million gay men who would be diagnosed with AIDS by 1993? No one had an answer.

Hand in hand with AIDS came the threat of repression, the growing power of the anti-gay religious right. At this writing, the federal and state governments had by and large resisted efforts to apply more coercive social policies—mass testing, quarantine, and the like—to the AIDS epidemic. Yet, reports of delegates to the 1988 Republican National Convention in New Orleans physically attacking gay protesters, shouting "AIDS is not a disease—it's the cure!" vividly illustrated the extent of homophobia that the epidemic had brought to the surface. Sari (Bootsie) Abelson, a fifty-six year old lesbian from Birmingham, Alabama, who had gone through two marriages, shock treatments, even institutionalization, before she could make peace with her sexuality, had said to me, "The world is fully capable of bringing on the homosexuals the same thing we allowed to happen to the Jews of the world. I see us acting the same way that my grandparents and my aunts and uncles did in Europe, who told themselves, 'They are not going to bother me.' And they bothered them. They bothered them in a big way. I fully believe it can happen again."

I preferred to take a more optimistic view—that gays and lesbians were creating a power base that would make such a scenario unlikely. But the gay community had serious weaknesses as an interest group. One was an inability to overcome the hostility of the dominant elements of the Republican party. In 1988, ninety-eight openly gay people were delegates to the Democratic National Convention in Atlanta; the following month, at the Republican National Convention, not a single openly gay or lesbian delegate was to be found. Gay Republican activist Bruce Decker had told me that openly gay people were "as welcome as a turd in a punchbowl" in the Grand Old Party. Yet, some degree of influence on both parties, from the inside and outside, was crucial. The same went for other institutions and environments usually viewed as uncongenial to gays, from churches to union halls to police forces. Gays and lesbians had to neutralize (if not win over) hostile segments of society by establishing some kind of presence. That was a major challenge. For that reason, I believed that Rose Mary Denman, the Methodist minister who stood up to her church, was a hero; that was why I admired openly gay people who stayed on in small towns; that was why Bob Almstead, the first openly gay cop in Washington, D.C., was a hero, too.

And that was why I admired David Hernandez. A twenty-five year old sophomore at UCLA who came from a working-class Chicano family, David was one of the founders of the gay fraternity at his school. He worked part-time at a warehouse with two hundred other men, many of whom were members of minority groups. All were members of the Teamsters, as he was. The day after a photograph of the gay fraternity brothers appeared in the daily newspaper, David went to work. "Gigantic guys," as he described them, whom he had worked with day after day, were staring at him or coming up and asking, with a mixture of incredulity and menace, "Was that you in the paper?" or "You're gay? *You're* gay?" or "Aren't you afraid of AIDS?" Many others, including his boss, refused even to look in David's direction. David was terrified. "Those were the most difficult hours of my life," he said. "My head, my stomach were spinning. I kept saying to myself, 'I wish I could take it back.' Here was this mob of Teamsters. I didn't know if someone would drop a box on me or run over me with a machine. Your fears go wild."

Still others who had never talked to him before greeted him in a friendly way as he walked past. Within a few days, the storm had passed; the other men went back to treating him as they always had, as the smart college kid who wouldn't wind up spending the rest of his life in the warehouse, as they most likely would. "If you can come out in that atmosphere, you can come out anywhere," David said.

Taking risks is the key to continued momentum. If collective action is essential to gay progress, so are individual acts of courage such as David's. Perhaps, in the end, sexual pluralism is something society will never accept. Perhaps demoralization and repression represent the scenario of the gay future, after all. But I believe otherwise. I have seen too many changes in a very short time, met too many people who have taken tremendous risks by becoming open about their sexuality and who will never return to the constricted lives of the past. For them, for all of us, there is simply no going back.